Mandelstam the Reader

Parallax Re-visions of Culture and Society

Stephen G. Nichols, Gerald Prince, and Wendy Steiner, Series Editors

Mandelstam the Reader

Nancy Pollak

The Johns Hopkins University Press
Baltimore and London

© 1995 The Johns Hopkins University Press
All rights reserved. Published 1995
Printed in the United States of America
on acid-free paper
04 03 02 01 00 99 98 97 96 95   5 4 3 2 1

The Johns Hopkins University Press
2715 North Charles Street
Baltimore, Maryland 21218-4319
The Johns Hopkins Press Ltd., London

Library of Congress Cataloging-in-Publication Data
will be found at the end of this book.
A catalog record for this book is available from the
British Library.

ISBN 0-8018-5006-1

For Louis and Katherine Pollak

❖ ❖

Our father's speech and our mother's speech—isn't our language nourished all its long life on the confluence of these two, don't they compose its character?

Osip Mandelstam, "The Judaic Chaos"

Contents

Acknowledgments

Mandelstam the Reader is the relict of so many years and revisions that much of it remains only in the form of the "drafts [that] are never destroyed," present in this latest version of the work as Dante's nonextant manuscripts are an inalienable part of his poem. For the same reason, the contributions of numerous people may no longer be apparent. Thus even these acknowledgments are just a partial case, a synecdoche for everyone I would thank.

I should note, first, the place where it all started: Victor Erlich's Post-Symbolist Poetry course at Yale in the spring of 1974. It continued as my senior essay under the direction of Omry Ronen in 1975–76, as a paper for him in the fall of 1977, and as my dissertation, still at Yale, under the direction of Victor Erlich and the late Lowry Nelson.

Savely Senderovich, Judith Vowles, Eric Naiman, and Pavel Nerler commented on proto-versions of chapters 1, 2, 3, and 4.

Omry Ronen was ever-generous with references, connections, and explanations.

I am especially grateful to Vyacheslav Ivanov for his detailed reading of the manuscript and suggestions for further investigation.

I have had talks on topics ranging from relativity to mycology to neuropathology with Edwin L. Goldwasser, Wallace Sherlock, and Jay Yasen respectively.

Over the years, discussions with Wayles Browne, Rabbi Laurence Edwards, Susanne Fusso, Leonid Ivanov, Stephen Nichols, Marena Senderovich, Gavriel Shapiro, Jonathan Shames, and Ward Winton have contributed to the making of this book. Peter Dreyer performed an immense service with his painstaking, insightful, learned, and good-humored copy-editing. I am indebted, too, to Slava Paperno for his heroic efforts on behalf of these pages.

My colleagues in the Cornell Department of Russian Literature, Patricia Carden, George Gibian, and Michael Scammell, along with Savely Senderovich and Gavriel Shapiro, have been most supportive and understanding throughout. So have the patient department staff, Diane Williams and Anne Marie Kniser.

My students at Yale, the University of Michigan, the University of Pennsylvania, and Cornell have been a source of inspiration and ideas.

The American Association for the Advancement of Slavic Studies has given permission to print, as the second chapter, a revision of my article "Mandel'shtam's *Mandel'shtein:* Initial Observations on the Cracking of a Slit-Eyed Nut, OR, A Couple of Chinks in the Shchell," which appeared in its original form in *Slavic Review* 46, 3/4 (Fall/Winter 1987).

Finally, I want to mention two people who are accountable for nothing I have said: David R. Goldmann, M.D., without whom I could not have written this book; and, once again, Omry Ronen, without whom it would not have been written.

A Note on the Text

Translation. All English versions of foreign-language verse, prose, and critical passages are mine unless otherwise noted. All Russian passages are given in English in the immediate vicinity, either in a translation following or preceding the quotation or, in rare cases, in contextual paraphrase. Subsequent quotations of the same passage, in particular titles or first lines of poems, are given in English, unless the discussion makes a point of the Russian. Occasionally, I do not give the translation of a title when the Russian is almost identical to the English ("Ariost," "Armeniia," "Poet"). In other words, those who do not know Russian should keep reading: you have all the information possible under the circumstances.

Transliteration. I use the (modified) Library of Congress system; it is less economical and more ambiguous than the international scholarly system but also more intuitive and vernacular. It is on the one hand unwieldy—letters pile up—but on the other descriptive and evocative, revealing more palpably the sound texture of the Russian. There is one major exception. I have chosen Mandelstam, as the poet's name is commonly spelled in English, rather than Mandel'shtam, though the latter form is consistent with the transliteration system used throughout the book and properly renders pronunciation (cf. also Gogol, Tolstoy rather than Gogol', Tolstoi).

Emphasis. Italics are mine unless the attribution is clear from context or otherwise noted.

Mandelstam the Reader

◤ The Reader and the Writer

This is a study of the late verse and prose of Osip Mandelstam (1891–1938). The final period of Mandelstam's work dates from 1930, when he began to write again after five years of poetic silence. It ends with the end of his Voronezh exile seven years later. Just a few poems have survived from the period between May 1937 and Mandelstam's death in a Siberian transit camp in December 1938.[1]

Critical treatment of Mandelstam has followed the evolution of his work. In general, earlier scholarship was devoted to his earlier writings. This is not surprising, since, with few exceptions, Mandelstam's late poetry was not published during his lifetime.[2] The first posthumous edition, the 1955 *Sobranie sochinenii* (*Collected Works*), included only twenty-three poems written between 1930 and 1932 (the "Armenia" poems account for twelve of these), and none later. As M. L. Gasparov points out in his article on the "evolution of Mandelstam's metrics," the Mandelstam corpus was hardly complete at the time of Kiril Taranovsky's 1962 article on the same subject, which considers the verse to 1925.[3] Yet Mandelstam's accessibility depends not just on external factors; readers have arrived gradually at his late work, learning to read it through an understanding of his earlier verse and through his critical and autobiographical prose.

Of the major monographs on Mandelstam, only Jennifer Baines's *Mandelstam: The Later Poetry* (1976) and Peter Zeeman's *The Later Poetry of Osip Mandelstam: Text and Context* (1988) are devoted to the work of the 1930s. Baines takes a comprehensive approach, treating each poem, and to some extent the prose of those years, in chronological order. She relies to a large degree on testimony, unpublished at the time of her study, by Mandelstam's wife, which has since appeared in Nadezhda Mandelstam's *Kniga tret'ia* (*Third Book* [1987]). Zeeman is more selective, and his orientation is somewhat theoretical. The present book focuses on a small body of work, and the approach is philological rather than biographical or philosophical.[4]

Mandelstam's late period is traditionally divided into the Moscow years (1930–34) and the Voronezh years (1935–37), though the two *Moskovskie tetradi* and three *Voronezhskie tetradi* (*Moscow Notebooks* and *Voronezh Notebooks*) are joined under the common title *Novye stikhi* (*New Verse*)—the "domestic" name of the unpublished verse of the 1930s,[5] and in the double focus of my book the "notebooks" are linked chronologically and thematically. In Chapter 2, I consider not only the verse but also the prose of the Moscow years, primarily *Puteshestvie v Armeniiu* (*Journey to Armenia*), written in 1931–32 (published in 1933), and also *Razgovor o Dante* (*Conversation about Dante*), written in the spring of 1933 (published in 1967). In Chapter 3, I examine "Vos'mistishiia" ("Octaves"), eleven eight-line poems written between 1932 and 1935, which are an exploration of poetry in process—the poetic "impulse," as Mandelstam called it in the contemporaneous prose. The center of Chapter 4 is the "Gudok" ("Whistle") cycle, five poems of December 1936. The cycle marks the return of poetry after another, briefer silence, and here Mandelstam returns to some of the images that preoccupied him in the "Octaves," taking up where he had left off in July 1935, when the "Octaves" were among the last poems he was working on.

Two related problems run through the book. The first is the dialogue between Mandelstam and Pasternak, which began with the appearance of Pasternak's *Sestra moia zhizn'* (*My Sister Life*) and *Temy i variatsii* (*Themes and Variations*) in 1922 and 1923, and with Mandelstam's immediate enraptured response to those books in his essays. The second is the Russian poets' relation to his Jewish origins, which emerged as a subject of the poets' dialogue in the 1930s, though it is prepared in the exchanges of the previous decade. Both problems are connected to the proposition implicit in the title of the book.

Differences between Mandelstam's and Pasternak's poetics have been the subject of frequent mention, if less analysis. Among those who consider the problem, Henry Gifford seconds Nadezhda Mandelstam, who calls the two poets "antipodes"; Mikhail Epstein reveals a similar perspective.[6] Mandelstam and Pasternak found each other uneasy colleagues. Neither was entirely comfortable with the presence of the other, as poet or as moral example. Readers find them uneasy contemporaries.

Commentary on Mandelstam's relation to his Jewishness ranges from attempts, notably Nikita Struve's, to make Mandelstam a Christian poet, to Clare Cavanagh's examination of the historical and cultural context of his Judaism, where she addresses his ambivalence about his origins as crucial and creative.[7] Baines suggests that Mandelstam's interest in Judaism had nothing to do with his own background: "It is important to realise that Mandelstam came to Judaism not through his blood but through the medium of Judaeo-Christian culture, approaching it in the same spirit as any other educated European did."[8] The twofold limitation of this view—it disparages both Mandelstam's relation to Judaism and his relation to the life of the mind, which can hardly be distinguished from "blood"—is not mitigated by the fact that Baines is probably relying on something said by

Mandelstam's wife. Nadezhda Mandelstam may not always be the most reliable witness, in matters of religion among others.[9] Yet even Nadezhda Mandelstam, whose family were converts and who was herself a devout Christian, acknowledged that Mandelstam never ceased to consider himself a Jew.[10]

In Mandelstam's "Jewish" poems of 1910, both Omry Ronen and Taranovsky show, the identification of the poet as a Jew means his separateness from the Russian homeland.[11] In this respect Mandelstam in the periods of his first two books, *Kamen'* (*Stone,* 1913, 1916) and *Tristia* (1922), is close to Pasternak, who, to the end of his life, felt that his Jewish birth kept him from fully participating in Russian poetry. Ronen points out that Mandelstam's interest in Catholicism and Russian Orthodoxy in the 1910s was part of a search not for a faith, but for order and system as such.[12] Charles Isenberg comments: "The young Mandelstam saw in Christianity the principle of authority that underlay and inspired modern Russian and European culture."[13] Robert Alter offers a useful corrective to critics who rush to represent Mandelstam as one kind of ideologue or another: "Osip Mandelstam did not believe either in Judaism or Christianity: he believed in poetry. For a time, he was inclined to associate poetry with Christianity because of his notions of Christian order and of the apparent spiritual seriousness of Christianity."[14]

By 1933, however, Mandelstam associated poetry—and authority—with a "Judaic" principle. In 1929, in *Chetvertaia proza* (*Fourth Prose*), he announced his pride in the "honorable calling" of Jew, which, he believed, distinguished him from the official "writers' tribe."[15] His conception of order was correspondingly transformed. The late poetry departs from the classical verse forms and lexicon that characterized the earlier periods; poetry comes to be equated with the raw material rather than the finished product.[16] Among the first of the Voronezh poems is "Eto kakaia ulitsa?" ("What street is this?" [April 1935]), with eleven lines and irregular and imprecise rhymes, where the imagined "Mandelstam Street" has the disreputable, "cursed" and "crooked" character of its namesake. At the same time, the acute sense of the opposition between the poet's Jewish origins and the orderly Russian milieu is tempered. In the earlier poems the opposition might appear a fatal one, but in the 1930s, Mandelstam realized what Ronen describes, with reference to the 1920 poem "Vernis' v smesitel'noe lono" ("Return to the incestuous bosom"), as the inevitability of the return to Jewish roots.[17]

Taranovsky finds in the 1933 octave "Skazhi mne, chertezhnik pustyni" ("Tell me, draftsman of the desert") evidence of a "new interest in the fate and destiny of the Jewish people."[18] His very concrete and topical reading of the poem ("it describes the endeavor of the Jews in Palestine to conquer the desert") is open to question. But his broader understanding is consistent with a premise of the present study: that Mandelstam reevaluated his relation to Judaism in the 1930s, as he reconsidered the origins and ends of the poet's word.

He did so, moreover, in light of Pasternak's own reflections on the same subject. For Pasternak, as for Mandelstam, the question of the poet as Jew became particularly acute in the early 1930s. That issue was joined between them when Pasternak objected to Mandelstam's Stalin epigram of November 1933, "My zhivem, pod soboiu ne chuia strany" ("We live, not sensing the country beneath us"), with the cryptic comment to Nadezhda Mandelstam, "How could he have written this poem—after all, he's a Jew!"[19] Pasternak's question is part of a larger polemic with Mandelstam about the poet's task, a polemic colored by Pasternak's fear that, as a Jew, he could never truly participate in Russian poetry. But features of the inarticulate language Mandelstam inherited from his father are also typical of Pasternak's verse as Mandelstam describes it in his 1923 essays.

For all their poetic and personal incompatibility, Pasternak was the contemporary Mandelstam most admired, and as Mandelstam's frequent references indicate, was much on his mind. It was in part through his thought about Pasternak that Mandelstam resolved the problem of the Jewish Russian poet. And Mandelstam's thought about Pasternak is his thought about poetry. Perhaps all the more in the 1930s, aware of his own approaching end, Mandelstam returned to the Pasternak he had called, in his essays of the early 1920s, the inevitable legacy of Russian poetry.

❖ ❖

The conception of the poet as reader has its beginnings in Mandelstam's early verse. Congenial to this conception is the pioneering work of Kiril Taranovsky and Omry Ronen on subtext as a key to Mandelstam's poetics.[20] With reference to the very early poem "Est' tselomudrennye chary" ("There are chaste charms" [1908]), Ronen writes about the "constant shifting of the 'eidola' of the poets in the subtextual array of historical affinities and unexpected typological correspondences."[21] He describes "Ia na slykhal rasskazov Ossiana" ("I haven't heard Ossian's tales" [1914]) as the poem where Mandelstam "first formulates the principle of the recurrence of the poetic word."[22] If, in Akhmatova's later epigram, "poetry itself is one enormous quotation,"[23] the poet, as the one who quotes others' words, is a reader. In the mid 1920s, in "Komissarzhevskaia," the penultimate chapter of *Shum vremeni* (*The Noise of Time* [1925], Mandelstam describes the biography of the *raznochinets,* that is, the poet, as a list of the books he has read.[24] He thus defines the poet as a reader. In *Journey to Armenia,* he compares the "book at work" to a "canvas stretched on a frame."[25] He is discussing not writing but the "physiology of reading." The comparison of the reader to the painter suggests the reader's active role in determining what is read.[26] This reader is another hypostasis of the poet who proceeds by quotation; his relation to the poet is like the poet's relation to the voices of the past. Whether from the perspective of the present or the future, the poem is not an "original" word but commentary, response.

In his 1922 essay on the anniversary of Blok's death, Mandelstam refers to *rodstvo* 'kinship', 'ancestry' and *proiskhozhdenie* 'origins' as the object of the critic's investigation. This is not the impressionistic criticism he calls "lyrics about lyrics" (the creative critic is hardly appropriate to the uncreative writer): "The critic need not answer the question of what the poet wanted to say, but he is obliged to respond to the question of where he has come from."[27] In the last chapter of *The Noise of Time,* "V ne po chinu barstvennoi shube" ("In a Fur Coat above One's Station"), he establishes a literary genealogy for the poet, describing the lesson of his teacher, V. V. Gippius:[28] to conceive of literature, specifically the literature of nineteenth century Russia, "not as a temple, but as a clan [*rod*]."[29] The adoption of literary forebears as family can be compared to the rejection of the personal principle in "Komissarzhevskaia" ("My memory is hostile to everything personal"), by the poet whose life is books.

The poet's biography has also a less articulate aspect. In "I haven't heard Ossian's tales," more than a decade before *The Noise of Time,* Mandelstam rejects *rodstvo* as the poet's object. Yet disdain for kin refers not to ancestors (the recipients of the poet's "treasure" are called "great-grandchildren"), but to contemporaries; "skuchnoe sosedstvo" ("tedious neighbors") echoes "skuchno peresheptyvat'sia s sosedom" ("it's tedious to exchange whispers with a neighbor") in "O sobesednike" ("On the Interlocutor" [1913]),[30] Mandelstam's early and fundamental essay about the relation between the poet and the reader. The childhood bookcase of "Knizhnyi shkap" ("The Bookcase"), another chapter of *The Noise of Time,* is emblematic of the importance of personal origins:

> The bookcase of early childhood is a person's lifetime companion. The disposition of its shelves, the selection of books, the color of the spines is perceived as the color, height, disposition of world literature itself. And those books that did not stand on the first bookshelf can never squeeze through into world literature, as into a cosmos. In the first bookcase, every book is perforce a classic, and not one spine can be discarded.[31]

The disorganized, Tiutchevian "womb world" that Mandelstam calls the
"Judaic chaos" contrasts with the harmonious and elegant order of imperial
Petersburg, where the Jewish poet as a boy felt himself an awed stranger.[32]
The bookcase reflects this juxtaposition of apparently incompatible
cultures:

> The lowest shelf I remember as always chaotic: the books did not stand spine to
> spine, but lay like ruins: reddish Pentateuchs with torn bindings, a Russian
> history of the Jews, written in the awkward and timid language of a Russian-
> speaking Talmudist. This was the Judaic chaos, cast into the dust [*povergnutyi
> v pyl' khaos iudeiskii*]. Here, too, quickly fell my ancient Hebrew primer,
> which after all I never mastered.[33]

The acknowledged volumes of German and Russian literature rise above
the incomprehensible Judaica tumbled at the bottom: "Above the Judaic
ruins began a bookish order [*stroi*]: that was the Germans. . . . Still higher
stood the maternal Russian books."[34] But in the childhood bookcase,
where each book is essential ("not one spine can be discarded"), Judaica is
the foundation for the orderly others.[35] Beginning with *The Noise of Time,*
Mandelstam reconsiders "the question of where [the poet] has come from."
    Nadezhda Mandelstam acknowledges that she did not understand
Mandelstam's growing interest, toward the end of the 1920s, in his father's
kin; she understood better the genealogy of the *raznochinets.*[36] That understanding may be reflected in her comment: "But he didn't, after all, believe
in his rabbinic birth and sought the Russian *raznochintsy.* It was from them
that he derived his origins."[37] In fact, Mandelstam's derivation of his
origins is more complicated; the attraction to Russian culture is only one
side of the story. Recounting the visit to a Yalta watchmaker who was, it
turned out, a Mandelstam and was able to show them the family tree,
Nadezhda Mandelstam notes: "It seemed to me that [Mandelstam] envied
the watchmaker and his old and kind wife because they still had a sense of
origins [*rod*] and of a link to their forebears."[38] In the chapter of *The Noise
of Time* called "Khaos iudeiskii" ("The Judaic Chaos"), Mandelstam calls
his language a "fusion" of the paternal and the maternal speech, associating
his father's unidentifiable "tongue-tie" with the "Judaic chaos," by contrast
with his mother's too-perfect Russian.[39] The biography of the reading
raznochinets depends as much on the poet's "rabbinical birth" as on his
Russian prototypes.
    Judaism provides a peculiarly apt model for the word of Mandelstam
the reader. In "The Bookcase," where the account of the childhood bookcase is the account of the textual origins of his word,[40] Mandelstam identifies the poet as a reader in a tradition. This is a tradition, moreover, in which

the book is central: a tradition based on the conception of the universe as
text, and as created out of text; a tradition sustained by reading and commentary.[41] Epstein writes that "Mandelstam . . . [turned] poetry into an
idiosyncratic Talmudic discipline of the interpretation of the signs of world
culture."[42] The shelves of the bookcase, which Mandelstam describes as
geological layers,[43] resemble the layers of earth cut through by the plow of
poetry, Mandelstam's image for the relation of poetry to time in the 1921
essay "Slovo i kul'tura" ("The Word and Culture"). The tradition is constituted of a ceaseless depositing of layer upon layer—the plow cutting
through the accumulations of the years does not eliminate the intervening
strata, but redeploys them, in "space" rather than in time ("Poetry is a plow,
cutting through time so that the deep layers of time, its black earth, appear
on top").[44] In "O prirode slova" ("On the Nature of the Word"), an essay of
1922, Mandelstam similarly describes Bergson's idea of relation, the product of the philosopher's "profoundly Judaistic mind":[45]

> Bergson examines phenomena not in the order of their subordination to the law
> of temporal sequentiality, but as if in the order of their *spatial extension*. This
> relation he frees from time and examines separately. Thus, related phenomena
> form a kind of fan, the folds of which can be unfurled in time, but at the same
> time it is subject to speculative furling.[46]

The conception of history implied in this description is close to the
perspective of rabbinic scholarship. Barry Holtz writes: "The interpreters
were accustomed to see all biblical moments as simultaneous: verses could
be compared or contrasted entirely out of context; the whole of Scrip-
ture . . . was seen as a vast sea of tiny, discrete insights . . . and Jewish
interpreters often appealed to the dictum 'There is no 'before' or 'after' in
Torah.'"[47] Mandelstam's poet works on the word much as the rabbinic
scholars did, making connections across time, perceiving distant events as
simultaneous. His poet is a reader in the Talmudic tradition.

The counterpart to the autobiography of the poet as reader in *The Noise
of Time* is the portrait of the poet as a scribe in *Conversation about Dante*.
Mandelstam never sat down to write.[48] The exception that proves the rule[49]
is the Stalin "Ode" ("Oda" is the domestic name of the poem),[50] also
known as "Stikhi o Staline" ("Verses about Stalin" [January—February
1937]), which, installing himself at the table, he forced himself to compose.[51] He rarely copied out his poems; that was a mechanical operation
(the fact that Nadezhda Mandelstam was the scribe in the family confirms
this), as distinct from the "calligraphy" that Mandelstam associated with
Dante—with poetry.[52] Thus the portrait of the poet as a scribe is the other
exception. The relation of Mandelstam's scribe to the word recalls the

rabbinic tradition, where the truth of the divine utterance depends on the faithful transcription of texts. George Steiner discusses the centrality of the text for the Jewish tradition:

> The mystery and the practises of clerisy are fundamental to Judaism. No other tradition or culture has ascribed a comparable aura to the conservation and transcription of texts. In no other has there been an equivalent mystique of the philological. This is true of orthodox praxis, in which a single erratum, the wrong transcription of a single letter, entails the permanent removal of the relevant scroll or page from the holy books. It is true . . . in the kabbalist's exhaustive scrutiny of the single Hebrew letter in whose graphic form and denomination manifold energies of meaning are incised.[53]

Mandelstam's image of the scribe resonates in Steiner's description, perhaps not accidentally; elsewhere in the essay Steiner cites *Conversation about Dante* (as one of the two greatest pieces of modern literary criticism).[54] Attentiveness to the letter is Mandelstam's perspective too:

> If we take this amazing work from the standpoint of the written language, from the standpoint of the independent art of the letter, which in 1300 was entirely equal to painting, music, and was one of the most respected professions, then to all the analogies proposed we must add a new one—writing to dictation, transcribing, copying. . . . Transcribing is not even it—this is calligraphy to the dictation of the most menacing and impatient dictors. The dictor-overseer is much more important than the so-called poet.[55]

The account of the awful dictors,[56] suggesting the danger of the least mistake in copying, recalls Talmudic injunctions against scribal error. The Talmud provides a comprehensive set of rules for copying. The alteration of a stroke transforms the meaning of the text, rendering it, in rabbinic terms, unholy—in Mandelstam's, false.[57]

As the poet-scribe, Mandelstam invokes the authority of tradition for his work.[58] Authenticity depends not on the "originality" of the work and its origins in life, but on its origins in the word, already spoken. Rabbinic interpretation reveals the same relation between "tradition" and the "individual talent": "For the rabbis all interpretations are essentially old—they are already known at Sinai after all."[59] Mandelstam, who esteems authority, emphasizes in the architecture poems of his first book, *Stone,* the fact of building where buildings have been.[60] In "Notre Dame" (1912), he begins his construction by noting what had stood on that site earlier: "Gde rimskii sudiia sudil chuzhoi narod, / Stoit bazilika . . . " ("Where a Roman judge judged an alien people / A basilica stands . . ."). He builds with an eye to what has come before as well as what is to come: "I chem vnimatel'nei, tverdynia Notre Dame, / Ia izuchal tvoi chudovishchnye rebra, / Tem chashche dumal ia—iz tiazhesti nedobroi / I ia kogda-nibud' prekrasnoe

sozdam" ("And, stronghold of Notre Dame, the more attentively / I studied your monstrous ribs, / The more often I thought—from unpropitious
weight / I too will create something beautiful some day") (cf. the description of the construction of Hagia Sophia out of fragments of other temples
in "Aiia-Sofiia" ["Hagia Sophia"]). The word invokes its past contexts;
every utterance presumes a long history.[61]

In representing the poet as a scribe subject to the dictors' will, Mandelstam writes: "Dante and fantasy—but they are incompatible! . . . Where's
his fantasy? He writes to dictation, he is a copier, a translator."[62] That
comment is characteristic of a poet who does not speak in terms of "imagination" or "creativity"; and, as is the case throughout *Conversation about
Dante,* Mandelstam might be speaking of himself. Nadezhda Mandelstam
writes, with reference to the passages about dictation: "This could be said
only by a poet who has come to know the categorical nature of the inner
voice through personal experience. . . . in poetic labor, arbitrariness, invention, fantasy are inconceivable."[63] But Mandelstam never seeks to deny
responsibility. Characteristic of him is the repeated "Because I . . ." ("Za
to, chto ia . . ."; cf. "I za eto . . . ia . . .").[64] Nadezhda Mandelstam juxtaposes as "polar opposites" the actor, with whom she associates Pasternak,
and the poet. The actor does not answer for his words: they are learned by
rote, and belong to the character. The poet is different: "But the poet always
answers for everything. He speaks only for himself and in his own name."[65]

Thus fidelity to tradition entails the revision of the work of the past.
The idea of reading that began with the childhood bookcase is close to what
Alter calls "the Jewish notion of inexhaustible revelation through words
and their exegesis."[66] The life of the letter depends on interpretation—on
reading. Like the Talmudic conception of the word, Mandelstam's conception is no mere literalism: "Writing and speech are incommensurable. The
letters correspond to intervals"; the "technique of writing with its clamps
and curves [well-rounded periods] grows into the aerobatic flight of flocks
of birds."[67] A decade before *Conversation about Dante,* Mandelstam had
written, in the "Semitic" *Egipetskaia marka (Egyptian Stamp)*:[68] "Destroy
the manuscript, but preserve what you have inscribed at the side."[69] This
recognition of the importance of commentary recalls, again, Talmudic
scholarship, where the page, with commentaries spiralling from the center,
is a metonymically deployed palimpsest—as if here the plow of poetry had
done its work.[70]

The present poet's work is just such a marginal commentary to the
work of the past (and what is written in the margins preserves what lies in
the center). Thus the account, in *Conversation about Dante,* of the functioning of the poetic word as quotation provides another parallel to the

graphic arrangement of the Talmudic page: "I want to say that the composition is put together not as the result of the accumulation of details, but as a
consequence of the fact that one detail after another tears away from the
thing, departs from it, darts off, unhitches itself from the system, departs
into its own functional space, or dimension [*ukhodit v svoe funktsional' noe
prostranstvo, ili izmerenie*]."[71] There is a vital connection between authority and responsibility, between tradition and interpretation. Mandelstam the
scribe is Mandelstam the reader.

❖ ❖

Yet the poet's Jewish birth could have antithetical consequences, as it
did in the case of Pasternak. Lazar Fleishman juxtaposes Mandelstam's
account of the childhood bookcase to a passage in a letter Pasternak wrote
to his parents in 1914. Pasternak notes that, having spent his youth preparing to be a musician, having "sacrificed the word to sound," as he put it later
in *Okhrannaia gramota* (*Safe Conduct* [1931])—in other words, having
grown up without reading—he was compelled, when he switched to the
idiom of the word, to be original.[72] For both Mandelstam and Pasternak,
childhood is not only the time of the poet's formation; it remains a basis for
comparison, a measure of authenticity, throughout the later years. It is with
reference to childhood first of all that Mandelstam acknowledges other
texts in establishing the poet's genealogy, and that Pasternak rejects them.
Pasternak's "originality" contrasts with Mandelstam's "tradition."

As the quality Pasternak assigns to himself, the nonreading writer,
originality entails faithfulness to life, to things as they are, without the
distorting hierarchies imposed by language. In *Safe Conduct,* Pasternak
describes his journey to Marburg, where he encountered the "authentic"
Middle Ages. He found the Marburg school of philosophy attractive for its
interest in knowledge in its "ceaseless authorship, at the hot sources and
outcomes of universal discoveries"; attractive because it was "original, it
dug up everything down to the foundation and built on a clear space."[73]
The poet encounters a world unencumbered by culture. In a letter to his
cousin Ol'ga Freidenberg of July 23, 1910, Pasternak makes the creative
state a perception of the world as unorganized content.[74] The work is
continuous with nature, with the landscape.[75] It is fact; it is the way the
world is; it is in the nature of things: "Moi drug, ty sprosish', kto velit / Chtob zhglas' iurodivogo rech'? / V prirode lip, v prirode plit, / V
prirode leta bylo zhech'" ("My friend, you ask who orders / The holy
fool's speech to burn? / It was in the nature of the lindens, in the nature of
the flagstones, / In the nature of the summer to burn [it]") ("Balashov").

The poem is much more valid than any work that can be ascribed to some author.[76]

Pasternak's account of the genesis of his book *My Sister Life* is an example of the way he asserts the validity of his work:

> With the appearance of *My Sister Life,* in which entirely uncontemporary aspects of poetry found expression, revealed to me through the revolutionary summer, it became a matter of absolute indifference to me what the force that gave the book was called, because it was immeasurably larger than me and the poetic conceptions surrounding me.[77]

The reflexive, passive, and impersonal constructions, the absence of nominal forms of the first person singular pronoun and of first person forms of the verb—all demonstrate the poet's point: the book is much more than the product of an individual "I." The author invokes the highest authority for his work: nature, life itself (the superlatives confirm the superiority, the uncontestability of the phenomenon described).

Thus Pasternak denies responsibility, as, for example, in "Posleslov'e" ("Afterword"), where "No, it was not I that caused you sadness," "No, it was not I" ("Net, ne ia vam pechal' prichinil," "Net, ne ia . . .") is a repeated refrain (the addressee, her "beauty," is the subject and cause of the poem: "Net, ne ia—eto vy, eto vasha krasa" ["No, it was not I—it was you, it was your beauty"]). But those denials, offered in support of the absolute authenticity and authority of the work, cannot acquit the poet.

For Pasternak, the detail is everything. Iu. Tynianov writes that Pasternak achieves the strongest "logical" connections through the juxtaposition of incidental detail.[78] The big picture is not in our purview: "Ne nado tolkovat' / Zachem . . ." ("One should not try to figure out / For what reason . . ."); we contemplate the particulars: "Ne znaiu, reshena l' / Zagadka zgi zagrobnoi, / No zhizn', kak tishina / Osenniaia,—podrobna" ("I don't know whether they've solved / The puzzle of the dark beyond the grave, / But life, like the autumn / Stillness, is detailed") ("Davai roniat' slova" ["Let's let words fall"]). Moreover, the particulars are synonymous and interchangeable. Any of the various contiguous features of the object might be chosen to represent it; or, on a different scale, any of a number of objects might be chosen to represent the universe. In *Safe Conduct,* Pasternak defines his autobiography in terms of accidents: "I characterize my life during those years deliberately accidentally [*sluchaino*]. I could multiply these signs or replace them with others."[79] A myriad of details is the protagonist's mode in "Marburg." The details might seem haphazard, chaotic, incomprehensible:[80] "Odnikh eto vse osleplialo. Drugim / Toi t'moiu kazalos', chto glaz khot' vykoli" ("Some were blinded by all of this. To

others / It appeared such a multitude [darkness] that it was pitch dark").
But there is an alternative interpretation. It is not, apparently, the subject,
but the detail that matters: "Kazhdaia malost' / Zhila i, ne stavia menia ni
vo chto, / V proshchal'nom znachenii ee podymalas'" ("Every trifle /
Was alive, and holding me of no account, / Rose in its farewell significance"). The detail is what matters, in its capacity as representative of the
whole that is not named: "Vse eto bylo podob'ia"; "I vse eto tozhe—
podob'ia" ("All this was likenesses"; "And all this, too, was likenesses").
The detail is not random, but purposeful:

> The details gain in clarity, losing in independent significance. Each one could
> be replaced by another. Any one is valuable. Any one you choose could testify
> to the state that grips the entire shifted reality.[81]

Here, in this prose counterpart to "Marburg"—the story of the protagonist's rejection by the beloved and the poet's coming into being—the
specific content of the detail is not important (Pasternak adds, in a note to
this passage: "I am speaking not about the material content of art . . . but
about the meaning of its manifestation").[82] The protagonist is blissful even
after rejection, because the significant factor is passion, not as a particular
emotion, but as a force. Each detail is vital as testimony to the protagonist's
altered state.[83]

   Iu. M. Lotman proposes that the writer envisions a range of choices,
and might substitute one word for another.[84] Thus, Pasternak's conception of detail presumes the perspective of an author, the one for whom
all possibilities are equally appropriate, equally significant representations of the one, authorial, universe: "Ty sprosish', kto velit, / Chtob av-
gust byl velik, / Komu nichto ne melko . . . // Vsesil'nyi bog detalei . . ."
("You ask who orders / August to be great, / For whom nothing is petty
. . . // The omnipotent god of details" ["Let's let words fall"]). In Pasternak's verse, the ubiquitous author himself is the unique authority.[85]

   Pasternak links his originality to another rejection of tradition, in a
letter written forty-five years after the 1914 letter to his parents. According
to this account of origins, the poet, who was born a Jew,[86] had a formative
childhood experience of another religion:

> J'ai été baptisé par ma bonne de prime enfance, mais à cause des restrictions
> contre les Juifs et surtout dans un famille qui en était exempte et jouissait d'une
> certaine distinction acquise par les mérites artistiques du père, le fait s'était un
> peu compliqué et restait toujours mi-secret, mi-intime, objet d'une inspiration
> rare et exceptionnelle plutôt que d'une calme habitude. *Mais je pense que c'est
> la source de mon originalité.* Je vivais le plus de ma vie dans la pensée
> chrétienne dans les années 1910–1912, où se formaient les racines, les bases
> principales de cette originalité, la vision des choses du monde, de la vie.[87]

Pasternak casts off his own heritage, choosing instead to create himself anew. He sees his origins in this "originality," in the conversion to another faith, and not in the tradition into which he was born. In the early poem "Kak bronzovoi zoloi zharoven'" ("As the brazier [scatters] bronze cinders"), he defines the process of poetry itself in terms of a conversion: "I, kak v neslykhannuiu veru, / Ia v etu noch' perekhozhu" ("And, as into an unheard-of faith, / I am converted [I cross over] into this night"). Turning away from Judaism, moreover, Pasternak casts off a system in which tradition is a constructive principle.

Lotman distinguishes the reader's from the writer's perspective: the reader can conceive of no alternative to the text as given; his word is essential and irreplaceable. A new word introduces a new content: "for the reader there are no synonyms" and "there is nothing accidental in the text perceived as artistically complete."[88] Pasternak, who cites a plethora of possibilities, suggests in *Safe Conduct* that telling *"only* the truth" is not sufficient, nor does he hesitate to define poetry as fibbing.[89] Mandelstam's purpose is the discovery of the one right word; the poet's torment is the famous difficulty of the task: "Ia slovo pozabyl, chto ia khotel skazat'. / Slepaia lastochka v chertog tenei vernetsia" ("I've forgotten the word that I wanted to say. / The blind swallow returns to the palace of shades") ("Lastochka" ["The Swallow"]); "Kakaia bol'—iskat' poteriannoe slovo" ("How painful it is to search for the lost word") ("1 ianvaria 1924" ["1 January 1924"]). For Mandelstam, the typical reader, there is only one way of saying something. If the right word is not found, the poem cannot be finished; on a larger scale, without the sense of poetic rightness, the poet falls silent. Between 1925 and 1930, Mandelstam wrote virtually no verse. Returning from Armenia, he acknowledged in the drafts to his new prose the "impossibility of choice, the absence of all freedom"[90] as the lesson of the sojourn in the place he called in *Journey to Armenia* the "little sister of the Judaic land" ("mladshaia sestra zemli iudeiskoi").[91] This understanding, close to the Judaic conception of the word (cf. the counterpart to the Judaic word in the unyielding and obligatory Armenian language),[92] affords Mandelstam the consciousness of his own rightness, the consciousness that allows him, after five years of silence, to write again.

◢ Mandelstam's *Mandel'shtein*

After the five years during which Mandelstam wrote almost no verse,[1] poetry returned to him in October 1930, in Tiflis, on the way back from Armenia. The "Armenia" poems are among the first of the "new verse," and, with their theme of penance for unproductivity, and their attempt to transform the factors of disturbance—the sense of limitation, confinement, deprivation[2]—into sources of new energy, they testify to Mandelstam's current concern with the operations of his word. At this juncture, Mandelstam gives programmatic attention to the principles of his writing. Iu. I. Levin proposes classifying *Conversation about Dante* as a Mandelstamian poetics as well as a "Dante treatise" and a poetic work in its own right.[3] *Journey to Armenia,* the prose that grew out of the Armenian sojourn, might be described in similar terms.

Mandelstam records a journey that arises at a time corresponding to Dante's "mezzo del cammin," a time of spiritual crisis; he goes, therefore, in search of a renewed sense of the poetic rightness without which he was unable to write.[4] In 1913 he had linked that sense with the certainty of the interlocutor, the future reader whose existence must confirm the poet's own. In the 1930s, the period for which Ronen notes a reorientation towards the poetics of the addressee,[5] the problem of the transmission of the poet's message becomes acute; the cry of the Voronezh verse is typical: "—Chitatelia! sovetchika! vracha! / Na lestnitse koliuchei—razgovora b!" ("[I want] a reader! an advisor! a doctor! / A conversation on a prickly staircase!").[6] The importance of the interlocutor is underscored in *Journey to Armenia,* an example of the genre to which Mandelstam assigns the *Divine Comedy:* it is a "conversational journey."[7] The journey occurs in conversation with philologists and linguists, artists and scientists—with the "Germans" (poets) and the "naturalists" to whom Mandelstam was "introduced" by the addressee of *Journey to Armenia,* the neo-Lamarckian entomologist B. S. Kuzin:[8] "I gratefully [*s blagodarnost'iu*] recollect one of the Erevan conversations."[9] Here, considering the journey that culminated in the reemergence of his poetic voice, Mandelstam explores the origins of his word in an attempt to ensure its vitality for the interlocutor, the future reader. Here, too, he is concerned with fundamental principles.

Those crucial Armenian conversations, which "help us to sense ourselves in the tradition,"[10] were an exchange with Kuzin, and the particular conversation that Mandelstam "gratefully recollect[s]," a discussion of

Alexander Gurwitsch's "embryonic field theory," is a key to the investigations of *Journey to Armenia*.[11] With reference to Gurwitsch's organismic conceptions, Mandelstam invokes a model prevalent in Soviet biological thinking in the 1920s and 1930s, according to which organisms are neither reducible to their component parts nor imbued with a nonphysical significance independent of those parts (cf. mechanism and vitalism, which Bergson, too, rejected),[12] but are defined by the functioning of the whole.[13] Revealing regularities at various levels of organization, systems must be studied both intrinsically, at each level and in terms of the connections between levels, and also in the context of interactions with the larger environment.[14] Organismic theory, which has parallels in the semioticians' view of the poetic text as a structured hierarchy of relations,[15] is the basis for the "vari[ations on] the theme of a nasturtium leaf" in "Moskva" ("Moscow"), the third chapter of *Journey to Armenia*,[16] an investigation of processes in the diverse spheres of plant physiology, human psychology, geometry, chess, impressionist painting.[17] In each of these spheres Mandelstam describes the growth of a force field, which takes the shape of a "salience" (*vypuklost'*), an accretion of space palpable to the physical or intellectual faculties:

> The embryonic leaf of the nasturtium has the form of a halberd or the bivalve of an extended pouchlet, turning into a tongue. It is also like a paleolithic flint arrow. But the tension of forces raging around the leaf transforms it at first into a figure with five segments. The lines of the troglodyte ending acquire an arched extension [*dugovaia rastiazhka*].[18]

The salience is entirely an outgrowth of the system generating it,[19] but it cannot be accounted for within that system and must be described from outside: "The problem is resolved not on paper, and not in the camera obscura of causality [*prichinnost'*], but in the vital impressionistic medium, in the temple of air and light and glory of Eduard Manet and Claude Monet."[20] The "solution" of the problem—the investigation of the medium of the salience—is the poet's task in the verse that is contemporary with *Journey to Armenia* and *Conversation about Dante*.

Gurwitsch's field theory grew out of his conception of the embryonic leaf,[21] which, in turn, has a Goethean prototype. Along with Kuzin, Mandelstam's other guide in these investigations is Goethe, who considered his scientific endeavors to be at least as important as, and of a piece with, his literary works. As a German and a naturalist, Goethe is central to Mandelstam's thinking in the early 1930s.[22] In the drafts to the last chapter of *Journey to Armenia*, "Alagez," Mandelstam points to Goethe's account of his Italian travels as the most important subtext of his work: "The only

book I had with me was Goethe's *Italienische Reise,* leather-bound for the
road and bent like a Baedeker."[23] He takes Goethe's Italian journal as his
guide to Armenia.

For Mandelstam, as for Goethe, the project of the journey is a rectification of vision; *Journey to Armenia* is about ways of seeing. He writes, in a
letter dating to the period of the composition of his travel journal: "My
book talks about the fact that the eye is an implement of thought, about the
fact that light is a force and that ornament is thought."[24] In "Kantsona"
("Canzone"), which recapitulates the desire for the journey, and its landscape, six months after the return, the first verb is *uvizhu* 'I will see'; the
poem is dominated by the metaphor of the extraordinary field glasses, and
vision is "rectified" as the seer adjusts them: "To Zeves podkruchivaet s
tolkom, / Zolotymi pal'tsami krasnoderevtsa, / Zamechatel'nye lukovitsy-
stekla, / Prozorlivtsu dar ot psalmopevtsa" ("Now Zeus tightens up deft-
ly, / With a woodworker's skillful fingers, / The remarkable bulb lenses,
/ The psalmist's gift to the seer").[25] The progress of the journey is mea-
sured in terms of what is visible: "Krai nebritykh gor eshche neiasen"
("The land of unshaven mountains is still unclear").

The rectification of vision entails the discovery of the proper object.
For Goethe, the functioning of the eye depends on its substantial likeness to
what it sees; the eye is formed with reference to the object:

> Das Auge hat sein Dasein dem Licht zu danken. Aus gleichgültigen tierischen
> Hülfsorganen ruft sich das Licht ein Organ hervor, das seinesgleichen werde;
> und so bildet sich das Auge am Lichte fürs Licht, damit das innere Licht dem
> äußeren entgegentrete. . . .
>
> Jene unmittelbare Verwandtschaft des Lichtes und des Auges wird niemand
> leugnen, aber sich beide zugleich als eins und dasselbe zu denken, hat mehr
> Schwierigkeit.[26]

Thus for the renewal of his vision Goethe went to the place where he could
learn to see from the beginning. He went to train his eye on the "original"
forms of Italy; to contemplate, in their native habitat and natural state, the
art works he had known only from reproductions, plants such as he had
seen artificially cultivated in the north.[27] His dearest dream was the discovery of the *Urpflanze,* the original plant that he conceived of not only as the
prototype for all vegetable forms, but also as a model according to which
phenomena in every sphere of life might be organized and comprehended.[28]

In another Goethean formulation Mandelstam reveals that he, too,
goes in search of original, organic forms. In the drafts to the sixth chapter of
Journey to Armenia, "Vokrug naturalistov" ("Around the Naturalists"),
recording his own approach to first things, he echoes one of Goethe's
progress reports. Goethe's statement, made with reference to the natural

sciences, occurs in the course of a discussion of activities in the visual arts, and of his literary efforts: "Ich glaube dem Wie der Organisation sehr nahe zu rücken" ("I believe I have come very close to the *how* of organization").[29] Mandelstam's remarks occur in the context of observations on the naturalists and the impressionists:

> Мы приближаемся к тайнам органической жизни. Ведь для взрослого человека самое трудное—это переход от мышления неорганического, к которому он приучается в пору своей наивысшей активности, когда мысль является лишь придатком действия, к первообразу мышления органического.[30]

> (We are getting close to the secrets of organic life. After all, the hardest thing for an adult is the shift from inorganic thinking, to which one grows accustomed in the period of one's greatest activity, when thought appears just an appendage of action, to the prototype of organic thinking.)

Mandelstam renders "sehr nahe zu rücken" as *priblizhat'sia;* he retains the dative of "dem Wie" in *tainam;* and he replaces "Organisation"with its paronym *organicheskii.* He confirms the Goethean inspiration of the passage with *pervoobraz,* for, if "das Wie der Organisation" does not refer to the protoplant as such, Goethe has in mind the general conception of original form that holds for phenomena in various spheres. Mandelstam, too, recognizes the broad applicability of the principle. In this passage, Mandelstam returns to his "dream of creating an organic poetics . . . of a biological character."[31] The "prototype of organic thinking," his discovery in *Journey to Armenia,* is an original form in the spheres of nature and culture. It is the prototype for the processes that are the variations on Mandelstam's theme: the determination of the poet's "place in the tradition," and "man's place in the universe."[32]

Like Goethe, therefore, Mandelstam conceives of his journey as a training of the eye that discovers the original form.[33] That form is discovered in "Around the Naturalists." In the drafts to the Darwin essay that was published in 1932 under the same title,[34] Mandelstam indicates a relation between the naturalist's eye and his "poetics": "his *eye,* his *manner of seeing* is a key to his methodology."[35] In the chapter called "Around the Naturalists," Mandelstam suggests that in reading the works of the eighteenth-century systematizers, he has learned how to see, achieving the twin Goethean purpose of the journey—spiritual and creative renewal: "Reading the naturalist-systematizers (Linneus, Buffon, Pallas) has an excellent influence on the disposition of the senses, [it] rectifies the vision [*vypriamliaet glaz*] and imparts to the soul a mineral, quartz calm."[36] A nearly identical formulation—the only difference being the subject of the proposition, "reading this naturalist"—occurs in the drafts, in a section devoted, not to either of the more renowned pair, but to the German naturalist Peter Simon Pallas (1741–1811). Catherine II named Pallas professor of natural history at the Imperial Academy of Sciences in 1768, and he made extensive journeys through Russia in the late eighteenth century. Mandelstam gives the German Pallas a Goethean " 'police' file":[37] "he was a geographer, and a pharmacist, and a dyer, and a tanner, and a currier, he was a botanist, a zoologist, an ethnographer."[38] An enumeration of items that attract Pallas's attention would have much in common with a list constructed for Goethe, to whom similar labels apply.[39] Pallas is another traveler with a universal scope. Like Goethe, too, he sees in depth and in detail: "[He saw a whole lot] He saw accurately, jotted down pointedly."[40] Pallas's eye is the prototypical organ of vision in *Journey to Armenia*.

Pallas has the capacity to comprehend a vast space in a tiny compass: "Kartina ogromnosti Rossii slagaetsia u Pallasa iz beskonechno malykh velichin. . . . Pallasu vidima i simpatichna tol'ko *bliz'*. Ot blizi k blizi on viazhet viaz'. Kriuchkami i petel'kami nadstavliaet svoi gorizont" ("The picture of Russia's vastness is composed in Pallas of infinitesimals. . . . Pallas sees and sympathizes with only what is *near*. From the near to the near he fastens a ligature. With small hooks and loops he adds on to his horizon").[41] Mandelstam derives such oxymoronic vision in the "Octaves," where five of the six lexical items in the first sentence of the prose passage (*ogromnost'* 'vastness', *slagaetsia* 'is composed', *beskonechnyi* 'infinite', *malyi* 'small', *velichina* 'quantity') occur in some form (the sixth, *kartina* 'picture', is given through a synonym, *risunki* 'drawings'; forms related to *bliz'* '[the] near' and *kriuchki* 'small hooks' occur too). The plot of those poems involves a move from "sunny . . . reality,"[42] bright three-dimensional space, into a central and infinitesimal "inner darkness" that is revealed to exist in an extraspatial and limitless dimension. The imperative of the "Octaves" is the penetration of the new dimension; the "inner excess" is the type of the salience formed in the process of growth: "Poniat' prostranstva vnutrennii izbytok / I lepestka i kupola zalog" ("To comprehend the inner excess of space / And the guarantee of the petal and the cupola"). Penetration is the task of an eye that resembles its obdurate object: "Preodolev za*tverzh*ennost' prirody / Golubo*tverd*yi glaz pronik v ee zakon" ("Overcoming the induracy of nature, / The blue-hard eye penetrated its law"). Mandelstam makes this eye his own.[43]

Another Mandelstamian observer has a sensibility similar to Pallas's: Kashchei ("Ottogo vse neudachi" ["The cause of all failures"]), with his cat and his "cat's eye" (*koshachii glaz*), an organ of vision that is also a stone. The "metonymic" vision of the cat's eye, which "magnifies the detail (at the expense of the whole, as physiologists tell us)," is, Ronen shows, the "source of wealth" for Mandelstam: it is poetic vision.[44] Pallas describes several cats in the journals of his Russian travels,[45] and Mandelstam's Pallas, too, has a cat: "It seems to me that he managed to cover all Russia from Moscow to the Caspian—with a large spoiled Siberian cat on his knees. . . . The cat was most likely deaf [*glukhoi*],[46] graying behind the ear."[47] Mandelstam treats Beethoven's deafness as a symptom and a cause of his musical genius.[48] The owner of the "deaf" cat has his own compensatory capacity, extraordinary vision.

For Mandelstam, who realizes literally the implications of Goethe's optics, the naturalist's probing eye must be formed on the model of what it sees.[49] What Pallas discovers with his cat's eye, therefore, is a mineral formation, moreover a stone that is also an organ of vision. "Overcom[ing] nature's induracy" is a task important to the author of *Stone*—the poet who would approach Dante "with a geological hammer" ("Nikto ne podkhodil k Dantu s geologicheskim molotkom"). Mandelstam is especially interested in Pallas's geological finds. Pallas uncovers a wealth of life in unexpected places:

> No one succeeded as Pallas did in removing from the Russian landscape the gray shroud of coachman's ennui. In its [imaginary] monotony, which has driven our poets sometimes to despair, sometimes to mournful ecstasy, he spied an unheard-of [variety of grains, of materials, of seams] a rich vital content. Pallas is a talented soil scientist. Streaked feldspar and dark blue clays go to his heart. . . .
>
> He experiences a natural pride on the occasion of the marine origins of the white and yellow Simbirian mountains and rejoices in their geological nobility.[50]

Pallas reads history in the stone. His work has a counterpart in the activity of the "blue-hard eye" that "penetrates [nature's] law," revealing the species beneath the earth's crust ("V zemnoi kore iurodstvuiut porody" ["In the earth's crust the rocks act the holy fool"]) and the shape of things to come ("I tianetsia glukhoi nedorazvitok, / Kak by dorogoi, sognutoiu v rog" ["And the obscure embryo stretches, / Like a road bent into a horn"]). Mandelstam gives another version of this activity in *Journey to Armenia*: "Telesnuiu kruglost' i liubeznost' nemetskoi muzyki on perenes na russkie ravniny. Belymi rukami kontsertmeistera on sobiraet rossiiskie griby. Syraia zamsha, gniloi barkhat, a razlomish'—vnutri lazur'" ("The corporeal roundness and courtesy of German music he transferred to the Russian plains. With the white hands of a concertmaster he collects Russian mushrooms. Damp chamois, rotting velvet, but if you break it open—there's azure inside").[51] The last image, which suggests the tendency of the white boletus mushrooms to show a bluish tinge when broken open,[52] encapsulates the discursive draft description of Pallas's ability to perceive the riches beneath the earth and, "cracked open," reveals the implications of his geological finds. *Lazur'*, in its original sense, is stone, 'lapis lazuli'; it is also the sea ("Sol'em tvoiu lazur' i nashe chernomor'e" ["We'll mingle your azure and our Black Sea"]) and the sky ("Lazur' da glina, glina da lazur'" ["Azure and clay, clay and azure"]).[53] The epithets *syroi*[54] and *gniloi* suggest damp, humid weather; both refer also to inorganic matter: *gniloi kamen'* is a cracked specimen of smoky topaz; *syroi* applies to unworked metal. Mandelstam represents the process by which atmospheric changes are encoded in the geological record, the conjunction of the meteorological and mineralogical spheres.[55]

In the "autobiographical confession" of *Conversation about Dante,* where he admits to having "consulted" with stones in conceiving that prose, Mandelstam identifies the conjunction of spheres, taking stone, which chronicles atmospheric change, as an analogue to Dante's revolutionary construction of time. The mineral form he calls a "diary of the weather," disclosing the "synchronism of events sundered by the ages," is another version of the layers of time turned up by the plow of poetry. Mandelstam represents Dante's "union of what cannot be united" in terms of quartz: "The interior of quartz, the Aladdin's space [*prostranstvo*] concealed in it, the luminescence, the incandescence, the chandelier's suspension of the fish rooms heaped in it—is the best of keys to the comprehension of the Comedy's coloration."[56] Dante's future-oriented vision has the structure of Pallas's: that oxymoronic compound of decaying vegetable matter and a precious mineral substance. The other geological metaphor for the poet's temporality finds a concrete embodiment in Pallas's unidentified discovery in the Russian plains.

That discovery can, after all, be identified. The stone discovered is substantially like the subject who finds it. In his Russian *Travels,* Pallas refers to mineral formations resembling the one Mandelstam describes as the traveler's find in "Around the Naturalists" and consults in *Conversation about Dante:* he observes "globular pieces [of sandstone] of various sizes, which, on breaking them, were partly hollow, and contained sand not unlike geodites"; elsewhere he mentions "amygdalite" formations.[57] The mineralogist A. E. Fersman, another source Mandelstam would have consulted, identifies similar formations in his comprehensive catalogue of stones found in Russia, calling them by various names: *zheoda, mindal'nye porody, mindal'nyi kamen', mindalina, mandel'shtein.*[58] Brokgauz-Efron has an entry for *mindal'nyi kamen',* alternatively *mandel'shtein:*

Porous varieties of ancient rocks in which the pores are filled with new mineral formations. These fillings of pores and empty places often have the form of almonds [*mindalin*] (and also of spheres, cylinders), whence their name. They appear especially often in the family of agate porphyries and melaphyres.

The geode, like the eye that discovers it, functions metonymically, its unprepossessing shell containing a crystalline treasure. It is one of Mandelstam's "oxymoronic images of inner wealth and outer poverty."[59] As *mindalina,* which has the second meaning "almond," the geode is linked to a fruit of which the antithetical varieties (bitter and sweet, hard-shelled and soft-shelled) originate in a single species (cf. Mandelstam's treatment of the oxymoronic almond in the drafts to the fifth chapter of *Journey to Armenia*).[60] Discovered by Mandelstam, who takes Pallas's cat's eye (the eye of *Felis* **manul**) as the prototypical organ of vision, *mandel'shtein* is the poet's name, his first word, and thus, as Mandelstam suggests in discussing the naturalist's eye, itself an organ of vision: the poet's way of cognizing and describing the universe. The implications of the discovery are enormous. The geode "rewards the reader's effort a hundredfold."

An almondate eye appears at the end of "Around the Naturalists," the figure for a Persian miniature in a volume of Firdusi's *Book of Kings:* "Persidskaia *min*iatiura kosit ispugannym gratsioznym *mindale*vidnym okom" ("The Persian miniature squints with a frightened graceful almond eye").[61] The description is motivated by another sense of *mindalina*— "tonsil." An illustration in a book in which the "earth and sky are sick with goiter—. . . ravishingly exophthalmic [*pucheglazy*]," and thus linked to the geode also through that glandular condition, the miniature is another example of the salience (*vypuklost'*) formed in the process of growth.[62] The skewed dimensions of the painting make the salience, with its inner excess, the spatial realization of the temporal perspective Mandelstam attributes to Persian poetry, which contains "longevity" and endows its reader with millennia.[63] The geodal miniature illustrates the temporality Mandelstam describes as Dante's in *Conversation about Dante* and ascribes to poetic language more generally in "The Word and Culture," with the Dantean vision of the poets of the past as contemporaries in the future (cf. *Inferno* 4): "This is a characteristic of all poetry, inasmuch as it is classical. It is perceived as what must be, and not as what already has been."[64] This is the fullness of time Mandelstam represents in "Alagez," where he takes, as the "prototype of our entire culture," the Latin gerundive, the future passive participle, an imperative of a more ancient speech.[65] Mandelstam's Odysseus achieves a state of fullness, in his first hypostasis in Mandelstam's work, in the 1917 poem "Zolotistogo meda struia iz butylki tekla" ("A

stream of golden honey flowed from the bottle"): "I, pokinuv korabl',
natrudivshii v moriakh polotno, / Odissei vozvratilsia, prostranstvom i
vremenem polnyi" ("And, abandoning ship, wearing out the sail in the
seas, / Odysseus has returned, full of space and time"). *Journey to Armenia,* which can be read as a Dantean canticle, traces a journey into that ideal
time. Mandelstam's travel journal follows the *Purgatorio* in particular, as
the record of a journey from an island (Sevan, in the first chapter) up a
mountain (Alagez, in the last). In "Sevan," Mandelstam describes life on an
island as a state of "noble expectation,"[66] suggesting the anticipation of the
purgatorial ascent. Mandelstam's mountain, moreover, resembles Dante's:
apparently inaccessible from the base, it reveals itself to be progressively
easier along the way: "It [Alagez] seemed to me a monolithic ridge. In fact
it is a plicated system and unfolds gradually—with the ascent the barrel
organ of the diorite strata unwound like an Alpine waltz."[67] The pilgrim
ascending the Armenian mountain enters a purgatorial temporality.[68]
Training his eye in Armenia, he envisions a new dimension.

❖ ❖

In the penultimate chapter of *Journey to Armenia,* "Ashtarak," Mandelstam alludes to the attainment of a new dimension with reference to
Ararat, the prototypical Armenian mountain and the legendary location of
the Garden of Eden and the Earthly Paradise. Describing the "cultiva[tion
of] a sixth—'Araratian'—sense: the sense of the attraction of the mountain" ("Ia v sebe vyrabotal shestoe—'araratskoe' chuvstvo: chuvstvo pri-
tiazheniia goroi").[69] Mandelstam invokes a version of organic processes
that is a model for the conception of growth explored in *Journey to Armenia:* a view associated with Lamarck's evolutionary theory, where the
organism, responding to need, "acquires" a characteristic that becomes,
over time (through habit), instinctual. But Mandelstam implies the conscious elaboration of the characteristic response ("vyrabotal"). He suggests
a deliberation that is absent, according to Lamarck, in animals.[70] In
Lamarck's conception, instinct arises "from the needs and propensities
which arouse immediately the individual's inner feeling and make him act,
*without any choice or deliberation, or, in short, any participation of the
intellect.*"[71] Thus thought has no place in the response to the "note" of
the "Octaves": "I na nee nemedlenno otvet'" ("And one must answer it
right away").[72] Elsewhere in *Journey to Armenia,* Mandelstam distinguishes people from "lower" forms of life in terms of the capacity of
consciousness not just to respond mechanically to the environment but to
control it. Unlike the salamander, which is not aware that the patterns on its
spine change according to its surroundings, a person "attempts to guess

[*ugadyvaet*] tomorrow's weather—so as to determine [*opredelit'*] his coloration himself."[73] Here Mandelstam uses *opredelit'* as "determine" in the sense of "fix" and not just "discover."[74]

The traveler's sixth sense, his instinct, is "second nature," that is, culture: "ono uzhe umozritel'no, i ostanetsia" ("it is already theoretical, and it will remain"). Mandelstam takes Lamarck's idea of "cultivation" in another sense. His motivation is a moral compulsion, thus human, not animal (not food, sexual fertilization, avoidance of pain, search for pleasure).[75] Yet by putting this compulsion in the context of Lamarck's instinct, Mandelstam suggests that it is as much a need as those physiological responses; the mechanism is similar, but the situation acquires a metaphysical level appropriate to the "higher" level of human consciousness.

The reference to Ararat is followed by the account of another move into an extraordinary dimension: the "first sensory encounter with the material of an ancient Armenian church"—stone:

> The little Ashtarak church is the most ordinary and, for Armenia, humble. So—a tiny church with a six-faceted *kamelaukion,* a rope ornament along the cornice of the roof and similar stringy brows over the stingy lips of the chink-like windows.
>
> The door is quiet as a mouse. I stood on tiptoe and peeked in; but there's a cupola, a cupola!
>
> A real one! Like in Rome at St. Peter's, beneath which there are crowds of many thousands and palms, and a sea of candles, and litters.
>
> There the hollowed spheres of the apses sing like shells [*rakoviny*].[76] There, the four bakers: north, west, south, and east—with punched-out eyes poke into the funnel-shaped niches, stumble about the hearths and the areas between them, and can't find a place for themselves.
>
> Who got the idea of enclosing space in this pitiful little vault, this miserable dungeon—in order to render it, there, homage worthy of the psalmist?[77]

Mandelstam's church is a concretion of space in stone; it is another growth, an instance of the protoform.[78] Concealing enormous capacity in a tiny compass, the church, like the geode, embodies the sense of "inner wealth and outer poverty" that characterizes Mandelstam's spiritual strivings at the time. The image of the church arises in the context of deprivation and loss; it is recollected from Zamoskovorech'e (where Mandelstam considered himself, "thanks to [his] birth . . . just an accidental guest").[79] The "comprehen[sion of] the inner excess," the imperative of the "Octaves," counters that experience of the "watermelon emptiness of Russia." Comparable to the ascent of the mountain, it is the correlative function, the "need" to which the acquisition of a sixth sense responds.

In a draft to the "Ashtarak" passage, Mandelstam describes the infernal preparation for the purgatorial ascent. Again the language is his touchstone:

> Я хочу познать свою кость, свою лаву, свое гробовое дно, [как под ним заиграет и магнием и фосфором жизнь, как мне улыбнется она: членистокрылая, пенящаяся, жужжащая]. Выйти к Арарату на каркающую, крошащуюся и харкающую окраину. Упереться всеми [границами] фибрами моего существа в невозможность выбора, в отсутствие всякой свободы. Отказаться добровольно от светлой нелепицы воли и разума. [Если приму, как заслуженное и присносущее, звукоодетость, каменнокровность и твердокаменность, значит, я недаром побывал в Армении]
>
> Если приму как заслуженное и тень от дуба и тень от гроба и твердокаменность членораздельной речи, — как я тогда почувствую современность?
>
> [Что мне она? Пучок восклицаний и междометий! А я для нее живу . . .]
>
> Для этого-то я и обратился к изучению древнеармянского языка. Структура нашего. . . .[80]

> I want to get to know my bone, my lava, the bottom of my grave [how beneath it life will begin to sparkle with magnesium and phosphorus, how it will smile at me: arthropteric, frothing, droning]. To go out onto Ararat, to its croaking, crumbling, expectorating margins. To take a stand, with all the [boundaries] fibers of my being, on the impossibility of choice, the absence of all freedom. To renounce voluntarily the bright absurdity of will and reason. [If I accept, as time-honored and everlasting, being clothed in sound, stone-blooded, and hard as stone, then my time in Armenia has not been wasted]
>
> If I accept as time-honored the shade of the oak and the shade of the grave and the hard stoniness of articulate speech—what happens then to my sense of contemporary life?
>
> [What is it to me? A bundle of exclamations and interjections! And that's what I live for . . .]
>
> It's for this reason that I turned to the study of the ancient Armenian language.[81] The structure of ours. . . .)

The "bright absurdity of volition and reason" is of a piece with the "bundle of exclamations and interjections," the mode of speech associated with "contemporary life." Mandelstam qualifies the definition in "Sukhum": "It's terrible to live in a world consisting entirely of exclamations and interjections!" ("Strashno zhit' v mire, sostoiashchem iz odnikh vosklitsanii i mezhdometii!").[82] He opposes the fearful, ephemeral contemporary mode to the Armenian sojourn, the condition of which is learning the ancient *grabar.*

A description of that unpromising and uncompromising tongue is interpolated in the account of Karmravor:[83] "The Armenian language does not get worn out—it's stone boots. Well, of course, a thick-walled word, seams of air in the semivowels."[84] The structure of inner excess implicit in the language description reflects the archaic origins of the word. In "Ashtarak," Mandelstam indicates that he made use of N. Ia. Marr's grammar in his study of Armenian ("Sometimes I awaken [*prosypaius'*] at night and repeat [*tverzhu*] to myself conjugations from Marr's grammar"),[85] and in "Ashot Ovanesian," the second chapter of *Journey to Armenia*,[86] mentioning his attempts to arrange instruction in Armenian, he takes up the problem of Marr's etymologies. He suggests an intellectual genealogy, a derivation of *Marr* from L*amar*ck. He discusses the Japhetic theory of the origins of all languages in four primordial roots in terms of a Lamarckian phylogeny of language, where speech, existing, as Marr suggests, at a preconceptual stage, is contemporary with the needs and inclinations of the primitive organism: "At the very deepest stages of speech there were no conceptions, just tendencies, terrors, and desires, just needs and apprehensions."[87] At the instinctual level of organization, the word appears as a single complex, a salience: "Seeing, hearing, and understanding—all these meanings were mingled at one time in a single semantic bundle [*puchok*]."[88] Its embryonic form remains evident in the functioning of the word. In *Conversation about Dante,* Mandelstam calls the word a "bundle [*puchok*] . . . [from which] meaning protrudes in various directions."[89] In "Moscow," he describes organic growth as the formation of a salience, much as he describes the word: "Take any point and connect it through a bundle [*puchok*] of coordinates with a straight line. Then continue these coordinates, intersecting the straight line at various angles, at a segment of identical length, connect them to each other, and you will get a salience [*vypuklost'*]."[90] *Vypuklost'* echoes *semanticheskii puchok* (the antithesis of "puchok vosklitsanii i mezhdometii," the "bundle of exclamations and interjections" that is contemporary life for the poet). The word as growth or salience retains its original multiplicity of meanings. Its structure is cognate with consciousness. It functions as the poet penetrates the layers of experience—as memory recreates the initial conditions of its formation, when all senses functioned together. To that extent, the word remains archaic, primitive. An extraordinary instinct is required for its comprehension: the development of the sixth sense in Armenia is essential to the return to archaic speech. This is a journey into the unconscious,[91] to the preconceptual stage of language; "embryological experience" is the corresponding physiological realm.

The preparation for the ascent of the mountain involves tracing life to its archaic origins,[92] to the paleontological remains, to encounter what

Mandelstam calls in "Sukhum" the "substantial evidence of existence."[93] Like Lamarck, he distinguishes between the ephemeral manifestations of life and a countervailing force. The Lamarckian coordinates of the scene are illuminated by a passage in René Berthelot's 1932 study of Goethe in relation to Lamarck and Hegel. The author of *Science et philosophie chez Goethe* quotes an account, by the hero of Sainte-Beuve's autobiographical novel *Volupté,* of the "impression Lamarck's lectures made on him" (cf. Mandelstam's own descriptions, in "Around the Naturalists," of Lamarck as a teacher, and of a butterfly located, he implies, on Lamarck's "staircase," as a "French academician"):[94]

> Dans l'ordre organique, une fois admis *ce pouvoir mysterieux de la vie,* aussi petit et aussi élémentaire que possible, il le supposait se développant luimeme, se composant, se confectionnant peu à peu avec le temps; le besoin sourd, la seule habitude dans les milieux divers fasait naître a la longue les organes, contrairement au pouvoir constant de la nature qui les détruisait; *car M. de Lamarck séparait la vie d'avec la nature. La nature, à ses yeux, c'était la pierre et la cendre, le granit de la tombe, la mort!* La vie n'y intervenait que comme un accident étrange et singulierement industrieux, une lutte prolongée avec plus ou moins de succes ou d'équilibre ça et là, mais toujours finalement vaincue; l'immobilité froide était régnante après comme devant.[95]

The description of life "interven[ing] as an accident," with the adverbial "ça et là," corresponds to Mandelstam's image of life "sparkl[ing]"—occasionally, fortuitously—from the bottom of the grave. Lamarck's "nature," represented by "la pierre et la cendre, le granit de la tombe, la mort," is paralleled in Mandelstam's series "kost', . . . lava, . . . grobovoe dno."

Mandelstam characterizes these antitheses in "Around the Naturalists," in another Lamarckian passage: the "functions [of the medium] are expressed in a certain disposition, which is gradually and ceaselessly extinguished by the rigor [*surovost'*] binding the living body and rewarding it with death."[96] *Surovost'*[97] figures in the "Ashtarak" drafts as "nevozmozhnost' vybora, otsutstvie vsiakoi svobody" ("the impossibility of choice, the absence of any freedom"). The infernal path to the purgatorial mountain is a rigorous one. It promises the hard certainty, the "substantial evidence" the traveler goes in search of; hence his determination to take a firm stand here. The traveler reiterates his purpose in "Alagez," the last chapter of *Journey to Armenia,* where the descent becomes an ascent: "Ia khochu zhit' v povelitel'nom prichastii budushchego, v zaloge stradatel'nom—v 'dolzhenstvuiushchem byt'' " ("I want to live in the future imperative participle, in the passive voice—in 'what must be' ").[98] His interest in the future passive participle has nothing to do with desire, just as the need that results in the attraction to the mountain is not facultative but obligatory: *ia khochu* 'I want,' here as in "Ashtarak," is "mean," "intend."[99] A comparable usage occurs in "Grifel'naia oda" ("The Slate Ode"): "I ia khochu vlozhit' persty / V kremnistyi put' iz staroi pesni" ("And I want to insert my fingers / Into the flinty path from the old song"). Ronen comments: "What the protagonist of GO wishes to 'understand by tactual verification' is . . . the reality of martyrdom . . . , [the] reality of life and death."[100] *Ia khochu* is motivated by the sense that there is no other way for the traveler in Armenia: hence the imperative, "what must be." Mandelstam does not propose to embrace the fate he envisions, but he means to go out and confront it.[101]

In this intention Mandelstam remains true to his Acmeist origins. He had written in the final lines of his first prose manifesto: "we will learn to bear 'more lightly and willingly the mobile [*podvizhnye*] fetters of being.'"[102] Those mobile fetters find their counterpart in 1932 in Lamarck's "mobile staircase" (*podvizhnaia lestnitsa*), which, in the eponymous poem, the poet announces his intention to descend; the lightness and freedom with which they are to be worn correspond to the "voluntary" spirit (*dobrovol'no*) in which he renounces volition and reason. For Mandelstam this act is perfectly reasonable. *Volia,* renounced in the "Ashtarak" descent, becomes the imperative **velenie* (*povelitel'noe*) of the "Alagez" ascent. The poet deprived of the ordinary senses cultivates other, extraordinary ones.

The blind naturalist, like the deaf composer, is exemplary in this respect: "Lamarck cried his eyes out into a magnifying glass. His blindness is equivalent to Beethoven's deafness."[103] In "Lamark" the poet vows, in protest against the degradation of humanity,[104] to become an annelid or an amoeba, renouncing his warm-blooded existence. But the shift, after the fourth stanza, from the future tense to the past distinguishes the intention from the attempt:

ЛАМАРК

Был старик, застенчивый как мальчик,
Неуклюжий, робкий патриарх . . .
Кто за честь природы фехтовальщик?
Ну, конечно, пламенный Ламарк.

Если всё живое лишь помарка
За короткий выморочный день,
На подвижной лестнице Ламарка
Я займу последнюю ступень.

К кольчецам спущусь и к усоногим,
Прошуршав средь ящериц и змей,

По упругим сходням, по излогам
Сокращусь, исчезну, как Протей.

Роговую мантию надену,
От горячей крови откажусь,
Обрасту присосками и в пену
Океана завитком вопьюсь.

Мы прошли разряды насекомых
С наливными рюмочками глаз.
Он сказал: природа вся в разломах,
Зренья нет—ты зришь в последний раз.

Он сказал: довольно полнозвучья,—
Ты напрасно Моцарта любил:
Наступает глухота паучья,
Здесь провал сильнее наших сил.

И от нас природа отступила—
Так, как будто мы ей не нужны,
И продольный мозг она вложила,
Словно шпагу, в темные ножны.

И подъемный мост она забыла,
Опоздала опустить для тех,
У кого зеленая могила,
Красное дыханье, гибкий смех.

(LAMARCK

There was an old man, as bashful as a boy,
An awkward, timid patriarch . . .
Who is the fencer for nature's honor?
But of course, the ardent Lamarck.

If everything that lives is just a blot
For the short escheated day,
On Lamarck's moving staircase
I will occupy the last step.

I will descend to the annelids and the cirripeds,
Rustling amid the lizards and the snakes,
On the elastic gangplanks, in the hollows,
I will decrease, disappear, like Proteus.

I will put on a horn mantle,
I will repudiate warm blood,
I will grow suckers and stick
A tendril into the ocean foam.

We passed by ranks of insects
With liqueur tumblers for eyes.
He said: nature's all in tatters,
There's no vision—you see for the last time.

He said: enough sonorousness,
You loved Mozart in vain:
A spider's deafness is encroaching,
Here the gap is stronger than our strength.

And nature retreated from us—
As if it had no need for us,
And it inserted the longitudinal brain,
Like a sword, in a dark sheath.

And it forgot the drawbridge,
Was late lowering it for those
Who have a green grave,
Red breath, supple laughter.)

The break at the midpoint of the poem is emblematic of the "gap" in nature between man and other species. Descending with Lamarck his Virgil, the poet loses the use of his senses. Like Dante in the Inferno, however, he does not join the ranks he moves through.

The poet on the lower steps of Lamarck's staircase is deprived of sight and hearing not because, as he proposes in the first part of the poem, he is transformed into a creature lacking the proper organs of perception, but because those faculties are not needed in the primitive world. The poet "sees for the last time" because "there is no vision" ("Zren'ia net"); he has "loved Mozart in vain" because "a spider's deafness is encroaching" ("Nastupaet glukhota pauch'ia"). Cf. the imprisoned king Arshak in the tale at the end of *Journey to Armenia:* "3. His ears have grown stupid from the stillness, but once they listened to Greek music. 4. His tongue is covered with scabs from the jailors' food, but there was a time when it used to press grapes to his palate and it was adroit, like the end of a flutist's tongue."[105] The tragedy is that the poet, who cannot relinquish his human features, goes to a place where they are useless, as they would be in a "Darwinian" system—and that is the point of the protest.

It is the loss of the senses in full consciousness that makes the descent to lower forms an "inferno for man" ("Nizshie formy organicheskogo bytiia—ad dlia cheloveka").[106] Passages from Raymond Queneau's *Gueule de pierre* (1934), quoted by Viach. Vs. Ivanov in his comparison of "Lamarck" to Queneau's book,[107] illustrate the distinction between man's continued consciousness and the oblivion of lower creatures. For the human who descends, there is pain: "Avec les invertébrés, commence l'angoisse." For the simplest water creatures that inhabit those realms, there is none: "Cette cellule autonome . . . vit *aveugle, silencieuse et sourde. Et sans crainte: car elle ne connaît pas d'ennemis. Elle ne connaît qu'une autre unité, une unité nutritive et ne connaît pas les multiplicités dévorantes.*" These creatures lack just the capacities that Mandelstam's protagonist is deprived of as he descends.[108] But they also lack the consciousness of deprivation—a consciousness the human protagonist retains. The protagonist of "Lamarck" has failed in his stated purpose, in that he has not joined lower forms. He is prevented by consciousness, which persists in spite of blindness and deafness. But in thus continuing to live as if life were more than a temporary, intestate "blot," he is victorious: "In the reverse, descending movement with Lamarck down the staircase of living creatures is Dante's greatness."[109] Not sight and hearing but other capacities finally distinguish man from lower forms.[110]

In the last stanza of "Lamarck," nature rejects the one with "a green grave, red breath, supple laughter." Laughter, according to Bergson, is a uniquely human attribute; it is related to intelligence.[111] Breathing is Mandelstam's metonymy for the poet's activity. The "red breath," aerobic respiration, is characteristic of man as opposed to cold-blooded creatures. In *Journey to Armenia,* blood spilled is a measure of passion: "Skol'ko krovi prolito iz-za etikh nedotrog!" ("How much blood has been spilled over these touch-me-nots!"—with reference to Mandelstam's beloved Persian miniatures),[112] while in "Akh, nichego ia ne vizhu, i bednoe ukho oglokhlo" ("Ah, I can't see a thing, and my poor ear has grown deaf"), one of the "Armenia" poems, the failure to "spill hot blood" suggests a lack of engagement: "Ia bestolkovuiu zhizn', kak mulla svoi koran, zamusolil, / Vremia svoe zamorozil i krovi goriachei ne prolil" ("I have worn out a pointless life, as a mullah would his Koran, / I have frozen my time and I haven't spilled hot blood") (the poet's blindness and deafness, however, are attended by inner vision: "I pochemu-to mne nachalo utro armianskoe snit'sia" ["And for some reason I started dreaming of the Armenian morning"]). The dynamics of "Lamarck" reflect the dichotomy Berthelot observes: "car M. de Lamarck séparait la vie d'avec la nature." The naturalist is defending nature's honor; but he is therefore engaged in a struggle with nature, which rejects man, for the meaning of life. Nature retreats from this medieval combat, putting away its weapon (*otstupila; . . . vlozhila slovno shpagu v temnye nozhny;* cf. the other images of battle and attack: *fekhtoval'shchik* 'fencer', *nastupaet* 'is attacking [encroaching]', *shpagu* 'sword', *nozhny* 'sheath', *pod"emnyi most* 'drawbridge'). At the same time, in its indifference to man, nature "sheathes" the longitudinal brain,[113] giving notice that creatures from here on are deprived of the spinal cord.[114] In Berthelot's description, it is life that loses the Lamarckian battle ("une lutte prolongée . . . mais toujours finalement vaincue"). But in Mandelstam's poem, the "green grave" itself is an enduring monument, testament to the one interred.[115] Though nature abandons man, he remains, with his memory, language, consciousness. The poet in "Lamarck" confirms the truth, the denial of which he protests: the preservation of man's efforts beyond his lifetime. The descent is an affirmation of the qualities that determine humanity.

❖ ❖

The language learned on the journey is appropriate to the descent as a move back in phylogenetic and ontogenetic time. Mandelstam's Armenia is a land of beasts and infants: "[Ty] nianchish' zverushek detei" ("You nurse cub children") in "Ty rozu Gafiza kolyshesh'" ("You ruffle the rose of Hafiz"); Armenian is a beast's language: "Dikaia koshka—armianskaia rech'— / Khishchnyi iazyk gorodov glinobitnykh" ("A wild cat—the Armenian speech— / The rapacious language of pisé cities") in "Koliuchaia rech' araratskoi doliny" ("Prickly speech of the Ararat valley"). The "frothing" and "droning," "croaking" and "expectorating" encountered on the mountain sound like Mandelstam's version of the language of Dante's most infernal passages, where speech is "turned back," acquiring an "infantile orchestration."[116] Ronen compares the infantile language of Mandelstam's Dante with the guttural speech of his literature teacher V. V. Gippius.[117] In its hardness and inevitability ("Kak liub mne iazyk tvoi zloveshchii, / Tvoi molodye groba, / Gde bukvy—kuznechnye kleshchi, / I kazhdoe slovo—*skoba*" ["How dear to me your menacing language, / Your young graves, / Where the letters are smithies' tongs, / And every word is a clamp"]),[118] Mandelstam's Armenian resembles the prototype of his childhood babble, the speech of his father, with its counterpart in the "Judaic chaos" of the Hebrew volumes on the lower shelves of the bookcase.

Armenian enters a complex of imagery that has origins in Mandelstam's childhood language. The speech of beasts appears nearly a decade before *Journey to Armenia,* in the 1923 sketch about the Moscow bazaar, "Sukharevka": "bazarnaia rech', kak khishchnyi zverek, sverkaet malen'-kimi zubkami" ("the bazaar speech, like a rapacious beast cub, flashes its little teeth").[119] At the bazaar, where books lie scattered alongside hardware ("cherez rassypannyi na zemle *skob*ianoi tovar, cherez knigi"), Mandelstam redeploys items that appeared in the account of the bookcase: "Books. What books, what titles: *Beautiful Dark Eyes . . . The Talmud and* *the Jews,* unsuccessful collections of verse whose childish cry rang out fifteen years ago."[120] As in *The Noise of Time,* Mandelstam juxtaposes Judaica and poetry, books close to the ground and childhood. As in that prose, the smell of leather pervades the scene, and is associated with work: "to kvadratnyi *zapakh dublenoi kozhi, zapakh iarma i truda,*—i tot zhe, no smiagchennyi i plutovatyi zapakh sapozhnogo tovara" ("now the intense *smell of tanned leather, the smell of the yoke and labor*—and the same, but softened and cunning, smell of the cobbler's trade").[121] The same phrases reappear in "The Bookcase," where, among a number of objects in the study of Mandelstam's father, objects "bound together closely in [the poet's] consciousness," immediately preceding the bookcase is the leather that was the material of his father's trade: "Do sikh por mne kazhetsia *zapakhom iarma i truda* pronikaiushchii vsiudu *zapakh dublenoi kozhi,* i lapchatye shkurki laiki, raskidannye na polu, i zhivye, kak pal'tsy, otrostki pukhloi zamshi—vse eto, i meshchanskii pis'mennyi stol s mramornym kalendarikom, plavaet v tabachnom dymu i obkureno kozhami" ("To this day *the smell of tanned leather,* penetrating everywhere, seems to me *the smell of the yoke and labor,* and the web-footed kid hides, scattered over the floor, and the shoots of plump chamois, alive, like fingers—all this, and the bourgeois writing desk with the marble calendar, floats in tobacco smoke and is seasoned with the smell of hides").[122] These objects are "bound together closely," too, in the prose of the 1920s, and their traces are associated with the poet's work in the prose of the 1930s, when Mandelstam returns to the problem of infantile speech.

Mandelstam describes his father as virtually speechless: "U ottsa sovsem ne bylo iazyka, eto bylo kosnoiazychie i bez"iazychie" ("My father had no language, it was inarticulateness and languagelessness"); "Chto khotela skazat' sem'ia? Ia ne znaiu. Ona byla kosnoiazychna ot rozhde-niia,—a mezhdu tem u nee bylo chto skazat'. Nado mnoi i nad mnogimi sovremennikami tiagoteet kosnoiazychie rozhdeniia. My uchilis' ne gov-orit', a lepetat'—i, lish' prislushivaias' k narastaiushchemu shumu veka i vybelennye penoi ego grebnia, my obreli iazyk" ("What did my family want to say? I don't know. It was congenitally tongue-tied—yet it had something to say. Congenital tongue-tie hangs over my head and the heads of many contemporaries. We learned not to speak, but to babble, and only listening to the swelling noise of the age and whitened by the foam of its crest did we acquire a language").[123] And while Mandelstam will not identify his father's speech with any particular language, he attributes to him, as Epstein notes, the "whimsical syntax of a Talmudist."[124] His father's tongue-tied speech depends on his Jewish roots.

Mandelstam "always tried to escape" the "Judaic chaos,"[125] and the influence of Judaism is correspondingly pervasive.[126] In "The Bookcase," he attributes to the Jewishness of his home the same fundamental significance he finds in the childhood bookcase: "As a crumb of musk fills a house, so the slightest influence of Judaism fills to overflowing an entire lifetime."[127] Jewishness is linked to an unorganized, unsystematic universe—to time out of joint—in *The Noise of Time:* the Jewish year began in September, by contrast with the "round Russian year," which "rolled along according to the calendar."[128] In the 1930s, the idea of the reverse course of time, associated negatively with Judaism also in the Scriabin essay,[129] acquired different connotations. Nikolai Otsup, who contrasts the "captive chaos" beneath Mandelstam's "crystalline clarity" (linking him to Tiutchev) with Pasternak's merely "external chaos" and the essential "integrity and chasteness of his 'spiritual well-being,'" hears in "Lamarck" the "most profound theme of Mandelstam's lyrics"; a "new manifestation of [his] fascination with 'primordial chaos,' this pull back from culture to prehistory."[130] F. B. Uspenskii links the descent in "Lamarck" with the return to the origins of language in the 1909 poem "Silentium."[131] Thus, too, the paternal Judaism, perceived initially as a limitation, a handicap, becomes a source of extraordinary power. Inarticulateness (*kosnoiazychie*) is a constructive element of Mandelstam's poetics. Nor is the opposition Mandelstam establishes in *The Noise of Time,* between articulate Russian and the hereditary tongue-tie, an opposition between speech and muteness.[132] It is an opposition between the historical "language" and the eternal "babble," and the recognition of the entrance of prophetic language into time. "Babble," the poet's original speech, is the origins of the poet's speech: "On opyt iz lepeta lepit, / I lepet iz opyta p'et" ("He fashions the experiment from babble, / And drinks babble from the experiment").[133]

The "outcast" (*otverzhennye*) sounds of ancient Armenian recall Mandelstam's "first" word, Tiutchev's stone, fallen from the mountaintop (*nizvernut,* in the version of "Problème" that Mandelstam quotes), the stone rejected by the builders, which, Ronen indicates, Mandelstam sets in the foundation of the Acmeist edifice in "The Morning of Acmeism."[134] Those sounds, recalling, too, the tomes of Judaica, the "Judaic chaos cast down into the dust" ("*povergnutyi* v pyl' khaos iudeiskii"), are "at some deep level, shameful" ("i, na kakoi-to glubine, postydnye").[135] In one of Mandelstam's early Jewish poems, "the depths" are associated with Judaism: "I glubina, gde stebli tonut, / Torzhestvovala svoi zakon" ("And the depth, where the stems sink, / Celebrated its law").[136] In Armenia the poet returns to the "deep stages" of language—preconceptual stages ("Na sa-

mykh glubinnykh stadiiakh rechi ne bylo poniatii").[137] Thus the shame of
speech is not the sense that compels Mandelstam's Hebrew teacher to "hide
his pride [in his Jewishness] when he goes out into the street."[138] It is the
sense associated with the descent to the origins of language, to the place
where the word is born. It appears as the shyness of the heart in "Silentium," a function of the return to the primordial medium: "I serdtse serdtsa
u*stydi*s', / S pervoosnovoi zhizni slito" ("And heart, shy away from
heart, / Fused with the first principle of life"). It appears again as the poet's
heightened sensibility in "The Swallow," one of the poems that Ronen
labels "Lethean Lines" for their characteristic plot of descent (*ka-
tabasis*):[139] "O esli by vernut' i zriachikh pal'tsev *styd,* / I vypukluiu
radost' uznavan'ia" ("Oh, if only one could bring back the shame of
sighted fingers, / And the salient joy of recognition"). The protagonist is
distinguished from "mortals," who live without the poet's consciousness
("Dlia nikh i zvuk v persty prol'etsia" ["For them even sound will flow into
the fingers"]) and therefore without the possibility of such loss ("A
smertnym vlast' dana liubit' i uznavat'" ["Now mortals are given the
power to love and to recognize"]).[140] The outcast and shameful language
learned on the mountain is poetic language by definition, as Gumilev
described it in his programmatic "Vos'mistishie" ("Octave"): "I, simvol gornego velich'ia / Kak nekii blagostnyi zavet, / Vysokoe kosnoiazych'e / Tebe daruetsia, poet" ("And, symbol of the heavenly majesty, / Like some righteous testament, / Sublime tongue-tie / Is given to
you, poet"). The "sublime slow tongue," Ronen notes, is the language that
the "poet shares with Moses."[141] Mandelstam's language is the language of
the tongue-tied prophet.

The connection between the paternal speech and the prophet's language is reinforced in the case of Mandelstam. The name Mandelstam
inherited from his father joins *Mandel* 'almond' (cf. *mindal'*) with *Stamm*
'trunk', 'stem'; 'family', 'clan', 'lineage'; 'root (of a word)'.[142] The image
of the oxymoronic almond has other childhood connections; Mandelstam
links it to the Judaic chaos in his autobiographical prose. The visits to his
paternal grandparents in Riga were steeped in the atmosphere that Mandelstam associated with the "bitter almond taste" (*gor'kii mindal'nyi vkus*) of
his grandmother's sweets.[143] Ronen writes that the "Biblical image of the
rod of almond tree (*Numbers* 17; *Jer.* 1) may have had a special meaning for
the author of 'Posox moj, moja svoboda.'"[144] He is referring to the staff of
Moses's brother Aaron, which flowered with almond blossoms, confirming
Aaron's right to represent the tribe of the Levites before God (Num. 17:8;
see also 17:5); Aaron was called on to interpret Moses's word to the people
(Num. 4:14–16), for Moses was, by his own admission, "tongue-tied":

"I skazal Moisei Gospodu: o, Gospodi! chelovek ia ne rechistyi . . . ia tiazhelo govoriu i kosnoiazychen" ("And Moses said unto the Lord, O my Lord, I *am* not eloquent . . . but I *am* slow of speech, and of a slow tongue") (Exod. 4:10; cf. 6:12).[145] The straightness and rightness associated with the rod of almond is juxtaposed to the "crookedness" of the prophet's speech, which Mandelstam reinterprets in "What street is this?" in terms of the "crookedness" of the name that means "rod of almond" ("Ulitsa Mandel'shtama. / Chto za familiia chertova! / Kak ee ni vyvertyvai, / Krivo zvuchit, a ne priamo" ["Mandelstam Street. / What a cursed name! However you turn it, / It sounds crooked, not straight"]). This is the prophetic situation—the tongue-tied speech that reveals the true word.

❖ ❖

The capacious cupola recurs in the "Octaves," as the likeness of a poetic period: "Kogda, unichtozhiv nabrosok, / Ty derzhish' prilezhno v ume / Period bez tiagostnykh snosok . . . / On tak zhe otnosit k bumage, / Kak kupol k pustym nebesam" ("When, destroying the draft, / You hold diligently in mind / A period without weighty notes . . . / It relates to the paper exactly / As the cupola does to the empty skies"). The cupola organizes the expanse of the skies; the period does the same for the paper and, by extension, the mind. In "Stikhi o neizvestnom soldate" ("Verses about the Unknown Soldier"), Mandelstam represents the human skull as a cupola: "Ponimaiushchim kupolom iasnitsia, / Mysl'iu penitsia, sam sebe snitsia— / Chasha chash i otchizna otchizne— / Zvezdnym rubchikom shityi chepets— / Chepchik schast'ia—Shekspira otets" ("It grows clear like a comprehending cupola, / It froths with thought, dreams of itself— / Cup of cups and homeland's homeland, / Cap sewn with a starry seam, / Little cap of happiness—Shakespeare's father"). In "Octaves," the same figure is implicit: "Byt' mozhet, my—Aiia-Sofiia / S beschislennym mnozhestvom glaz" ("Maybe we're Hagia Sophia / With a countless multitude of eyes"). That figure suggests the limitless visionary potential of the mind's eye. The skull, the brainpan, is the first instance of the geodal configuration in *Journey to Armenia,* as the object of the archaeological expeditions that are the preparation for Armenia in "Sevan."[146] Yet it is not just the generalized human brain that concerns Mandelstam. The skull is "Shakespeare's father." Mandelstam's purpose in Armenia is a discovery of origins, and the move into a new space is a journey, first of all, into the poet's own brain: the landmarks are peculiarly Mandelstamian.

Mandelstam classifies the visionary organ in "Ne iskushai chuzhikh narechii . . ." ("Do not attempt foreign tongues . . ."—Ronen's translation).[147] The language of Ariosto and Tasso has the salience, the hardness ("Ved' vse ravno ty ne sumeesh' stekla zubami ukusit'!" ["Anyway you can't bite glass with your teeth!"]) of the Armenian stone (into which Mandelstam had also tried to sink his teeth: "Zuby zreniia kroshatsia i oblamyvaiutsia, kogda smotrish' vpervye na armianskie tserkvi" ["Vision's teeth crumble and break off when you look at Armenian churches for the first time"]).[148] The Italian poets themselves appear to be stone: "Chto esli Ariost i Tasso, obvorozhaiushchie nas, / Chudovishcha s lazurnym mozgom i cheshuei iz vlazhnykh glaz" ("What if Ariosto and Tasso, bewitching us, / Are monsters with an azure brain and scales of moist eyes"). *Lazur'*, as I have noted, is lapis lazuli. *Mozg* is current in mineral terminology: *gornyi mozg* is a type of kaolin. *Cheshuiki* refer to the particles in a mineral conglomerate as well as to the scales of reptiles or fish. In his "autobiographical confession," Mandelstam describes the geodal formation with a comparable formulation: the crystals deposited in the stone are "fish rooms" (*ryb'i komnaty*). These monsters resemble Pallas's mineralogical find: the unsightly though—here, clearly—sighted exterior; the inner azure. The stone brain is a geode, *mandel'shtein*, realized externally, visually as an organ of vision (**lazurnyi mozg**—**glaz**; cf. **razlomish'**). In the context of a foreign language ("V poslednii raz pered razlukoi chuzhoe imia ne spaset" ["For the last time, just before parting, a foreign name is no salvation"]), Mandelstam discovers his own name (the antithesis of *chuzhoe imia, mindal'* occurs—the only instance in his verse—in "Staryi Krym," the other poem of May 1933 written in the Old Crimea: the almond, with its early profusion of blossoms, is a figure of loveliness inappropriate to that sorrowful landscape). As in Armenia—in "Ashtarak," with the descent to lower forms to find his own bone and stone, and in "Around the Naturalists," with the unexpected access of mineral wealth amid dross—in an alien, even hostile place, Mandelstam discovers what is native and his own.

In the land where "people's skulls are equally beautiful in the grave and at work,"[149] the descent to the grave turns into the ascent of the mountain. *Vyiti k Araratu* 'To go out onto Ararat' follows *poznat' svoiu kost'* 'to get to know my own bone' in the sequence of projected activities, for Ararat is the site of the redeemed Earthly Paradise, the end of time, as it is man's original home. The path through the Inferno brings the pilgrim to the center of the earth—whence, traveling in the same direction, he emerges on the other side, at the foot of Purgatory. This feature of the Dantean journey is reflected in *Inferno* 26, a focus of Mandelstam's discussion in the fifth section of *Conversation about Dante*. Mandelstam com-

ments on Odysseus's final enterprise, the voyage beyond the Pillars of
Hercules, which mark, for Dante, the limits of the inhabited world:

> Эта песнь о составе человеческой крови, содержащей в себе
> океанскую соль. Начало путешествия заложено в системе крове-
> носных сосудов. Кровь планетарна, солярна, солона. . .
>
> Всеми извилинами своего мозга дантовский Одиссей презирает
> склероз, подобно тому как Фарината презирает ад.
>
> «Неужели мы рождены для скотского благополучия и остающу-
> юся нам горсточку вечерних чувств не посвятим дерзанию выйти
> на запад, за Геркулесовы вехи—туда, где мир продолжается без
> людей? . . . »[150]

(This is a canto about the composition of the human blood, which contains
ocean salt. The principle of the journey is located in the system of blood
vessels. Blood is planetary, solar, salty. . . .

With all the convolutions of his brain, Dante's Odysseus despises sclerosis,
in the same way that Farinata despises the inferno.

"Surely we were not born for the well-being of beasts, and won't we dedi-
cate our last remaining fistful of evening senses to daring—to go out to the
West, beyond the Pillars of Hercules—where the world continues without
people?". . .)

The journey to probable death is undertaken to avert another, more fear-
some end—the end of consciousness: sclerosis, amnesia (cf. the Lamarckian notion of the force of death as a gradual rigidification, a narrowing and
hardening of the vessels and organs).[151] This is the protest of the protagonist of "Lamarck," who would risk sight and hearing rather than embrace
a system according to which nothing accomplished in man's lifetime en-
dures into subsequent generations. Like Odysseus, the poet elects to "dedi-
cate [his] last remaining fistful of evening senses" to the journey to the
place "without people." The descent to lower forms is an "inferno for
man," but for the traveler who undertakes that sacrifice, it leaves open the
possibility of a different way. Dante's damned hero perishes in sight of
Purgatory, but Mandelstam, envisioning Lamarck as a butterfly, is seized
with a "wild desire to look at nature through the painted ocelli of that
monster [*chudovishche*]"[152] (again, as in the poem about "the Italians,"the
eyed monster is the organ of vision). In the context of Mandelstam's
Armenia, sensual deprivation becomes a sign and a condition of vision. The
voyage "out" suggests an expansion rather than a narrowing of horizons.

The perspective of "Alagez" is what Mandelstam achieves in his
speculative travels—in consultation with the naturalists, an activity he
describes in terms of the same move "out," into another dimension: "S tekh

por, kak druz'ia moi—khotia eto slishkom gromko, ia skazhu luchshe priiateli—vovlekli menia v krug estestvennonauchnykh interesov, v zhizni moei obrazovalas' shirokaia progalina. Peredo mnoiu raskrylsia *vykhod* v svetloe deiatel'noe pole" ("Since my friends—although that is too emphatic, I should say pals—drew me into the circle of the natural sciences, a wide glade has taken shape in my life. A way out into a bright field of activity has opened up before me").[153] *Vykhod* 'a way out', echoed in *vyiti* 'to go out' of the "Ashtarak" drafts and the "Odysseus" canto,[154] corresponds to the rectification of the eye Mandelstam ascribes to the influence of Pallas and company; *svetloe deiatel'noe pole* 'a bright field of activity' recalls Gurwitsch's embryonic field and Mandelstam's variations on it, including the Persian miniature—and the vast, luminous space the visionary Pallas discovers in the Russian plains. The geode is comparable to yet another mineralogical "monstrosity," the crystal with thirteen thousand sides, which Mandelstam, "in the capacity of the grateful reader," derives from the *Divine Comedy* and in the formation of which "space seems to go out of itself" ("prostranstvo kak by *vykhodit* iz sebia samogo").[155] The almond-date eye of the miniature, a symptom of the illness that makes the poetry long-lived, is the rectified organ of vision, and it provides a glimpse of the new space. With this prospect in view, Odysseus sets sail, and Mandelstam sets his sights on the mountain.

3

✍ Judaic Chaos, Judaic Cares

Aber vielleicht dürfen wir den Naturforscher, der das Gebiet der lebendigen Anschauung verläßt, um die großen Zusammenhänge zu erkennen, vergleichen mit einem Bergsteiger, der den höchsten Gipfel eines gewaltigen Gebirges bezwingen will, um von dort das Land unter ihm in seinen Zusammenhängen zu überschauen. Auch der Bergsteiger muß die von den Menschen bewohnten fruchtbaren Täler verlassen. Je höher er kommt, desto weiter öffnet sich das Land seinem Blick, desto spärlicher wird aber auch das Leben, das ihn umgibt. Schließlich gelangt er in eine blendend klare Region von Eis und Schnee, in der alles Leben erstorben ist, in der auch er selbst nur noch unter großen Schwierigkeiten atmen kann. Erst durch diese Region hindurch führt der Weg zum Gipfel. Aber dort oben steht er in den Momenten, in denen in vollster Klarheit das ganze Land unter ihm ausgebreitet liegt, doch vielleicht dem lebendigen Bereich nicht allzu fern.

> Werner Heisenberg,"Die Goethesche und die Newtonsche Ferbenlehre im Lichte der Modernen Physik"

(Perhaps we can liken the scientist who leaves the field of direct sense-impression in order to see nature as a whole, to a climber who wants to master the highest peak of a mighty mountain in order to survey the country below him in all its variety. The climber too must leave fertile inhabited valleys. As he ascends, so more and more of the country unfolds below him, but also life around him becomes more and more sparse. Eventually he reaches a dazzling, clear region of ice and snow in which all life has died and where he can only breathe with great difficulty, and only by traversing this region can he reach the top. But once he has reached it, in the few moments in which the whole country below him is visible with absolute clarity, he may not be so distant from life.)

The new space that opens up in *Journey to Armenia* reappears in *Conversation about Dante,* where Mandelstam locates poetry in an extraordinary dimension: "poeziia . . . vodvoriaetsia na novom, vneprostranstvennom pole deistviia"; "kogda vpolne pereseliaesh'sia na deistvennoe pole poeticheskoi materii . . ." ("poetry . . . establishes itself in a new, extraspatial field of activity"; "when you move completely into the active field of the poetic material . . .").[1] In the "Octaves," the eleven eight-liners contemporary with *Conversation about Dante* and *Journey to Armenia*, Mandelstam locates the poet himself in that dimension.[2] The "Octaves" might be considered a lyric counterpart to the poetics that he attempts to formulate in the two great prose pieces of the early 1930s.

Toward the end of 1933, Mandelstam made a comment to Akhmatova that confirms his current concern for the principles of his work: "Stikhi seichas dolzhny byt' grazhdanskimi" ("Now we must write only civic verse"), and he recited "We live, not sensing the country beneath us."[3] Mandelstam wrote several civic poems in November of that year. In addition to the ill-fated Stalin epigram, they include "Kvartira tikha, kak bumaga" ("The apartment is quiet as paper") and two eight-line poems that broke off from it,[4] "U nashei sviatoi molodezhi" ("Our holy youth have . . .") and "Tatary, uzbeki i nentsy" ("The Tatars, the Uzbeks, and the Nenets"). Taranovsky suggests that "The Apartment"[5] was a response to Pasternak's comment about the Mandelstams' new living quarters: "Now you have an apartment, you can write,"[6] and to Pasternak's own "apartment" poem, "Krugom semeniashcheisia vatoi" ("With the cotton wool seeding all around" [1931]); the meter was prompted by Pasternak's poem and by Khodasevich's "Ballada" ("Ballad" [1921]), both in amphibrachic trimeter.[7] M. L. Gasparov observes the predominance of ternary meters in Mandelstam's verse of 1930–34, anomalous by comparison with the earlier and later periods; he connects this shift to the civic thematics.[8] Mandelstam names Nekrasov in "The Apartment" ("I stol'ko muchitel'noi zlosti / Tait v sebe kazhdyi namek, / Kak budto vkolachival gvozdi / Nekrasova tut molotok" ["And each allusion is charged / With so much tormenting malice, / As if Nekrasov's hammer / Were driving in nails here"]), confirming the key in which that poem was written.

For all the concreteness of their imagery, the "Octaves" are extremely abstract, and in this regard they contrast with the "occasional" poems that are the context of their composition. A list of items that appear in the "Octaves" might suggest a series of scenes. There are a seascape, a desert, a wooded mountain path, babbling brooks and birds twittering, butterflies and cathedrals, lizards, snails and rocks, crystal goblets, a game of pick-up-sticks, an overgrown garden, a note, drafts and notes, three books, two children, and more.[9] But such a list would be deceptive. As Levin points out in his study of "V igol'chatykh, chumnykh bokalakh" ("In needlelike, plague-filled goblets"), these poems must be read image by image and word by word; their material is not "situational."[10]

"The Apartment" is a protest against the services required of the poet in exchange for the appurtenances of social life, by one who rejected the trappings of comfort and respectability. As an abstract "underside" of "The Apartment," the "Octaves" are a peculiar example of the genre of civic verse. Mandelstam wrote nine of the "Octaves" in November 1933, eight of which, like "The Apartment" and its associated octaves, are in amphibrachic trimeter. The primary impulse of "The Apartment," "I nekuda bol'-

she bezhat' " ("And there's nowhere left to run"), is an echo of the recurrent cry of the 1920s: compare "I nekuda bezhat' ot veka-vlastelina"; "Kuda? na ulitse temno" ("And there's nowhere to run from the sovereign-age"; "Whither? it's dark outside"),[11] and it is a key to the appearance of the "Octaves," the November poems in particular. One of these is "I ia vykhozhu iz prostranstva" ("And I go out of space"), where the poet resolves the issue of where, now, to run. In "The Apartment," the need to escape is represented in terms of the realia of a Moscow apartment, though in grotesque perspective; in the "Octaves," the departure from accustomed dimensions is given in the context of metapoetic speculation. The last stanza of "The Apartment" points to the difference: "I vmesto kliucha Ipokrena / Davnishego strakha struia / Vorvetsia v khalturnye steny / Moskovskogo zlogo zhil'ia" ("And instead of Hippocrene's spring, / A stream of the ancient fear / Bursts into the hackwork walls / Of the evil Moscow lodging"). Fear is not absent in the "Octaves" (cf. "O babochka, o musul'-manka" ["O butterfly, o Muslim woman"]), but it is not the last word. The relation between "The Apartment" and the "Octaves" might be compared to the relation between the "Verses about Stalin," written in January 1937, and the Voronezh poems of the same weeks: another instance of "civic" verse engendering its contemporaneous antithesis, its own darker—and brighter—side.[12]

The "Octaves" themselves are a response to Pasternak—the response of the poet who needs no pen and paper for his poetry; the poet who knows that poetry "establishes itself in an extraspatial field of activity." The verb *chitaiu* 'I read' is common to the "Octaves" and "The Apartment." In "The Apartment," the object of the verb is *paikovye knigi:* "ration books," the most mundane reading matter, appear an equivalent of "literature," the "permitted" writing that Mandelstam rejected in *Fourth Prose*.[13] In "And I go out of space," the object of *chitaiu* is *uchebnik beskonechnost[i]* 'infinity's textbook', also not a "real" book, and certainly not "literature." This is a book with no pages ("bezlistvennyi" ["leafless"])—as opposed to ration books, where the page is everything—and, it seems, no words, only roots (of words or of numbers: "zadachnik . . . kornei" (["problem book of . . . roots"]). In the "Octaves," Mandelstam traces the origins of his verse and locates it in the cosmic scheme; here is the antithesis to the topical imagery of "The Apartment," a setting as far as possible from the "hackwork walls" of the apartment.

While eight of the "Octaves" are in amphibrachic trimeter, three are in iambs: "Shestogo chuvstva kroshechnyi pridatok" ("The minute appendage of the sixth sense"), written in May 1932, in iambic pentameter; and "Preodolev zatverzhennost' prirody" ("Overcoming nature's induracy") and "I Shubert na vode, i Motsart v ptich'em game" ("Schubert on the water, and Mozart in birds' commotion"), both of which Mandelstam worked on in January 1934, in variable iambs (pentameter with one hexameter line and hexameter with two pentameter lines). But eight lines in alternating feminine and masculine rhyme, the chief formal feature unifying the eleven poems in the absence of metrical consistency, is not a sufficient condition for inclusion in the "Octaves." In each of the periods in question, Mandelstam composed other eight-line poems: "Vy pomnite, kak beguny" ("You remember how the runners") in May 1932 (completed in Voronezh in 1935); the two octaves that accompany "The Apartment" in November 1933; and, in January 1934, "A posredi tolpy—zadumchivyi, bradatyi" ("While amid the crowd—pensive, bearded") and "On dirizhiroval kavkazskimi gorami" ("He conducted the Caucasus Mountains");[14] in July 1935, when Mandelstam wrote the second version of "Liubliu poiavlenie tkani" ("I love the appearance of the fabric") and copied down "In needlelike, plague-filled goblets" and "And I go out of space," as if acknowledging them for the first time,[15] he wrote the eightliner "Ispolniu dymchatyi obriad" ("I'll perform a smoke-colored rite").[16] The coherence of the eleven poems finally called "Octaves"—which, like the Armenia poems, Nadezhda Mandelstam considers not a cycle but a selection (*podborka*)[17]—depends on still other features of the octave.

In the "Octaves," which seem a kind of "last" poem, Mandelstam looks back to his beginnings as a poet, to the founding of Acmeism and to the ties formed then and never broken. In August 1928, the seventh anniversary of Gumilev's death, Mandelstam wrote to Akhmatova that his conversation with Gumilev had not ended.[18] The conversation with Gumilev continues in the "Octaves." Mandelstam refers to Gumilev's programmatic "Octave," and not only in his title.[19] He follows Gumilev's representation of the poet's extraordinary situation and his obscure language.[20] The thematic parallels indicate that "Octaves" is more than a formal description.

Gumilev himself examines the octave form in a review of Gorodetskii's 1914 collection *Tsvetushchii posokh* (*The Flowering Staff*).[21] The volume was subtitled *Verenitsa vos'mistishii* (*A Chain of Octaves*), and was advertised under that name as a publication of the Guild of Poets (*Tsekh poetov*) for 1912, and of the fictitious house Acme, where Mandelstam published *Stone* in 1913.[22] Gumilev suggests two possibilities for realizing the potential of the octave. One is "recording the most fleeting thoughts and sensations, which could never crystallize in a real poem. A collection of such 'eights' [*'vos'merki'*] gives the impression of a completely spontaneous diary, and behind it one can so easily see the face of the poet himself, hear his tone of voice.[23] This first possibility for the octave is consistent, in turn, with two aspects of Mandelstam's "Octaves": his reluctance to acknowledge them as finished poems; and the very personal presence in evidence here. First, Mandelstam considered the "Octaves" to be the beginnings of a larger whole. As Nadezhda Mandelstam writes: "Mandelstam absolutely did not want to collect and record the octaves. He tried for a long time to convince me that an octave is simply a failed attempt at a large-scale poem."[24] Thus he committed two of the "Octaves" to paper only in 1935. Second, the abstractness of the poems (these are "sketches compos[ed] of butterflies' specks"), along with the infrequency of the first person singular, indicates that the universe of the "Octaves" is an inner world.

Gumilev's other possibility for realizing the potential of the octave is the "astonishing" juxtaposition of apparently irreconcilable antitheses; "for this one would need to reveal complex antinomies of consciousness, again to feel the world as dangerous and somewhat hostile."[25] Gumilev presents this possibility as an alternative to the first, but it, too, is relevant to Mandelstam's poems. A series of oppositions is part of the procedure of the "Octaves": these include singular/plural; straight/curved; small/large; internal/external; life/death; illness/cure. The most explicit instance of such oppositions is the butterfly, which Mandelstam calls "large"; it is the sign of metamorphosis (*zhiznianochka*) and the harbinger of death (*umiranka*), and it evokes the exclamation "boius'!" ("I'm afraid!"). The element of danger appears again in the oxymorons of the penultimate "Octave": "V igol'chatykh, chumnykh bokalakh, / My p'em navazhden'e prichin, / Kasaemsia kriuch'iami malykh, / Kak legkaia smert', velichin" ("In needle-like, plague-filled goblets, / We drink the delusion of causes, / Touch, with lading hooks, small / Quantities, like light death").

The title of Gorodetskii's volume, R. D. Timenchik writes, had Acmeist associations, referring to and elaborating on the Acmeist logo.[26] In keeping with the implications of the octave as described by Gumilev, *The Flowering Staff* combines the two basic, and antithetical, senses of "acme": in Timenchik's description, as " 'the highest degree of something, flower, flowering time, sometimes—peak' " and as "edge, tip, point."[27] Similar composite words had been proposed, by Marr among others, as typical of the early stages of language;[28] and the "Octaves," constructed on oppositions, concern a move in the direction of primitive speech. The appearance of the octave form is connected to the plot of the return to origins, as it recalls the beginnings of Acmeism and of Mandelstam's path as a poet.

The appearance of the octave marks, too, a return to the origins of Mandelstam's word. The title *The Flowering Staff* is a reference to the biblical rod of almond. The unique instance of *mindal'* in Mandelstam's verse occurs just half a year before the composition of the major portion of the "Octaves," and in another civic poem: "Vse tak zhe xorosha rasseiannaia dal'— / Derev'ia, pochkami nabukhshie na malost', / Stoiat, kak prishlye, i vozbuzhdaet zhalost' / Vcherashnei glupost'iu ukrashennyi mindal' " ("The absent-minded distance is still just as pretty— / The trees, bursting with buds at the slightest trifle, / Stand like newcomers, and the almond, adorned / In yesterday's folly, arouses pity").[29] *Mindal'* is not only Mandelstam's signature. In Gumilev's "Persidskaia miniatiura" ("Persian Miniature"), the poet is to become, after death, a Persian miniature that represents, among other things, a prince with "almond eyes" ("I prints, podniavshii ele-ele / Mindalevidnye glaza").[30]

Mandelstam completed the identification between the miniature and the almond eye in *Journey to Armenia,* in the description of the Persian painting as "sick with goiter"; the miniature "looks aslant" with its "almond-shaped eye" (the "Octaves" themselves, as implements or organs of cognition, are "eyes").[31] In the 1922 essay "Deviatnadtsatyi vek" ("The Nineteenth Century"), Mandelstam contrasts another verse form, the Japanese *tanka,* with the miniature: "It is not miniature, and it would be a great mistake to confuse it with a miniature on the basis of its brevity. It has no scale, because there is no movement in it."[32] The *tanka* is static, motionless; the miniature, on the contrary, is notable for it dynamism. The proportions of the miniature belie its content: "The horizon has been abolished. There is no perspective. An enchanting slow-wittedness."[33] In the "Octaves," where the protagonist's task is "to comprehend the inner excess of space," objects conventionally conceived of as small (a butterfly, a child) are described as large, and an object called "enormous" turns out to be infinitesimal ("ogromnye korni" ["enormous roots"]). Dimensions are oxymoronically skewed: along with small and large, the values of inner and outer, curved and straight, one and many, are reconsidered (cf. the Cracker Jack toy, where the picture changes when it is turned in a different direction).[34]

In a 1913 octave dedicated to Mandelstam (one of a series of octaves in *The Flowering Staff* dedicated to colleagues and fellow poets), Gorodetskii takes up the theme of space and time that Mandelstam will pursue in the "Octaves." The first stanza–"On verit v ves, on chtit prostranstvo, / On nezhno liubit mater'ial, / On veshchestva ne ukorial / Za medlennost' i postoianstvo" ("He believes in weight, he honors space, / He tenderly loves material, / He didn't reproach matter / For slowness and constancy")[35]—contains a rhyme that reappears in Mandelstam's 1915 poem "O svobode nebyvaloi" ("About fantastical freedom"): "Nam li, broshennym v prostranstve, / Obrechennym umeret', / O prekrasnom postoianstve / I o vernosti zhalet'?" ("Is it for us, abandoned in space, / Doomed to die, / To regret beautiful constancy, / To regret loyalty?"). In this poem, Ronen suggests, Mandelstam refers to constancy (*postoianstvo*) along with loyalty (*vernost*)[36] as an Acmeist virtue.[37] In the "Octaves," where Mandelstam again rhymes space (*prostranstvo*) with time (*postoianstvo*), the exit from space is not a departure from but a return to roots.[38]

The context of the Gumilev reminiscences in the "Octaves" is illuminated by Mandelstam's comment during a walk in February 1934, as recalled by Akhmatova: "My shli po Prechisten'ke. Svernulis' my na Gogolevskuiu bul'var, i M. skazal, Ia k smerti gotov" ("We were walking along Prechistenka. We turned onto Gogol Boulevard, and M. said, 'I am ready for death'").[39] Ronen has identified the source of the comment in Gumilev's dramatic poem *Gondla;* he shows that Akhmatova was aware of the allusion, since she referred to *Gondla* in quoting Mandelstam's words in *Poema bez geroia* (*Poem Without a Hero*).[40] But as is typical for *Poem Without a Hero,* several lines cross here. Blok, too, plays a prominent role in Akhmatova's treatment of those words, where the phrase "Ia k smerti gotov" appears to belong to a speaker out of "Shagi komandora" ("The Steps of the Commander")—or out of the story of Don Juan, which, Mandelstam wrote with reference to that poem, Blok transformed into myth.[41] The coincidence of the deaths of Blok and Gumilev in August 1921 was enough to link the two apparently antithetical figures in the minds of contemporaries.[42] Blok, along with Gumilev, was on Mandelstam's mind when he composed the "Octaves."[43] In January 1934, moreover, Mandelstam composed another series of "occasional" poems, including the eight-liners "While amid the crowd—pensive, bearded" and "He conducted the Caucasus Mountains"; the occasion was the death of Andrei Belyi. These poems approach the "Octaves" from the other side: where "The Apartment" introduces the theme of escape, the Belyi poems suggest the theme of death. The domestic name of those poems, "Rekviem" ("Requiem"), referred first of all to the poet himself. In this context, Belyi might be included among the poets associated with Mandelstam's remark.

Mandelstam conceived of the poet's death as the culminating act, the final word without which neither the life nor the work makes sense ("Pushkin and Scriabin").[44] Hence, perhaps, his interest in poets' last poems.[45] He was working on the "Octaves" even as he composed his "Requiem," and he fell silent in February 1934, having written, in "Masteritsa vinovatykh vzorov" ("Mistress of guilty glances"), "Ty, Mariia, gibnushchim podmoga, / Nado smert' predupredit', usnut'. / Ia stoiu u tverdogo poroga" ("You, Maria, give succor to those who are perishing, / One must forestall death, fall asleep. / I stand at a firm threshold"). The intrusion of poems from the "Requiem" into the "Octaves" confirms the theme of the poet's death as a key to the plot of those eight-liners. For Mandelstam, the sense of the "Octaves" as a last poem seems especially acute.[46]

❖ ❖

According to Nadezhda Mandelstam, Mandelstam established a definitive order only for the first three "Octaves": the later and earlier variants of "I love the appearance of the fabric," and "When, destroying the draft."[47] The first (chronologically the later) "I love . . ." variant is the only one of the "Octaves" set, as I have noted, in "sunny . . . reality":

> Люблю появление ткани,
> Когда после двух или трех,
> А то четырех задыханий
> Прийдет выпрямительный вздох.
>
> И дугами парусных гонок
> Открытые формы чертя,[48]
> Играет пространство спросонок—
> Не знавшее люльки дитя.

> (I love the appearance of the fabric,
> When after two or three
> Or even four gasps
> The rectifying sigh comes.
>
> And tracing green forms
> With regattas' arcs,
> Space plays half-awake—
> A child that has not known a cradle.)

The "appearance of the fabric" (*poiavlenie tkani*) is equivalent to an event in three-dimensional space. After that event, in the opening line of the "Octaves," the poems trace, in reverse, the course of its accomplishment. Nadezhda Mandelstam, citing Mandelstam, calls the "Octaves" "poems about cognition."[49] The first three "Octaves" represent the culmination of the process of cognition, as the emergence of the word or work. In the remaining eight, Mandelstam follows the work back from its appearance in space to its origins in some other place and medium.[50]

This reverse process begins in the second (earlier) version of "I love the appearance of the fabric," which has the same opening quatrain as the first:

Люблю появление ткани,
Когда после двух или трех,
А то четырех задыханий
Прийдет выпрямительный вздох.

И так хорошо мне и тяжко,
Когда приближается миг,
И вдруг дуговая растяжка
Звучит в бормотаньях моих.

(I love the appearance of the fabric,
When after two or three
Or even four gasps
The rectifying sigh comes.

And it's so good and so hard for me
When the moment's near,
And suddenly an arched extension
Sounds in my mutterings.)

The common opening quatrain suggests a parallel between the two second quatrains, linked to the first by a coordinating conjunction and to each other by common lexicon. But in the second quatrain of the second "Octave" events are not projected in space; they remain in a metaphysical realm. The "Octave" Nadezhda Mandelstam would put third continues the internal scene:

Когда, уничтожив набросок,
Ты держишь прилежно в уме
Период без тягостных сносок,
Единый во внутренней тьме,
И он лишь на собственной тяге
Зажмурившись, держится сам,
Он так же относит к бумаге,
Как купол к пустым небесам.

(When, destroying the draft,
You hold diligently in mind
A period without weighty notes,
Single in the inner darkness,
And it, just on its own traction,
Screwing up its eyes, holds on itself—
It relates to the paper exactly
As the cupola does to the empty skies.)

The "period" emerges in an inner space, a "darkness," unlike the bright seascape of the first "I love the appearance of the fabric." The excess—"drafts" and "notes"—has been eliminated.[51] Here, as in "The Apartment," "paper" is least of all the locus of the poet's activity; cf. "Kvartira tikha, kak bumaga, / Pustaia, bez vsiakikh zatei" ("The apartment is as quiet as paper, / Empty, with no frills"). The paper of the "Octaves" is empty, like the apartment, and by analogy to the skies. In a poem of 1911 Mandelstam compared the sky to a blank piece of paper: "O nebo, nebo, ty mne budesh' snit'sia! / Ne mozhet byt', chtob ty sovsem osleplo, / I den' sgorel, kak belaia stranitsa: / Nemnogo dyma i nemnogo pepla!" ("O sky, sky, I'll dream about you! / It can't be that you've gone completely blind, / And the day's burned out like a blank page: / A little smoke, a little ash remain!"). The sky acquires definition only with the appearance of the cupola. Indeed, the function of the cupola is to define the sky. As Ronen points out,[52] in "The Morning of Acmeism," Mandelstam described the function of the Gothic bell tower in similar terms: "The good arrow of the Gothic bell tower is malicious, because its entire meaning is to prick the sky, to reproach it for being empty [*pusto*]."[53] In the process of composition, paper is an incidental, technical, but not essential, attribute of the work; the paper is defined by the word, while the accoutrements of writing can be abandoned in favor of the word independent of the page ("Period bez tiagostnykh snosok" ["A period without weighty notes"]).[54]

The sequence of the first three "Octaves" reveals a tendency out of brightness into darkness, out of three dimensions into another, internal one. The goal of the investigations in the "Octaves," as described in "Overcoming nature's induracy," accounts for this tendency: "Poniat' prostranstva vnutrennii izbytok, / I lepestka i kupola zalog" ("To comprehend the inner excess of space, / And the pledge of the petal and the cupola"). The inner darkness of the mind appears to be an external space; in "When, destroying the draft," the personal principle, signaled by the pronoun *ty* 'you' in the first quatrain, disappears in the second.[55] Like the place "outside of space," reached by a parallel move in the last "Octave," the inner space represents not the usual three dimensions but their speculative simulacrum.

As Mandelstam was reluctant to acknowledge them a completed work, the "Octaves" remain, in some sense, unfinished. Yet their "unfinished" nature may be a programmatic aspect of these poems. In *Conversation about Dante,* Mandelstam established raw material (*syr'e*) as the matter of poetry; in *Fourth Prose* he had written, "It's gotten to the point where I value, in the word trade, only proud flesh, only the insane excrescence."[56] The move into an internal, mental space is represented in the "Octaves" as a move from the completed work to an earlier stage—into the raw material of verse. But at the same time, consistent with the theme of cognition, this is a move towards enlightenment.

❖ ❖

The problem Mandelstam poses in the "Octaves" is one he had referred to as much as twenty years before in "The Morning of Acmeism," where he compared the poet's work to the work of the mathematician:

> The spectacle of the mathematician unthinkingly squaring some number in ten figures fills us with a certain amazement. But too often we lose sight of the fact that the poet raises the phenomenon to a power in ten figures, and the modest exterior of the work of art not infrequently deceives us as to the monstrously condensed [chudovishchno-uplotnennaia] reality it possesses. That reality in poetry is the word as such.[57]

The "monstrously condensed reality" concealed behind the "modest exterior" of the work appears in the "Octaves" as the "inner excess of space" that, as Mandelstam indicates in "Overcoming nature's induracy," it is the poet's purpose to fathom.[58] The difference lies in the stage of the process represented. Whereas the poet in 1913 sets in motion the exponential growth of the phenomenon, in 1933 he has the opposite task: to discover the principle on which the work is constructed; to move back from the work to its constitutive elements.

In the "Octaves," as in "The Morning of Acmeism," mathematical imagery provides the terms of the investigation. Numbers are prominent not just in the Gumilevian title. The "six" of *Shestogo chuvstva kroshechnyi pridatok* ("The minute appendage of the sixth sense") appears to follow directly from the last line of Gumilev's own "Shestoe chuvstvo" ("The Sixth Sense"): "Tak, vek za vekom—skoro li, Gospod'— / Pod skal'pelem prirody i iskusstva, / Krichit nash dukh, iznemogaet plot', / Rozhdaia organ dlia *shestogo chuvstva*" ("So, for ages and ages—will it be soon, Lord? / Beneath the scalpel of nature and art, / Our spirit screams, flesh grows faint, / Giving birth to the organ of the sixth sense").[59] But Mandelstam parted from Gumilev in his treatment of number. In the poem "Slovo" ("The Word"), Gumilev treats number as a poor, mundane substitute for the divine and affective word, which is meant not to inform but to perform: "V onyi den', kogda nad mirom novym / Bog sklonial litso svoe, togda / Solntse ostanavlivali slovom, / Slovom razrushali goroda. // A dlia nizkoi zhizni byli chisla, / Kak domashnyi, pod"iaremnyi skot, / Potomu chto vse ottenki smysla / Umnoe chislo peredaet" ("On that day when, over the new world, / God inclined his face, / The sun was stopped with a word, / With a word, cities were destroyed. // But for lowly life there were numbers, / Like domestic beasts of burden, / Because the clever number communicates / All the nuances of meaning"). Nadezhda Mandelstam remarks that Mandelstam "related coldly" to Gumilev's poem; he considered number, like the word, part of the cultural heritage. Mandelstam's consideration of the numerical aspects of his verse testifies to this attitude: he "always paid attention to the number of lines and stanzas in the poem and the number of chapters in prose."[60] In the "Octaves," the title of which introduces number as a motif, the total number of lines, 88, seconds the essential 8 (in this respect the "Octaves" represent the third stage in a numerical progression, following *Vtoraia kniga* [*Second Book*] and *Chetvertaia proza* [*Fourth Prose*]). Levin suggests that the number eleven is a "modulus" in Mandelstam's work.[61] That number recurs regularly in the 1930s, when in addition to the eleven "Octaves," Mandelstam wrote four eleven-line poems (the first is "What street is this?") and one poem with two stanzas of eleven lines each; the final part of the "Verses about the Unknown Soldier," too, is an eleven-line stanza; *Conversation about Dante* has eleven chapters—and *Journey to Armenia* has eight (Gumilev's "Sixth Sense" has six stanzas).[62] The "Octaves" are constructed on a combination of eight and eleven, and here Mandelstam refers to eight of the eleven integers between one and eleven: 1 ("And I go out of space," "When, destroying the draft"); 2, 3, 4 ("I love the appearance of the fabric"); 5 (implied in "I love . . ." by the "liberating breath" following the four gasps); 6 ("The minute appendage of the sixth sense"); 8 ("Octaves"), and 11 (the total number of poems).[63] In the last "Octave," the protagonist departs for an overgrown garden of numbers, where "roots" are numerical as well as verbal.

More than ten years earlier, in "The Word and Culture" and "On the Nature of the Word," Mandelstam considered two views of the future of culture in terms of two geometries. He had referred to those geometries in a letter to Viacheslav Ivanov of August 13 (26), 1909: "In your book there is one place from which two great prospects open out [*otkryvaiutsia*], as the two geometries—Euclid's and Lobachevsky's—do from the parallel postulate."[64] The interpretation of the parallel postulate distinguishes the Euclidean system, where parallel lines will never meet, from the Lobachevskian system, where they may.[65] Like the two geometries, Mandelstam suggests, Ivanov's "two great prospects" are variant descriptions of the same thing. So are the two essays of the early 1920s, which might be considered twins (cf. Mandelstam's "twin" poems).[66] "On the Nature of the Word" is about the word and culture, while the first paragraph of "The Word and Culture" represents the future of the word as a reversion to nature, a return to the primitive past: "The grass on the Petersburg streets is the first shoots [*pobegi*] of the virgin forest that will cover the site of present-day cities."[67] This "new inspired nature" ("novaia odukhotvorennaia priroda") is a "kingdom of the spirit *without man*" ("tsarstvo dukha *bez cheloveka*"). In the final passage of "The Word and Culture," by contrast with the first, the future does not exclude people. Contemporary culture is characterized as glossolalia, a "primitive" language corresponding to primitive growth, but motivated by the collective human breath or spirit; the seven-boled pipe of Pushkin's "Muza" ("The Muse") inspires Mandelstam's comparison of the word to a "thousand-boled pipe, animated with the breath of all ages at once."[68]

In "On the Nature of the Word," Mandelstam represents alternative conceptions of philological evolution in terms of the geometrical model: "Just as there are two geometries—Euclid's and Lobachevsky's—two histories of literature are possible, written in two different keys: one speaking only of gains, the other only of losses, and both will speak of the same thing." Through a series of quasi-mathematical metaphors, many of which (among other lexical items) are echoed in the "Octaves," Mandelstam describes the criterion of the unity of a national literature. That criterion— the medium of literary evolution—is the language. In this essay, the image of young growth (*pobegi* here echoes the same word in "The Word and Culture") suggests the beginnings of a revitalized language arising out of the decaying body of the ancient one:

> Язык же, хотя и меняется, ни одну минуту не застывает в покое, от точки и до точки, ослепительно ясной в сознании филологов, и в пределах всех своих изменений остается *постоянной величиной*, «константой», остается *внутренне единым* [cf. «*Единый во внутренней тьме*»]. Для всякого филолога понятно, что такое тождество личности в применении к *самосознанию* языка. Когда латинская речь, распространившаяся по всем романским землям, зацвела новым цветением и пустила *побеги* будущих романских языков, началась новая литература, детская и убогая по сравнению с латинской, но уже романская.[69]

(A language—although it changes, does not for one moment become fixed in repose—from one point to another, each one blindingly clear in the consciousness of philologists, and within the limits of its changes, remains a fixed quantity, a 'constant,' remains *internally unified* [cf. "*Single one* in the *inner darkness*"]. It's clear to any philologist what personal identity is as applied to the *self-awareness* of a language. When Latin, spreading throughout the Romanic lands, blossomed anew and put out the *shoots* of the future Romance languages, a new literature began, childish and impoverished by comparison with Latin, but already a Romance literature.)

In the garden of numbers of "And I go out of space," "culture" reverts to "nature"; the "Octaves" might be described as Otsup describes "Lamarck," with reference to the "pull back from culture to prehistory." The "neglected garden" of the last "Octave" is a place *without people* (*bez liudei*). But the garden offers "roots," among them *postoianstvo* 'constancy' and *samosoznan'e prichin* 'the self-awareness of causes'. The question posed by these alternative visions is the same, in the essays and in the "Octaves": is this a future with or without people?[70]

In the letter to Ivanov, Mandelstam had compared the parallel postulate to Ivanov's "image of amazing penetration—where the one who does not agree to participate in the choral ring quits the circle, covering his face with his hands." From the image of the individual leaving the choral ring, two conclusions—the "two great prospects"—can be derived: either the path returns to the circle, or it leads away, never again to intersect with the circle. Ivanov gives the alternatives in the final sentence of the passage Mandelstam refers to: "He [the individual] may die; but he cannot live apart."[71] The question is not, therefore, whether or not to leave the circle. In either case, the individual takes his solitary way "out of space," as Mandelstam puts it in the last "Octave." But in one case, the individual may return; in the other, he will not. The one who departs rejoins the choral ring—or he goes to death. Ronen quotes the letter to Ivanov in discussing Mandelstam's perpetual pull towards the chorus.[72] The course of the "Octaves" tends in the other direction. Yet in the extraspatial garden, in the absence of people, the possibility of new growth remains.

❖ ❖

The motif of geometry is explicit in "Tell me, draftsman of the desert." Mandelstam juxtaposes the lines of the geometer, who tries to measure the desert, to the circles traced by the wind in the sand:

Скажи мне, чертежник пустыни,
Арабских песков геометр,
Ужели безудержность линий
Сильнее, чем дующий ветр?
—Меня не касается трепет
Его иудейских забот—
Он опыт из лепета лепит
И лепет из опыта пьет. . .

(Tell me, draftsman of the desert,
Geometer of the Arab sands,
Could the unruliness of lines
Be stronger than the blowing wind?

—The trepidation of its Judaic cares
Is no concern of mine;
It fashions the experiment from babble
And drinks babble from the experiment.)

The poem is an address and response. The identity of the interlocutors, and even the distribution of lines between them, has been a matter of dispute. Anne Nesbet equates the geometer and the poet;[73] Clarence Brown equates the geometer, the poet, and the wind, opposing this composite figure to the questioner, whom he identifies as "Mandelstam or . . . his surrogate."[74] But if "the poet" is distinguished from "Mandelstam," or from the lyrical subject, then the identity of the first person, the one who addresses the geometer, remains uncertain.

The second octave in Gumilev's "Happiness," "Khochesh', gorbun, pomeniat'sia . . ." ("Hunchback, do you want to exchange . . ."), resembles "Tell me, draftsman of the desert" in structure: here, too, is a dialogue of two unidentified speakers, in which the first four lines represent a first person address to a second person, while the next four lines represent a scornful response. The opening query, here too, suggests a contrast between the mode of the addressee and the mode of the speaker. Gumilev's hunchback is offered the speaker's fate: "'Khochesh' shutit' i smeiat'-sia, /Byt' vol'noi ptitsei morei?'" ("'Do you want to joke and laugh, / To be a free bird of the seas?'"); Mandelstam's "blowing wind" corresponds to Gumilev's free seabird, also subject to the winds (cf. the seascape of the first "Octave"). But the hunchback prefers his crippled state to the poet's freedom: "'Ukhodi, ne stoi so mnoi riadom, / Ne khochu ot tebia nichego!'" ("'Go away, don't stand next to me, / I don't want a thing from you'").[75]

Similarly, Mandelstam's geometer, addressed in the first quatrain, responds in the second, equating the cycle of "experiment" and "babble" with "Judaic cares," and dismissing the activity of the third person singular as repetitive and pointless: "It fashions the experiment from babble / And drinks babble from the experiment." Nadezhda Mandelstam correctly identifies that third person (represented by the pronouns *ego* 'his,' 'its' and *on* 'he,' 'it') as the wind (*vetr,* a masculine noun), mentioned at the end of the first quatrain. But she accepts without question the geometer's dim view of the wind's activity: "'Judaic cares' refers to the wind. What the wind does. It is shallow furrows, superficial changes by comparison with the large design of the 'draftsman' and the 'geometer of the desert.'"[76] Her interpretation, too, fails to account for the respective roles of the two interlocutors.

The skeptical attitude towards the activity of the wind has a precedent in a subtext identified by Taranovsky, who compares the "blowing wind" (*duiushchii vetr*) to the circling wind observed by Ecclesiastes.[77] Ecclesiastes is concerned that what man accomplishes in his lifetime will be lost to future generations: no memory will remain (people are no more than beasts) (Eccles. 1:11; 3:18–19). Like the geometer, Ecclesiastes does not understand the wind's circling. But in the absence of positive identification to the contrary, the lyrical subject of "Draftsman of the desert,"[78] the first person singular in the first quatrain, must be associated with the first person singular of the other "Octaves"; and this subject is linked to the wind rather than to the skeptical geometer, Acmeist pronouncements about the poet as craftsman notwithstanding.[79] The geometer himself is hardly the builder of the architecture poems and "The Morning of Acmeism"; the "unruliness of lines" is closer to the "whim of a demigod" than to the "simple carpenter's rapacious measurement by eye" ("krasota ne prikhot' poluboga, / A khishchnyi glazomer prostogo stoliara").[80] In "When, destroying the draft," the period in the mind is the model of what the geometer fails to accomplish: it is self-sufficient, complete, not to be effaced, as opposed to the geometer's ephemeral lines. In "I love the appearance of the fabric," the wind itself "sketches," but it "traces open forms," with "arcs" ("I dugami parusnykh gonok / Otkrytye formy *chertia*"), while the geometer tries to account for the "shifting sands" ("Sypuchykh peskov," in a variant) with straight lines. Nadezhda Mandelstam discusses Mandelstam's antipathy to fantasy: "Mandelstam always spoke about fantasy as if the very word contained the epithets 'unbridled,' 'unruly' [*'bezuderzhnyi'*], and completely denied its role in the creative process."[81] Her habit of echoing Mandelstam's words makes the comment particularly telling.[82]

The masculine singular pronoun *on*, which refers first of all to the wind ("it"), also suggests a person ("he"). The geometer, responding to the question about the wind, dismisses the poet's activity at the same time. The repetitive "Judaic cares" are the wind's, but they might be the poet's. The alternation of "babble" and "experiment" is the creative cycle.[83]

In the first two decades of his work, Mandelstam had tried to escape the primitive and inarticulate element he calls the "Judaic chaos" ("kotorogo . . . bezhal, vsegda bezhal").[84] By the fall of 1933, as he realizes that the poet's activity is inextricably bound up with the fate of the Jew, "Judaic chaos" (*khaos iudeiskii*) has become "Judaic cares" (*iudeiskie zaboty*).

❖ ❖

The word *zabota* 'care' appears in only five of Mandelstam's poems; "Draftsman of the desert" is the last. The earlier instances are "Kak koni medlenno stupaiut" ("How slowly the horses go" [1911]), "Sestry—

tiazhest' i nezhnost'—odinakovy vashi primety" ("Sisters—heaviness and tenderness—identical are your signs" [1920]), "Komu zima—arak i punsh goluboglazyi" ("For some winter is arrack and blue-eyed punch" [1922]), and "O, kak my liubim litsemerit'" ("Oh, how we love to dissemble" [1932]). In all except the first poem, *zabota* refers to the most intimate and fundamental aspects of the poet's being.[85] The shift is characteristic. Others care for the delirious protagonist of "How slowly the horses go"; "Drugie liudi, verno, znaiut, / Kuda vezut oni menia, / A ia vveriaius' ikh zabote" ("Other people, surely, know, / Where they are taking me. / And I entrust myself to their care"); and this may be the last time the poet allows himself such a luxury. In "Oh, how we love to dissemble," however reluctantly, Mandelstam resolves the opposition between *obmorok* 'fainting spell' or 'swoon' and *zabota* in a different direction: "Liniaet zver', igraet ryba / V glubokom obmoroke vod, / I ne gliadet' by na izgiby / Liudskikh strastei, liudskikh zabot" ("The beast molts, the fish plays / In the deep swoon of the waters, / And if only one didn't have to look at the twists / Of people's sufferings, people's cares"). Mandelstam echoes the lines from Pushkin's *Tsygany* (*The Gypsies*) that he had quoted in "The Word and Culture" and "On the Nature of the Word": "Ne ponimal on nichego, / I slab, i robok byl, kak *deti,* / Chuzhie liudi dlia nego / *Zverei i ryb* lovili v seti. / Kak merzla bystraia reka, / I zimny vikhri bushevali, / Pushistoi kozhei prikryvali / Oni sviatogo starika" ("He didn't understand a thing, / And he was as weak and timid as children, / For him, strangers caught / Beasts and fish in nets. / When the rapid river froze, / And winter winds raged, / They covered the holy old man / With a downy hide"). The reference to Pushkin is mediated, too, through Annenskii's translation of Verlaine's "Pensée du soir,"[86] the last lines of which Mandelstam quotes in the same context in "On the Nature of the Word": "Na temnyi zhrebii svoi ia bol'she ne v *obide.* / I nag i nemoshchen byl nekogda Ovidii" ("I'm no longer aggrieved by my dark lot. / Ovid was once both naked and helpless"). Cf. "Eshche *obidu* tianet s bliudtsa / Nevyspavsheesia *ditia,* / A mne uzh ne na kogo dut'sia, / I ia odin na vsekh putiakh" ("The child that hasn't gotten enough sleep / Still imbibes injury from the saucer, / But I no longer have anyone to blame, / And I am alone on all paths"). The poet is "no longer a child." Unlike the Ovidian poet, sheltered by strangers, it is he who must care for others, speak for everyone ("Ia govoriu za vsekh s takoiu siloi"), however much he might like to remain silent ("Ia bol'she ne rebenok" [1931]).[87] "In the deep swoon of the waters" suggests the antithesis of the poet's conscious verbal activity. Thus in "Mistress of guilty glances," the poet distinguishes the first person plural from fish, "sound-lessly making *o*'s with their mouths" ("besshumno okaiushchikh rtami"). Speech is in danger of disappearing, the poet is in danger of succumbing to the undefined, tempting but fatal underwater world rather than remaining in the differently dangerous world of definition and death.[88] "Mistress . . ." began the silence that ended only the following April, in Voronezh.[89]

The poet's "Judaic cares" have a double aspect, as represented by the linked verbs *lepit'* 'to fashion' or 'to model' and *pit'* 'to drink'. The activities designated by these verbs correspond to invention and recollection (*izobreten'e, vospominan'e*), which, Mandelstam wrote in the 1922 essay "Literaturnaia Moskva" ("Literary Moscow"), "go hand and hand in poetry."[90] In the Voronezh poem "Fleity grecheskoi teta i iota" ("The Greek flute's theta and iota"), *vylepit'* refers to the artist's invention of his own world: "A fleitist ne uznaet pokoia: / Emu kazhetsia, chto on odin, / Chto kogda-to on *more rodnoe* / Iz sirenevykh *vylepil* glin" ("But the flutist knows no peace: / It seems to him that he's alone, / That once he fashioned a kindred sea / Out of lilac clay"). Drinking, one of Mandelstam's constant figures for the poetic process, and consistent with the representation of that process as reading (both *pit'* 'to drink' and *chitat'* 'to read' suggest "taking in"), is a counterpart to recollection.[91]

Zabota is associated contextually with drinking in each of the four poems in question. In "Draftsman of the desert," where *zabot* 'of . . . cares' rhymes with *p'et* '[he] drinks,' drinking is one manifestation of the poet's "Judaic cares."[92] (The activity of the multitude in "In needlelike, plague-filled goblets"—"My p'em navazhden'e prichin" ["We drink the delusion of causes"]—is a grotesque version of the poet's activity.) In "For some winter is arrack . . . , " the activity of the poet, called *zabota,* is contrasted with others' activity, which is characterized in terms of drinking: "Komu zima—arak i punsh goluboglazyi, / Komu—dushistoe s koritseiu vino"; "Komu zima—polyn' i gor'kii dym k nochlegu" ("For some winter is arrack and blue-eyed punch, / For some it is wine fragrant with cinnamon"; "For some winter is wormwood and bitter smoke for the night's lodging"). In "Oh, how we love to dissemble," the child's activity, drinking ("tianet s bliudtsa" ["imbibes from the saucer"]), contrasts with the poet's, which means involvement in "people's cares" ("liudskie zaboty"). In "Sisters—heaviness and tenderness," Mandelstam refers to the poet's task as *zabota:* "U menia ostaetsia odna zabota na svete, / Zolotaia zabota, kak vremeni bremia izbyt' " ("One care alone remains for me on earth, / A golden care—to get rid of the burden of time"). The accomplishment of the task—the discovery of the word, the moment of recognition ("Vremia vspakhano plugom i roza zemleiu byla" ["Time has been turned up by a plow, and the rose was the earth"])—is given in the following line as an act of drinking: "Slovno temnuiu vodu ia *p'iu pomutivshiisia vozdukh*" ("As if it were dark water I drink the turbid air").

Yet as a representation of the poet's activity, *zabota* suggests not only his care for another but also another's care for him (cf. "How slowly the horses go," where just the second meaning is relevant). The two meanings are evident in "For some winter is arrack . . . ": "Nemnogo teplogo kurinogo pometa / I bestolkovogo ovech'ego tepla; / Ia vse otdam za zhizn'—mne tak nuzhna zabota" ("A little warm chicken dung / And pointless sheep's warmth; / I'll give up everything for life—I need care so much").[93] Here Mandelstam introduces the "pointlessness," characteristic of the reciprocal relation of care, that is the theme of the inner stanzas of the poem. He juxtaposes *zabota* to the "senseless" act of communication (cf. "blazhennoe, bessmyslennoe slovo" ["the blessed, senseless word"]): "Tianut'sia s nezhnost'iu bessmyslenno k chuzhomu."[94] "Reaching out tenderly, senselessly to a stranger" describes the main tendency of Mandelstam's poetry ("On the Interlocutor"). The frequent forms of the second person singular indicate the prominence of the conative function;[95] the orientation towards the addressee is the force of Mandelstam's "experiment." Mandelstam's "babble" is evidence of the phatic function, which, Jakobson writes, is the "first verbal function acquired by infants . . . [who] are prone to communicate before being able to send or receive informative communication."[96] (Opposed to the phatic function in "For some winter is arrack" is the activity of *zagovorshchiki* 'conspirators', whose speech is not "pointless" [*bestolkovyi*], but "about something," and therefore not to the point.) In a letter to Tynianov of January 21, 1937, Mandelstam accounted for his life's work as "mixing what's important with trifles" ("meshaia vazhnoe s pustiakami").[97] The very pointlessness of the wind's circling, of the poet's "Judaic cares," is its deep meaning.

❖ ❖

Thus the "experiment" is dedicated to the unidentified "those" in "Schubert on the water, and Mozart in birds' commotion," where Mandelstam investigates the activity disparaged in "Draftsman of the desert":

И Шуберт на воде, и Моцарт в птичьем гаме,
И Гете, свищущий на вьющейся тропе,
И Гамлет, мысливший пугливыми шагами,
Считали пульс толпы и верили толпе.

Быть может, прежде губ уже родился шепот,
И в бездревесности кружилися листы,
И те, кому мы посвящаем опыт,
До опыта приобрели черты.

(Schubert on the water, and Mozart in birds' commotion,
And Goethe whistling on the winding path,
And Hamlet thinking with frightened steps,
Took the crowd's pulse and trusted the crowd.

Perhaps before the lips the whisper was already born,
And in treelessness leaves circled,
And those to whom we devote the experiment
Acquired features before it.)

Corresponding to the relation between *opyt* 'experiment' and *lepet* 'babble' in "Draftsman of the desert" is the relation, here, between *opyt* and *te* 'those' (or its metonym, *cherty* 'features'—another instance of the root *chert-* 'delineation', 'depiction', or 'portrayal',[98] which appears also in "Draftsman of the desert" and in "I love the appearance of the fabric"), the future hypostasis of *tolpa* 'the crowd'. The poet's task is to realize the "features" of the anonymous third person plural *te;* the future is constituted of this "those."[99] The paronomastic relation between *lepet* and *tolpa* (based on consonants, which Mandelstam had described as the productive unit— the "seed"—of the language in "Zametki o poezii" ["Notes on Poetry"])[100] supports this account of the cycle, where babble, or the unrealized "those," alternates with the experiment, or the present crowd. The dense orchestration of *On opyt iz lepeta lepit / I lepet iz opyta p'et* mimics the operations of the cycle, as "experiment" alternates with "babble" and the sounds *p, t, l* recur. The same sounds are repeated in "Schubert on the water": *pltlp* in *pul's tolpy* 'the pulse of the crowd', for example, is an instance of *lepet,* and another example of the cyclical structure that characterizes these poems on various levels. *Lepet* 'babble' is a synonym of *shepot* 'whisper', and like *te,* it is the unarticulated material of the experiment.[101]

Te reappears in the first poem of the Belyi "Requiem," again with reference to the future.[102] That plural subject, contrasting with the solitary poet, is also closely linked to him: "Da ne sprosiat tebia molodye, griadushchie—*te*— / Kakovo tebe tam—v pusto*te,* v chisto*te,*—siro*te*" ("May you not be asked, by the young, the future ones—those— / How things are with you there, orphan—in the emptiness, in the clearness").[103] In "Schubert on the water," as in "Golubye glaza i goriashchaia lobnaia kost'" ("Blue eyes and burning frontal bone"), *te* is a building block of the verse, entering its "fabric" or "tissue" (*tkan'*). It is the fundamental unit with respect to phonological and semantic organization. *Te* is *t* in vocalic form; that consonant saturates these lines. Along with *p* and/or *l, t* produces not only *tolpa,* the "crowd" that is the synonym of *te* (see also *lepet*), but also *opyt,* the "experiment" that is its antithesis. *T* is common to the names of the principals of the poem, Schubert, Mozart, Goethe, Hamlet (Shubert, Motsart, Gete, Gamlet), as *te* is to the "name" of the addressee in the Belyi poem (*sirote,* in the dative); and it appears in *ptichii gam* and *tropa, lepet* and *shepot, bezdrevesnost', listy,* and *cherty. Te* is an embryonic form, the material of the phenomena the poet attends to and relies on. It is an instance of *lepet;* as the minimal essence of the poetic material, *te* is a "blessed senseless word," a trans-sense element and the locus of future meaning.

The alternation of babble and experiment is an instance of the relation between subliminal and conscious creative activity. This is Mandelstam's concern also, as Ronen describes it, in "The Slate Ode."[104] Ronen refers to a shift from stupor to understanding and from the general to the individual; the latter, too, is relevant to the "Octaves," where the relation between the solitary protagonist and the crowd is important to the plot. The alternation has a counterpart in the division of labor between the right and the left hemispheres of the brain, devoted, respectively, to immediate, nonspeech comprehension and spatial relations, and to logical comprehension and linguistic relations.[105] Following the (perhaps mythopoetical) model proposed by the psychologist Julian Jaynes, "babble" corresponds to the inarticulate communications associated with the gods (a right brain function), while the "experiment" is the human articulation of the divine conception (by the left hemisphere). The poet commands not just articulate speech (cf. "lips") but also the inarticulate "whisper" associated with prophetic utterance.[106]

❖ ❖

As the alternations of the cycle indicate, the approach to future meaning does not proceed by lines; curves—arcs and spirals—describe the shape of thought. The inadequacy of linear conceptions of sequence is revealed in the second quatrain of "Schubert on the water. . . ." The first of three examples, "Maybe before the lips the whisper was already born," represents a single segment of the cycle, reversing the expected order of events, according to which articulation comes before speech: the "whisper" is not produced by the "lips," but precedes them. A similar idea of order, again with reference to the process of speech, had appeared in "The Word and Culture": "Not one word exists yet, but the poem already sounds."[107] In the second example, "And leaves circled in treelessness," with its invocation of the Goethean Leaf (cf. "Goethe whistling on the winding path"), the object again precedes its apparent begetter. In the last example, a picture of the complete cycle, the consequence comes both before and after the cause: "And those to whom we devote the experiment / Acquired features before it." The whisper that precedes the lips, like the features of the "futures," in Ronen's term,[108] can be attributed to the force that makes the leaves circle. This force is the "blowing wind," which, as breath or spirit, comes and goes, in all directions at once.

The desert of "Draftsman of the desert," a counterpart to the "inner excess of space" as the object of the poet's investigation, resembles the sea of the first "I love the appearance of the fabric" in its vastness and its difficulty of access by measurement. "Lines" cannot account for such a subject; the "open forms" of "I love the appearance of the fabric" might. The wind of "Draftsman of the desert" is an implicit presence, too, in the first "Octave," where, in the guise of space, it is the agent that moves the sails. Its activity is comparable to the geometer's: "Otkrytye formy *cherti*a" ("Tracing open forms"); cf. "*Chert*ezhnik pustyni" ("Draftsman of the desert"). But its mode is antithetical: the curves of the "open forms" contrast with the geometer's straight lines. Like those curves, whether "regattas' arcs" ("*Dug*ami parusnykh gonok") or "arched extension" ("*dug*ovaia rastiazhka")[109] (cf. "*du*iushchii vetr" ["the blowing wind"]), the "rectifying sigh"—"vy*priam*itel'nyi vzdokh"—marks the appearance of the word after struggle.[110] The model in each case is the lips, which curve even as they straighten (*priamoi* 'straight'; cf. *rect-*). In the "Requiem," Mandelstam describes the posthumous life or "growth" of the protagonist. The body of the dead poet resembles a parabola endlessly approaching the asymptote: "Tak lezhi, molodei i lezhi, beskonechno *priamias'* " ("So lie, grow younger and lie, endlessly straightening").[111] Lines in the Einsteinian space-time continuum are curves, as opposed to the geometer's lines, which extend into a Euclidean infinity. The disgruntled geometer notwithstanding, the course of the "Octaves" as a whole celebrates the poet's business, for which the circling of the wind is a model. The poet's lines are curves, "penetrating the dusk of future times" (*Conversation about Dante*).

In the Voronezh poem "Rozhdenie ulybki" ("The Birth of a Smile"), the lips are both straight and curved: "I raduzhnyi uzhe strochitsia shov / Dlia beskonechnogo poznan'ia iavi" ("And an iridescent seam is already being stitched / For the endless cognition of reality"). *Strochitsia* 'is being stitched' is related to *stroka* 'line', as in a line of verse (cf. the second, colloquial meaning of the verb, "to scribble"). *Raduzhnyi* 'iridescent', paronomastically echoing *rozhdenie* 'birth', evokes a rainbow, not just its colors but also its curve (in the description of the stitched skull in the "Verses about the Unknown Soldier," another image of a seam is connected to consciousness: "Zvezdnym rubchikom shityi chepets" ["Cap sewn with a starry scar"]). The function of the curved line is its access to the infinity of cognition. In the following stanza, the lips take the form of a helix: "Ulitki rta naplyv i priblizhen'e" ("The influx and approach of the helix of the mouth"). Helices appear in "The minute appendage of the sixth sense" among the tiny organs of perception and articulation: "Monastyri ulitok il' stvorchatok, / Mertsaiushchikh resnichek govorok" ("Monasteries of helices or valves, / The murmur of flickering lashes"). The spiral models Mandelstam's conception of recurrence, distinguishing it from Blok's vicious circle. The graphical representation of uniform circular motion in time,[112] the spiral suggests identity in change; the return to the starting point marks a new level of operation.[113] In the "Octaves," the object of the poet's cognitive activity, the "inner excess of space," elicits spiral growth (in *Journey to Armenia*, thought is a growth):[114]

Преодолев затверженность природы,
Голуботвердый глаз проник в ее закон.
В земной коре юродствуют породы,
И как руда из груди рвется стон.

И тянется глухой недоразвиток
Как бы дорогой, согнутою в рог,
Понять пространства внутренний избыток
И лепестка и купола залог.

(Overcoming nature's induracy,
The blue-hard eye penetrated its law.
In the earth's crust the rocks act the holy fool,
And like ore, a groan bursts from the breast.

And the obscure embryo stretches,
Like a road bent into a horn—[115]
Must comprehend the inner excess of space,
And the pledge of the petal and the cupola.)

The "blue-hard eye," with its penetrating vision, is the ideal protagonist of the "Octaves." It recalls the "Requiem," where the blue-eyed (*golubye glaza*) Belyian skater traces curves on the "blue-hard river" (*golubotverdaia reka*). In the "Requiem," too, a curve or a spiral path is the way to measure the inner space: "Kogda dushe i toropkoi i robkoi / Predstanet vdrug *sobytii glubina,* / Ona bezhit *viiushcheiusia tropkoi,* / No smerti ei tropina ne iasna" ("When the depth of events suddenly appears / Before the timorous and timid soul, / It runs along a winding track, / But the path of death is not clear to it"). In "Schubert on the water," the experimenters' thought is manifested in the course of their meandering walk: "I Gete, svishchushchii na v'iushcheisia trope, / I Gamlet, myslivshii puglivymi shagami" ("And Goethe, whistling on the winding path, / And Hamlet, thinking with frightened steps"). Mandelstam composed "by ear" ("s golosa")[116] and while walking or pacing (thus writing—not the work of the scribe—was the mechanical recording of the already-completed poem; cf. "On tak zhe otnessia k bumage, / Kak kupol k pustym nebesam" ["It relates to the paper exactly / As the cupola does to the empty skies"]). The protagonist of the "Requiem" engages in the same active thought, both in the mountains and on ice: "I mashuchi stupal na tesnykh Al'p tropy, / I oziraiuchis', pustynnymi bregami / Shel, chuia razgovor beschislennoi tolpy" ("And gesticulating [he] stepped onto the paths of the close-ranked Alps, / And, looking around, along deserted shores / Went sensing the conversation of the countless crowd"); "Konkobezhets i pervenets, vekom gonimyi vzashei / Pod moroznuiu pyl' obrazuemykh vnov' padezhei" ("Ice skater and firstborn, whom the age threw out by the scruff of the neck, / To the accompaniment of the frost dust of cases formed anew"); ". . . gde priamizna rechei, / Zaputannykh, kak chestnye zigzagi / U kon'kobezhtsa v plamen' goluboi" (". . . where is the straightness of the speeches, / Convoluted like honest zigzags, / Of the ice skater in the blue flame").[117] Both the curving lips and the meandering steps, the poet's implements of cognition, reflect the convolutions of the brain; cf. "Vsemi izviliny svoego mozga" ("With all the convolutions of his brain") in *Conversation about Dante,* and "v ikh izvilinakh, razvivakh" ("in their convolutions, bifurcations") in the Voronezh poem "Ne u menia, ne u tebia—u nikh" ("Not I, not you—they have"). Mandelstam compares the skater's figure eights to the poet's speech; Annenskii understood the meaning of that shape: "Deviz Tainstvennoi poxozh / Na oprokinutoe 8" ("The Device of the Mysterious is like / An overturned 8"), he wrote in the opening lines of the poem called "∞." The "Octaves" are based on the same number and the same figure. These are eighty-eight lines, eight-liners—miniatures— that, when turned in a different direction, spell infinity.

The locus of infinity is the mind, identified as the inner space in "When, destroying the draft"; cf. the confirming rhyme "v ume" / "vo vnutrennei t'me" ("in the mind" / "in the inner darkness"). The noun *t'ma* accounts for two aspects of that space: its "darkness," associated with the internal location, and, in the second meaning of the word, its multitudinousness; the line "*Edinyi* vo vnutrennei *t'me*" ("Single in the inner darkness") juxtaposes the singular subject and the host from which he separates himself, having left external for internal space. The garden outside of space is "without people"; but it contains a potential multitude (*zadachnik kornei* 'problem book of roots').

In *Conversation about Dante,* indirection is the poetic mode. "Fear of direct answers" ("strakh pered priamymi otvetami") is a positive quality of the poet's speech.[118] Mandelstam represents the "evasiveness" of poetic speech with the metaphor of sails:[119]

> In order to reach the goal, it is necessary to take into consideration the wind blowing in a somewhat different direction. Just such is the law of tacking [*parusnogo lavirovan'ia*].
>
> Let us remember that Dante Alighieri lived in the age of the flowering of seafaring [*parusnogo moreplavan'ia*] and the highly developed art of sailing [*vysokogo parusnogo iskusstva*]. Let us not hesitate to keep in mind that he contemplated models of tacking and maneuvering [*parusnogo lavirovan'ia i manevrirovan'ia*]. Dante deeply honored the art of contemporary navigation. He was a student of this most evasive [*uklonchivyi*] and plastic sport, known to man from ancient times.[120]

Sails appear in the first version of "I love the appearance of the fabric" ("I dugami parusnykh gonok . . . " ["And with regattas' arcs"]); Mandelstam evokes them in another "Octave":

> И клена зубчатая лапа
> Купается в круглых углах,
> И можно из бабочек крапа
> Рисунки слагать на стенах.
>
> Бывают мечети живые—
> И я догадался сейчас:
> Быть может, мы Айя-София
> С бесчисленным множеством глаз.
>
> (And the maple's jagged paw
> Bathes in round corners,
> And one can compose pictures
> On the walls out of butterflies' specks.
>
> There are living mosques,
> And I've just figured it out:
> Maybe we're Hagia Sophia
> With a countless multitude of eyes.)

The "round corners" ("kruglye ugly") are the pendentives beneath the dome of the temple. The Russian architectural term *parusa* 'pendentives', literally, 'sails', appears not in the "Octaves" but in Mandelstam's earlier poem "Hagia Sophia": "Na *parusakh,* pod kupolom, chetyre / Arkhangela prekrasnee vsego" ("In the pendentives, beneath the cupola, four / Archangels are most beautiful of all") (cf. the vast space contained by the cupola of Karmravor, with its "four bakers").[121] The maple leaf ("paw") suggests the shape of the six-winged seraphim represented with wings outstretched in the pendentives of Hagia Sophia (jagged-edged leaves appear on the wall mounts in the gallery). The image of sails is reinforced in "Hagia Sophia" by the description of the cathedral "bathing [swimming] in the world" ("Prekrasen khram, kupaiushchiisia v mire"); in the "Octaves," the maple leaf "bathes [swims] in round corners" ("Kupaetsia v kruglykh uglakh"). Further linking the leaf with sails is the variant "green forms" ("zelenye formy"), which suggests vegetable growth, in "I love the appearance of the fabric." Like the "open forms" traced by the sails, the leaf describes curves; cf. "I v bezdrevesnosti kruzhilisia listy" ("And in treelessness leaves circled").

The cupola of "Hagia Sophia" is implied in "And the maple's jagged paw," where the "round corners" catch the curve of the dome and the "countless multitude of eyes" corresponds to the "forty windows—a triumph of light" ("sorok okon, sveta torzhestvo") that, as Mandelstam describes it in his 1912 poem, encircle its base. The arcs of the cupola again point to non-Euclidean geometry as the system according to which the inner space can be comprehended. The description of Hagia Sophia in the earlier poem as the "wise spherical building" ("mudroe, sfericheskoe zdan'e") anticipates the connection between circular structures and cognition in the "Octaves."[122] The cupola is a model for the thinking subject. In "And the maple's jagged paw," making the windows eyes, mentioning the possibility of "living mosques" (cf. the image of the skull as "Shakespeare's father" in the "Verses about the Unknown Soldier"), Mandelstam links this image with the cupola that he compares to the mind in "When, destroying the draft."

Unlike the mind in that poem, with its defining "period," the protagonist of "And the maple's jagged paw" is a collective subject. Multiplicities make up the mosque, just as the cathedral is constructed out of numerous plurals in the earlier "Hagia Sophia" ("sto sem' zelenykh mramornykh stolbov 'a hundred green marble columns', *apsidy i eksedry* 'apses and excedrae', *sorok okon* 'forty windows', *parusa* 'pendentives', *chetyre arkhangela* 'four archangels', *serafimy* 'seraphim'). In *Journey to Armenia,* Mandelstam compares the cupola of the Ashtarak church to the cupola of St. Peter's, which contains a startlingly vast multitude of things: "pod kotorym tysiachnye tolpy, i pal'my, i more svechei, i nosilki" ("beneath which are crowds of thousands, and palms, and a sea of candles, and litters").[123] The first person plural protagonist of "And the maple's jagged paw" is opposed not only to the singular subject of "When, destroying the draft": "*Edinyi* vo vnutrennei t'me" ("Single in the inner darkness"); in the last "Octave," too, a singular subject emerges from the collective: "I ia vykhozhu . . . *odin*" ("And I go out . . . alone").

The distinction between the individual and the collective intellect was a concern of the philosopher Averroes (1126–98), whom Mandelstam characterizes in *Conversation about Dante* as the "Arabic border" to the Aristotelian butterfly ("Aristotel', kak makhrovaia babochka, okaimlen arabskoi kaimoi Averroesa"). Averroes appears in Dante's Limbo along with a number of thinkers, including three who are important for the "Octaves": Euclid and, as this discussion will show, Ptolemy and Heraclitus (*Inferno* 4.138–44). Considering, apparently, Averroes's role in introducing Aristotle to the medieval world, alluding in particular to his famous commentaries on Aristotle (he quotes Dante's line, "Averrois, che il gran comento feo . . . "),[124] Mandelstam anticipates the butterfly imagery of the "Octaves": "Oni komponenty *odnogo risunka*. Oni umeshchaiutsia na membrane odnogo kryla" ("They are components of a single picture. They fit on the membrane of a single wing");[125] cf. "*risunki . . . iz babochek krapa*" ("pictures . . . out of butterflies' specks") in the "Hagia Sophia" octave. Averroes was born in Cordova during the period of the joint flowering of Muslim and Jewish culture in Spain; his works were translated into Hebrew.[126] His great contemporary, who praised Averroes's work, was the Sephardic Jewish thinker Maimonides, born scarcely more than a decade later in the same city; Maimonides's *Guide to the Perplexed* involved an attempt to reconcile Jewish faith with Aristotelian philosophy.[127] The description of Averroes as a marginal commentary to Aristotle recalls the image, in *The Egyptian Stamp,* of the notes "written on the side" ("to, chto napisano sboku"), which illustrate Mandelstam's conception of writing as reading and reveal its Talmudic roots. The mingling of traditions embodied by Averroes's life and work is reflected in the "Octaves," where the "Muslim" or "Arab" theme is not, pace Maiia Kaganskaia, antithetical to the poet's "Judaic cares."[128] The Arab and the Judaic are variants of a single theme.[129] (When Mandelstam took up the study of Spanish in Voronezh, the "Spanish" theme entered his poetry as another variant of the Jewish theme.)

The Lamarckian butterfly of *Journey to Armenia* inspired in the poet the "desire to look at nature through the big-eyed wings of this monster." In conjunction with the "countless multitude of eyes," the butterflies' specks in "And the maple's jagged paw," the mosaics of the cathedral murals, can be compared to the butterfly's wings conceived of as an organ of vision, a way of perceiving or representing the world. The reference to Hagia Sophia as a mosque, not a Christian cathedral with a pagan past as in the earlier "Hagia Sophia," links the butterfly with the Arab theme in the "Octaves"; in another "Octave," the butterfly is called a "Muslim": "O babochka, o

musul'manka, / V razrezannom savane vsia,— / Zhiznianochka i umiranka, / Takaia bol'shaia—siia!" ("O butterfly, o Muslim woman, / All in
a slit shroud, / Living one and dying one, / So big, this one!"). In the
context of the ancient association of the soul with a butterfly,[130] the representation of Averroes as the border of the Aristotelian butterfly recalls, in
particular, Averroes's commentary on Aristotle's *De anima,* and his discussion of Aristotle's arguments about the immortality of the soul. Mandelstam invokes this problem in calling the butterfly "zhiznianochka i
umiranka."[131]

The Arab theme persists in "Draftsman of the desert," in the line
"Arabskikh peskov geometr" ("Geometer of the Arab sands"), and in "In
needlelike, plague-filled goblets." It is concealed in the Pushkinian subtext
common to these two poems, *Pir vo vremia chumy* (*Feast in a Time of
Plague*), identified by Ronen and by Levin:[132] "Est' upoenie v boiu . . . / I
v araviiskom uragane, / I v dunovenii Chumy" ("There is rapture in battle . . . / And in the Arabian hurricane, / And in the breath of the
Plague"). The subtext confirms the other aspect of the theme: the "Arabian
hurricane," like the breath of the plague, like "[e]verything, everything that
threatens ruin," may be "charged, for the mortal heart, / With an ineffable
delight"—may contain the "guarantee of immortality" ("Vse, vse, chto
gibel'iu grozit, / Dlia serdtsa smertnogo tait / Neiz"iasnimy naslazhden'-
ia— / Bessmert'ia, mozhet byt', zalog"); cf. "I lepestka i kupola zalog"
("The guarantee of the petal and the cupola").[133] The poet who fears the
butterfly as a memento mori ("O flagom razvernutyi savan, / Slozhi svoi
kryl'ia—boius'!" ["O shroud unfurled like a flag, / Fold your wings—I'm
afraid!])[134] makes his business "Judaic cares," the alternation between
"babble" and "experiment." That alternation has a counterpart in a second
problem of Averroean philosophy, to which Dante refers in the *Purgatorio.*
In his understanding of Averroes's much-interpreted conception of the
"possible intellect" (*intellectus possibilis*), Dante rejects the idea that the
mind is immortal only to the degree that it possesses a fragment of a
universal and impersonal knowledge: such a view denies the immortality
of the individual.[135] The Arab theme in the "Octaves," suggesting the
problem of the individual mind in the context of the collective, is one
manifestation of the problem that Mandelstam addresses as "Judaic
cares": the relation between unconscious and conscious mental activity,
which leads to the poet's departure from the multitude and from three-
dimensional space.

❖ ❖

In "The Morning of Acmeism," revealing the antipathy to causality that would remain consistent throughout his work, Mandelstam calls for a new kind of proof: "Logic is the kingdom of the unexpected. To think logically is to be ceaselessly astonished."[136] Unexpected connections are the logic of the "Octaves." Levin observes that in the penultimate poem of the sequence, there is little logical or "real" connection between the first and second couplets, or between the third and fourth:[137]

В игольчатых чумных бокалах
Мы пьем наважденье причин,
Касаемся крючьями малых,
Как легкая смерть, величин.
И там, где сцепились бирюльки,
Ребенок молчанье хранит,
Большая вселенная в люльке
У маленькой вечности спит.

(In needlelike, plague-filled goblets
We drink the delusion of causes,
With large hooks we grasp small
Quantities, like light death.
While in the place where the jackstraws are joined,
The child keeps silent,
A big universe sleeps
In a small eternity's cradle.)

Syntax reflects the lack of connection: each pair of couplets is linked by juxtaposition but not by subordination or even by conjunction. Between both pairs of couplets, however, there is a metaphorical connection. Just as the child of lines 5–6 can be identified with the "large universe" of lines 7–8, so the "causes" of lines 1–2 have a counterpart in the "small quantities" of lines 3–4. The jackstraws of the second quatrain, resembling the small quantities of the first (cf. the "needlelike goblets"—and goblets are among the pieces in the game of *biriul'ki*),[138] continue the theme of causes. The connections that operate here are the antithesis of the "forced, mechanical accommodation, [the] mistrust of language" that Mandelstam associates, in "On the Nature of the Word," with "so-called Futurism."[139] In "The Morning of Acmeism," criticizing the Futurists for ignoring "conscious sense," Mandelstam refers to their words as jackstraws: "and, disdainfully discarding the jackstraws [*biriul'ki*] of the Futurists, for whom there is no greater delight than hooking [*zatsepit'*] a difficult word with a knitting needle, we introduce the Gothic into the relations between words."[140] With

their "knitting needles" the Futurists make "difficult word[s]" light and
insubstantial, by contrast with the material of the Acmeists, who "joyfully
accept [the weight (*tiazhest'*) of the word]." Just as inappropriate is the
activity of the first person plural in the penultimate "Octave," which, Levin
points out, tries to grasp small quantities with large hooks.[141] Mandelstam's beloved Gothic implies lightness, but it does so through the harmonious play of forces, through juxtapositions of mass: "iz tiazhesti nedobroi . . . prekrasnoe sozdam" ("from unpropitious weight . . . I will create something beautiful"); hence, too, "nosit' 'legche i vol'nee' " ("bear
'more lightly and willingly' ") in "The Morning of Acmeism." Thus the
Gothic cathedral, the epitome of medieval logic, today appears "monstrous": "What in the thirteenth century seemed the logical evolution of the
conception of organism—the Gothic cathedral—now gives the aesthetic
effect of monstrosity [*chudovishchnoe*]."[142] Monstrosity is an essential
property of the word that obeys the laws of the "kingdom of the unexpected." Mandelstam suggests the attraction of such monstrosity with reference to the "Italians": "Chto esli Ariost i Tasso, obvorozhaiushchie
nas, / *Chudovishcha* s lazurnym mozgom i cheshuei iz vlazhnykh glaz"
("What if Ariosto and Tasso, bewitching us, / Are monsters with an azure
brain and scales of moist eyes").[143] In the "Octaves," the jackstraws are not
subject to human manipulation (*stsepilis'* 'are joined'—no agent is given;
see also *derzhitsia sam* 'holds on itself' in "When, destroying the draft"; cf.
zatsepit' 'to hook' in "The Morning of Acmeism"), let alone understanding. The place where they are joined, where the connections are made,
which Mandelstam refers to as "there" (*tam*), is the new home of the orphan
poet; cf. "Kakovo tebe *tam* . . . " ("How things are with you there . . . ").
Hence the injunction "Da ne sprosiat tebia . . . " ("May you not be
asked . . . "). About that future, "the child keeps silent." From the perspective of the present, the connections are inscrutable, like the knowledge of
the child.

Thus the meaning of *biriul' ki* in the second quatrain goes beyond the
dangerous obsession with causes in the first. The phrase *igrat' v biriul' ki*
'to play jackstraws' has the idiomatic sense "to occupy oneself with trifles." This sense is evident in the Heraclitian subtext of the poem, identified
by Levin: "aiōn pais esti paizon, pesseuon; paidos hē basilēiē."[144] Levin
translates the epigram as "Vechnost'—ditia, igraiushchee v kosti,—tsarstvo rebenka" ("Eternity is a child playing dice—the kingdom of the
child").[145] M. Marcovich reads *pesseuon* as "playing dice (or draughts),"
and writes: "the implication of the verb: 'a *fortuitous* or *meaningless* action' . . . is much more likely than: 'a thoughtful and skillful one'; because
it is played by a [child], and because the issue of the game most probably

depended on the fortuity or chance of *dice* (since dice were used in the great majority of Greek games on play-board . . .)."[146] But a "meaningless" action may be evidence of the activity of poetry for Mandelstam (cf. "mixing what's important with trifles" in the letter to Tynianov). Child's play is the most serious business.

Hence Mandelstam's interpretation of Heraclitus's child. The child occurs in the "Octaves" in two hypostases. At the beginning of the sequence of poems, it suggests the end of a process; at the end of the sequence, it suggests the beginning—further evidence of the departure from the linear, "progressive" order of events. In "I love the appearance of the fabric," the child is a metaphor for space: "I dugami parusnykh gonok / Otkrytye formy chertia, / Igraet prostranstvo sprosonok, / Ne znavshee liul'ki ditia" ("And, tracing open forms / With regattas's arcs, / Space plays half-awake— / A child that has not known a cradle"). The curving lips substitute for the child-space in the second version of "I love the appearance of the fabric": "I vdrug dugovaia rastiazhka / Zvuchit v bormotan'iakh moikh" ("And suddenly an arched extension / Sounds in my mutterings"). In "The Birth of a Smile," it is the appearance of the child's smile ("Kogda zaulybaetsia ditia . . . " ["When a child begins to smile . . . "]), represented in terms of curves, that suggests the moment of cognition, which is also the moment of articulation. The "child that has not known a cradle" (hence "sprosonok" ["half-awake"]) is the newborn infant—the completed work, the uttered word. In the penultimate "Octave" the child is again associated with space: "bol'shaia vselennaia" ("a large universe"). But whereas the first child appears at birth, which is the end of embryonic development (cf. "I tianetsia glukhoi nedorazvitok" ["And the obscure embryo stretches"]), the second child appears in the cradle, and, still asleep, it is pointing elsewhere.

Mandelstam's second child contrasts with Blok's in "Ravenna": "Vse, chto minutno, vse, chto brenno, / Pokhoronila ty v vekakh. / Ty, kak *mladenets, spish'*, Ravenna, / *U* sonnoi *vechnosti* v rukakh" ("All that is momentary, all that is fleeting, / You have interred in the ages. / You, like an infant, sleep, Ravenna, / In the arms of sleepy eternity"). Blok's child-city is unchanging for all time. But the sleep of Mandelstam's child is not a perpetual deathlike drowsiness. The imminence of growth is acknowledged in a subtext identified by Ronen,[147] Lermontov's "Ditia v liul'ke" ("The Child in the Cradle"), a translation of Schiller's third epigram, "Das Kind in der Wiege": "Schastliv rebenok! i v liul'ke prostorno emu, no dai vremia / Sdelat'sia muzhem, i tesno pokazhetsia mir" ("Happy is the child! he has plenty of space even in the cradle, but give him time / To become a man, and the world will seem cramped").[148] Time enters the

picture, though Mandelstam, qualifying "eternity" as "small," both denies
its absolute existence and links it with space; the place "where the jackstraws are joined" is apparently subject to the laws of relativity (Mandelstam makes *vechnost'* comparable to *vselennaia:* it is not "eternity" but
"an . . . eternity," like "a . . . universe").[149] Specifically, with *malen'kaia
vechnost'* 'a small eternity', and not, for example, *korotkaia* 'short', he
interprets Heraclitus's much-disputed *aiōn* as the personal lifespan, rather
than "time" or "an age" or, as Levin gives it, simply "eternity."[150] *Malen'-
kaia vechnost'* is the lifetime of the child, which, because of his "small"
size or "young" age, seems to be forever.[151]

The child will awaken and grow. But limitation is not a negative
consequence of growth for this child, as it is for Lermontov's. The eternity
of Mandelstam's child is the "inner excess of space"—the internal realm
that, contained in a small compass, has the potential for infinite expansion.

Mandelstam explores the same internal realm in the last "Octave."
Again he describes the object of investigation, the dimension beyond
space, in spatial terms:[152]

И я выхожу из пространства
В запущенный сад величин
И мнимое рву постоянство
И самосознанье причин.

И твой, бесконечность, учебник
Читаю один, без людей,—
Безлиственный, дикий лечебник,
Задачник огромных корней.

(And I go out of space
Into the neglected garden of quantities,
And tear imaginary constancy
And causes' self-consciousness.

And, infinity, your textbook
[I] read alone, without people,
Leafless, wild book of cures,
Problem book of enormous roots.)

The first person singular is finally, definitively distinguished from the first
person plural, as "And I go out . . . " (see also "alone, without people")
follows "We drink . . . " in the preceding poem. Gumilev similarly distinguishes between the collective plural and the poet's singular: "My nikogda
ne ponimali / Togo, chto stoilo poniat'"; "I, simvol gornego velich'ia . . . / Vysokoe kosnoiazych'e / Tebe daruetsia, poet" ("We never

understood / What deserved to be understood"; "And, symbol of the heavenly majesty . . . / Sublime tongue-tie / Is given to you, poet"). Ronen mentions Gumilev's "Octave" as well as Fet's "Gory" ("Mountains") with reference to the "analogy between the revelation on the mountain and the act of poetic comprehension" in "The Slate Ode."[153] Mandelstam associates the journey "out" with the path onto the mountain, the place where revelation takes place. The poet, attempting to fulfill the injunction of "Overcoming nature's induracy," "goes out" for the purpose of cognition, in order to "comprehend the inner excess of space." The garden that implies infinity, like the cradle that contains a "large universe," is another bounded area with an infinite internal dimension—the dimension of growth, of the future.[154]

While the last "Octave," like the next to last, does not correspond to any "real" situation, the figure of the garden organizes the poem. Six of the thirty words in the poem belong to the semantic field of the garden: *sad* 'garden', *kornei* 'roots', *zapushchennyi* 'neglected', *bezlistvennyi* 'leafless', *dikii* 'wild', *rvu* 'I tear'). This garden has a number of features that link it with other Mandelstamian gardens, which, typically desolate and vast, are associated with illness, apocalypse, death. The garden in a 1913 poem is both forbidden and abandoned: "I za reshetkoi zapovednoi / Pusteet postepenno sad" ("And beyond the forbidden grille / The garden grows gradually empty").[155] In *Journey to Armenia,* an overgrown garden appears to the traveler a refuge from an official conversation: "Mne uzhe stanovilos' skuchno, i ia vse chashche pogliadyval na kusok *zaglokhshego sada* v okne" ("I was already getting bored, and more and more often I glanced at the bit of overgrown garden in the window"). In the same prose, Mandelstam tells of the schoolteacher who converted a little-used piece of orchard into a garden and was excluded from the collective as a result.[156] The isolation from people implied by the instructive Armenian tale appears already in 1917 as an attribute of the garden in "A stream of golden honey flowed from the bottle." The approach to this garden anticipates a similar move in the "Octaves": "Posle chaiu my *vyshli v* ogromnyi korichnevyi *sad*" ("After tea we went out into the enormous brown garden); compare "I ia vykhozhu . . . v . . . sad" ("And I go out . . . into . . . the garden").[157] D. M. Segal uses the term *bezliudnost'* 'unpopulatedness', 'desolation' (cf. Blok's "Bezliudnost' nizkikh ostrovov" ["The desolation of the low islands"]) to describe the scene in "A stream of golden honey";[158] in the garden of "And I go out of space," the poet, characteristically, is alone: "odin, bez liudei."

The first garden is enormous: "*ogromnyi korichnevyi sad.*" So is the second. "Infinity's textbook," if not a metaphor for the already metaphorical garden, is associated with it by contiguity (the poet in the garden reads the textbook); and the garden offers "enormous roots," echoing the earlier description: "Zadachnik *ogromnykh korn*ei." The total context of the attribute *ogromnoe* in Mandelstam's work includes the features "apocalypse, cataclysm, death." See, for example, "V ogromnoi komnate nad chernoiu Nevoi, / Dvenadtsat' mesiatsev poiut o smertnom chase" ("In the enormous room above the black Neva, / The twelve months sing about the hour of death"); "Vlachitsia traurnoi kaimoi / Ogromnyi flag vospominan'-ia" ("The enormous flag of recollection / Drags itself along with a funereal border"); "Nu chto zh, poprobuem: ogromnyi, neukliuzhii, / Skripuchii povorot rulia. / . . . My budem pomnit' i v leteiskoi stuzhe, / Chto desiati nebes nam stoila zemlia" ("Okay, let's try: an enormous, awkward, / Creaking turn of the tiller. / . . . We will remember, even in Lethean cold, / That the earth cost us ten heavens"); "I bessmertnykh roz ogromnyi vorokh / U Kipridy na rukakh. / . . . I blazhennykh zhen rodnye ruki / Legkii pepel soberut" ("And an enormous heap of immortal roses / Are in Cypris's hands. / . . . And the kindred hands of blessed women / Will gather the light ash"); "Ogromnyi park. Vokzala shar stekliannyi. / Zheleznyi mir opiat' zavorozhen. / . . . Na trizne miloi teni, / V poslednii raz nam muzyka zvuchit" ("The enormous park. The glass globe of the station. / The iron world is spellbound again. / . . . At the funeral feast of the dear shade, / For the last time, music sounds for us"); "Vytashchil gornyi rybak raspisnye lazurnye sani. / . . . Ves' vozdukh vypila ogrom-naia gora" ("The mountain fisherman has dragged out the decorated azure sleigh. / . . . The enormous mountain has drunk up all the air").[159] In "Sokhrani moiu rech' navsegda . . . " ("Preserve my speech forever . . . " [1931]), where the poet's situation is isolated in the extreme ("Ia, ne-priznannyi brat, otshchepenets v narodnoi sem'e" ["I, unacknowledged brother, apostate in the family of the people"]), the garden has associations of death ("Kak pritselias' na smert' gorodki zashibaiut v sadu . . . " ["As taking a deadly aim, they knock down the skittles in the garden"—based on Ronen's translation]).[160] V. N. Toporov comments on the consequences of the solitary state in Mandelstam's work: "space . . . widens, becomes rarified, transparent, apparently infinite, not correlated with everyday experience and therefore threatening, instilling sensations close to agorapho-bia."[161] Such sensations are part of the scene in the last "Octave."

The dimensions of the Mandelstamian garden suggest a distorted perspective. In "Ia k gubam podnoshu etu zelen' " ("I raise this greenery to my lips" [1937]), the disturbing magnificence of the garden gives it an apocalyptic coloration: "I ne slishkom li velikolepno / Ot gremuchego parka glazam?" ("And isn't the fulminating park / Too magnificent for the eyes?"). The landscape of yet a third garden in *Journey to Armenia,* the scene pictured in the Persian miniature of "Around the Naturalists," skewed as if it were ill with a glandular disease, is consistent with this pattern ("The horizon is abolished. There is no perspective. A charming slow-wittedness. The fox's noble staircase ascension and the sense of the gardener's [*sadovnik*] leaning against the landscape and architecture").[162] A shifting of boundaries occurs in "A stream of golden honey. . . " The ancient Tauris is conflated with the modern Crimea; the vines participate in two ages at once: "V kamenistoi Tavride nauka Ellady—i vot / Zolotykh desiatin blagorodnye, rzhavye griadki" ("In stony Tauris is the science of Hellas—and lo! / The noble rusted furrows of the golden acres"). The mountains appear from the garden through the miragelike shimmering of the air: "Gde vozdushnym steklom oblivaiutsia sonnye gory" ("Where the sleepy hills are drenched with airy glass"). The consequence of these temporal and spatial dislocations is the triumphant return of the classical hero: "Odissei vozvratilsia, prostranstvom i vremenem polnyi" ("Odysseus has returned, full of space and time"). In the "Octaves," the extraordinary perspective of the protagonist who "read[s] . . . infinity's textbook" implies the other "prospect" suggested by Ivanov's vision of the choral ring: the alternative fate of Odysseus, the relocation of the hero in the place outside of space.

In a "posthumous" declaration of January 1937, Mandelstam again implies the association of the poet's solitary situation with death: "Eshche ne umer ty, eshche ty ne odin" ("You have not yet died, you are not yet alone"). In "Stansy" ("Stanzas"), dated May–June 1935 (the same summer that Mandelstam completed the first and the last two "Octaves"), the protagonist's movement exactly reverses the departure from space, and the opposite association holds: "No, kak v kolkhoz idet edinolichnik, / Ia *v mir vkhozhu, i liudi* khoroshi" ("But as the private farmer enters the collective, / I enter the world, and people are good"); and "Ia dolzhen zhit', dysha i bol'sheveia, / I pered smert'iu khorosheia, / Eshche pobyt' i poigrat' *s liud'mi*" ("I have to live, breathing and bolshevizing, / And looking better on the point of death, / To be and play with people for a while still"). Being with people stays the poet's death sentence. Ronen suggests that the line "Chitaiu odin, bez liudei" ("I read alone, without people") may be motivated by Pushkin's "I odin, bez gostei, / P'iu za zdravie Meri" ("And alone, without guests, / I drink Mary's health"), from "Iz Barry Cornwall" ("From Barry Cornwall"), the translation of a lyric that appeared in the same volume as the original of Pushkin's *Feast in a Time of Plague.* In the "Octaves," the poet departs from the feast, to seek, alone, a cure for the plague of causal thinking in the garden and book of "And I go out of space."

In the last "Octave," the words that convey the desolation of the scene also indicate mortal illness. In addition to characterizing the garden as neglected, *zapushchennyi* can refer to a situation that has been ignored too long—for example, an illness that has become incurable. The attributes of the herbal (*lechebnik*) seem to deny the possibility of cure it implies. *Bezlistvennyi* eliminates the pages of the herbal and the leaves of the medicinal plants; *dikii,* which has the idiomatic sense of "painful, unhealthy, morbid," is close to *zapushchennyi* in suggesting the unchecked evolution of an illness. But this picture changes with each word.

The desolate garden that portends death points to the possibility of new beginnings. Real writing does not require leaves, sheets of paper (cf. "proud flesh, an insane excrescence" in *Fourth Prose*).[163] *Dikii* can refer also, like *zapushchennyi,* to unrestrained vegetable growth—a sign of vitality. The herbal offers an antidote to the "delusion of causes" by its very contradictory being. *Bezlistvennyi* and *dikii,* antitheses with reference to the garden, both describe a state prior to or following culture. The "leafless, wild herbal," like the "neglected garden," suggests culture turned back to nature; it is an artifact of culture, as a book, but wild and without "leaves" or pages. In "Schubert on the water" leaves appear in the absence of trees: "Byt' mozhet, prezhde gub uzhe rodilsia shepot, / I v bezdrevesnosti kruzhilisia listy" ("Perhaps before the lips the whisper was already born, / And in treelessness leaves circled").[164] Leaves without trees are the leaves of a book. And, like the whisper before the lips, leaves in treelessness suggest the immanence of culture in nature. In the last "Octave" the situation is reversed. A book without leaves is the book of nature.[165] The garden is a piece of nature that has been bounded,[166] nature become culture. But a "neglected garden," like a "leafless book," is in the process of reverting to nature—coming unbound. "Infinity's textbook" is at once bound, being a book, and unbounded, teaching about limitlessness.[167]

The protagonist of the "Octaves" "goes out" to observe the cycle of culture and nature in its entirety. The neglected garden embodies this cycle; it recalls the newly archaic Petersburg of "The Word and Culture," as another place where nature, having been cultivated by man, returns to its primitive beginnings. Nadezhda Mandelstam writes that the vision of a world without people that recurs in Mandelstam's work from 1921 on is a tormenting picture of the end of culture—while man, the human mind, "embodies the meaning of life."[168] But "And I go out of space," which she does not include in her catalogue of such future visions, challenges the inexorable bleakness of that interpretation.

❖ ❖

Even as the attributes of the garden continue to operate on one level, the entire situation of "And I go out of space" is transferred to an abstract plane, corresponding to the movement of the protagonist out of space. On this plane, where *sad velichin* 'the garden of quantities' is the organizing figure, mathematical models apply. The last of the series of integers mentioned or alluded to in the "Octaves" appears in "And I go out of space": *odin* means not just "alone"; it is also "one." The various oppositions of the "Octaves" can be derived from the fundamental Pythagorean opposition singular / multitude, and the "garden of quantities" itself is a Pythagorean realm, where number is the essence of things.[169] But according to Pythagorean doctrine, enumeration begins with two; as "one," the poet is prior to number. Like the period in the mind, no longer weighed down by draft and notes, the poet in the garden (who has a function analogous to that of the period and the cupola, or the Gothic spire of "The Morning of Acmeism"), having departed from the first person plural ("we drink"—"And I go out"), remains emphatically singular: "*odin, bez* liudei" ("alone, without people"); cf. "*bez* tiagostnykh snosok, / *Edinyi* vo vnutrennei t'me" ("without weighty notes, / Single in the inner darkness"). Derived, like the period, from the multitude, the poet is in turn the source from which number derives, the experiment (*opyt*) out of which the future crowd (*te*) will be generated. The circular structure of the cycle of babble and experiment recalls Heraclitus's "ek panton hen kai ex henos panta" (Marcovich translates "out of every thing there can be made a unity, and out of this unity all things are made").[170]

The future crowd is implicit in the last "Octave." The garden is created like a "mural out of butterflies' specks," or a "picture of Russia's vastness" out of "infinitesimals." Mandelstam indicates as much in calling it "sad *velich*in": it is those "*magn*itudes" that make the garden large. The poet would follow the cycle investigated in "Schubert on the water," moving from the completed work, the "experiment," as it appears in the present and in three-dimensional space, to its infinitesimal components: to "babble," to the prearticulate origins, persisting at a different point in the cycle. The move "back" follows the operations of the work itself. In *Conversation about Dante*, Mandelstam describes the poetic composition as a dynamic form, elaborated as one detail after another breaks off, "departs into its own functional space or dimension."[171] The comprehension of the work means tracing each part to its origins. This is the task of the poet who himself departs into a new dimension—there to become a reader.

The garden offers a perspective of the place where the "child keeps silent"—the place to which the "orphan" of the "Requiem" has departed (cf. "alone, without people"). The poet resembles Archimedes, who developed spherical as opposed to plane geometry (one of his books is *Peri elikōn [On Spirals]*; cf. the curve called the "spiral of Archimedes"), and whose famous request for a place to stand beyond the earth is the subject of Schiller's first two epigrams ("Ein Wort an die Proselytenmacher" [1795]; "An die Proselytenmacher" [1800]).[172] The spiral or helix is the model for growth in the "Octaves." In *Psammitēs (The Sand-reckoner)*, Archimedes determined a method of describing large numbers using grains of sand as a model; the object was a sphere the size of the universe. The significance of the work was not just the method but also the conception of calculation, through the accumulation of small quantities.[173] This principle is basic to the mathematics of the "Octaves." The poet outside of space must have the "capacity for accommodation" that Mandelstam attributes to the naturalist, whose eye, "like [the eye] of a predatory bird, ... turns first into binoculars, then into a jeweler's magnifying glass."[174] As Pallas does, the poet sees at close range, and at the same time he sees the whole picture.

That capacity is essential, too, for the reader attempting to discern the continually shifting outline of the garden. The place outside of space can be compared to the realm of imaginary mathematics described by P. A. Florenskii in his 1922 book *Mnimosti v geometrii (Imaginary Entities in Geometry)*. In an appendix, discussing the significance of the engraving on the title page by V. A. Favorskii,[175] Florenskii comments on the division of the representation into a geometrical figure and its "imaginary" obverse, which appears properly out of focus when the eye is fixed on the "real" figure. The imaginary plane is not visible but "palpable," "salient" (Florenskii gives as one analogy a transparent window, sensed by the forehead pressed against it). Its physical aspect is merely a convention:[176]

> The page, as such, of course is not white, but colorless: it is the abstract possibility of representations. It would be a mistake to see in this page a piece of paper, matter, when that [paper] in itself is neither a plane nor any other geometrical figure; by page, one must understand the infinitely fine space of representations, something like a transparent film placed on the paper. This film, in itself, is yet not one or another *side* of the representational plane, but the entire plane, with both of its sides and all of its thickness, though in fact it is infinitesimal.[177]

Mandelstam's garden has just such an abstract existence. That "leafless" book is a locus of "imaginary" values ("*mnimoe* postoianstvo / I samosoznan'e prichin"),[178] and its dimensions are infinitesimal.

Characterizing time in the imaginary realm as "flow[ing] in *reverse, so that consequence precedes cause*" (his emphasis), Florenskii links this most modern, relativistic conception with what he calls the Ptolemaic-Aristotelian-Dantean ontology: "In other words, here efficient causality is replaced . . . by final causality, by teleology." At the point where this order takes over, the length and mass of physical bodies become "imaginary" (*mnimyi*).[179] In "On the Nature of the Word," published the same year as Florenskii's book, Mandelstam, invoking the theory of relativity, considers a different order of events, where, as in the "Octaves," the "whisper" may precede the "lips." Mandelstam, too, associates Dante's cosmology with the discoveries of modern physics (*Conversation about Dante*);[180] and he anticipates his Dante study by nearly a decade in embracing Bergson's idea of duration, which entails the deployment of events in their spatial extension rather than their temporal sequence: "He [Bergson] is interested exclusively in the inner relation of events. He frees this relation from time and examines it separately."[181] The "fan of phenomena" unfurled by the Bergsonian poet recalls the causal chain of "The Morning of Acmeism": Mandelstam does not deny its existence, but he indicates the need for a new relation to it: "Budem zhe dokazyvat' svoiu pravotu tak, chtoby v otvet nam sodrogalas' vsia tsep' prichin i sledstvii ot al'fy do omegi, nauchimsia nosit' 'legche i vol'nee podvizhnye okovy bytiia'" ("We will prove our rightness so that the entire chain of causes and consequences from alpha to omega trembles in response to us, we will learn to bear 'more lightly and willingly the mobile fetters of being'").[182] In each case, the linear—temporal—sequence is no longer predictive.

The deployment of events in space suggests a different relation to time: "Chtoby spasti printsip edinstva v vikhre peremen i bezostanovochnom potoke iavlenii . . . " ("In order to preserve the principle of unity in the whirl of changes and the ceaseless stream of phenomena . . . "). Bergson's purpose, as Mandelstam describes it, is close to the problem of Schiller's fifth epigram, "Das Unwandelbare," which, like the first four, concerns the shape of the universe and the possibility of comprehending it. Here the temporal dimension enters the picture, as it does in the last two "Octaves": "'Unaufhaltsam enteilet die Zeit.'—Sie sucht das Beständ'-ge. / Sei getreu, und du legst ew'ge Fesseln ihr an." *Printsip edinstva* 'the principle of unity' corresponds to Schiller's "Das Beständige"; *v vikhre peremen i bezostanovochnom potoke iavlenii* 'in the whirl of changes and the ceaseless stream of phenomena' to "Unaufhaltsam enteilet die Zeit" (cf. *bezuderzhnost' linii* 'the unruliness of lines'). The Bergsonian "teaching" itself ("In order to preserve the principle of unity . . . ") is reminiscent of Schiller's injunction "Sei getreu." The result of the effort, "ew'ge Fessel'n," has a counterpart in the "mobile fetters of being" that the poet had learned to accept in subordinating the causal chain to a different logic.[183] In "On the Nature of the Word," Mandelstam gives "infinity" a negative recommendation: "Dvizhenie *beskonechnoi tsepi* iavlenii bez nachala i kontsa est' imenno durnaia *beskonechnost'*, nichego ne govoriashchaia umu, ishchushchemu edinstva i sviazi" ("The movement of an infinite chain of phenomena without beginning or end is precisely a bad infinity, saying nothing to the mind that seeks unity and relation").[184] The "infinite chain of phenomena" is the causal chain; Mandelstam refers to this conception of causality with *navazhden'e prichin* 'the delusion of causes' in the penultimate "Octave." But *durnaia beskonechnost'* contrasts with *uchebnik [beskonechnosti]* 'the textbook of infinity' and the lessons of the garden. From the perspective of the place outside of space, infinity acquires a different aspect. It is self-enclosed: it is the inner space of the mind.

Just as the sequence of causes appears meaningless from an extraspatial perspective, so, too, the endless extension of the geometer's lines is superseded, outside of space, by a different constancy. In the "Octaves," Mandelstam looks back at Blok's geometry in "Na ostrovakh" ("On the Islands"). The protagonist of Blok's poem, regretting the lost world of "ancient loyalty" ("O razve, razve kliast'sia nado / V starinnoi *vernosti* navek" ["Oh, must one, must one swear / To ancient loyalty forever?"]), announces his determined participation in a different mode of activity, represented as counting: "Net, s *postoianstvom geometra,* / Ia chisliu kazhdyi raz bez slov, / Mosty, chasovniu, rezkost' *vetra,* / *Bezliudnost'* nizkikh ostrovov" ("No, with a geometer's constancy, / I enumerate each time without words, / The bridges, the chapel, the harshness of the wind, / The desolation of the low islands"). In "Draftsman of the desert," Mandelstam echoes Blok's rhyme *geometra* / *vetra* and also his *khrust peska* 'the crunch of sand'—cf. *Arabskikh peskov geometra* 'Geometer of the Arab sands'. Expressions in *bez-* 'without', frequent in "On the Islands," recur in "And I go out of space": *bez liudei* 'without people' corresponds to *bezliudnost'* 'desolation'; cf. also *beskonechnost'* 'infinity' and *bezlistvennyi* 'leafless'; *bez slov* 'without words' is implicit in this octave, the setting of which is a world of "roots" that precedes articulate speech. Mandelstam's *postoianstvo* 'constancy', too, echoes Blok's, juxtaposed in "On the Islands" to its companion *vernost'* 'loyalty'.

Blok's protagonist, in committing himself to the "geometer's constancy" and to a word of mechanical—meaningless—activity, says farewell to the values of the past: "Ved' grud' moia na poedinke / Ne vstretit shpagi zhenikha" ("My breast will not meet / The bridegroom's sabre in a duel"). Mandelstam returns to the old values, to the original Acmeist virtues, in entering the "more complex dimension" outside of space. In the last section of his book, Florenskii suggests that the theory of relativity has "rehabilitated" the Ptolemaic-Dantean cosmos; Ptolemy's geocentric construction of the universe appears as valid as the Copernican heliocentric model.[185]

Mandelstam welcomes this change, writing in *Conversation about Dante:* "Ptolemy has returned from the back porch! . . . Giordano Bruno was burned in vain!"[186] Bruno, author of philosophical works on the infinite, who rejected, heretically, the notion of absolute truth, is associated here, like Ptolemy, with the kind of dynamic description that is essential in poetry as in science. Mandelstam writes, in the preceding paragraph:

> We describe just what we should not describe, that is, the stopped text of nature, and have grown unaccustomed to describing the single thing that, by its structure, is subject to poetic representation, that is, impulses, intentions, and amplitudinal vacillations.[187]

The distinction between these two approaches recalls the poet's quarrel with the geometer, whose lines are inadequate to the "shifting sands"; only the wind can account for its "amplitudinal vacillations." The name of the great geometer *Ptolemy* is ciphered into "Draftsman of the desert" (see also "Schubert on the water") with the reiterated *ptlptlptlptptpt* that accounts for the alternation of babble with experiment.

❖ ❖

In the universe of modern physics, to which Mandelstam assigns Dante, the dimension beyond space is time.[188] Mandelstam attributes to Dante an extra sense with respect to time: "Uniting what cannot be united, Dante changed the structure of time, though perhaps it's the other way around: he was compelled to resort to a glossolalia of facts, to the synchronism of events, names, and traditions sundered by the ages precisely because he heard the overtones of time."[189] The response to the perception of time, in Mandelstam's case as in Dante's, is a new relation to space—a "playing" with space, which Mandelstam represents in the "Octaves" as the playing of space itself ("Igraet prostranstvo sprosonok" ["Space plays half-awake"]). Comparing Dante's poetry to a crystal, of which the multiple facets cannot be embraced by the eye all at once, Mandelstam likens the crystal, in turn, to a hive; bees work to create this "thirteen-thousand-sided figure": "Their collaboration becomes increasingly broad and complex in the process of hive-formation, by means of which *space seems to go out of itself* [*prostranstvo kak by vykhodit iz sebia samogo*]."[190] In *Journey to Armenia,* "going out" is associated with illumination, discovery, and, by implication, reading (the beloved "naturalists"—who have the ideal eye): "Since my friends . . . drew me into the circle of the natural sciences, a wide glade has taken shape in my life. A way out [*vykhod*] into a bright field of activity [*deiatel' noe pole*] has opened up before me." In *Conversation about Dante,* the poet, becoming a reader, "goes out of space," enters the dimension of poetry:[191]

When you read [*chitaesh'*] . . . with all your might and with complete conviction; when you move completely into the field of action of the poetic material
[*pereseliaesh'sia na deistvennoe pole poeticheskoi materii*] . . . then . . . the
hegemony of the conductor's baton takes over orchestrated space, tearing
[*rvushchaia*] it, projecting from the voice like a more complex mathematical
dimension out of three-dimensionality.[192]

The protagonist of the "Octaves," too, settles in that new dimension in
the process of reading. The verb *chitat'* (*chitaiu, chitaesh'* 'read') is
common to the last "Octave" and the Dante essay. "[V]ykhozhu iz prostranstva" ("go out of space") corresponds to and is complemented by
"pereseliaesh'sia na deistvennoe pole poeticheskoi materii" ("move completely into the field of action of the poetic material"); in the prose, the
place *to which* is given. *Rvu* 'tear' has a counterpart in the activity of the
conductor's baton, "tearing" space (*rvushchaia ego*). The extraspatial garden, where the same process of reading takes place, is the locus of the
activity of poetry.[193]

In the context of the garden, *rvat'* 'to tear' has a literal sense: the poet
plucks constancy and causality as if they were among the "quantities"
growing there. A form of that verb appears in "Overcoming nature's induracy": "I kak ruda iz grudi *rvetsia* ston" ("And like ore a groan bursts from
the chest"). This is a birth (cf. *glukhoi nedorazvitok* 'the obscure embryo'
in the second quatrain); as the response to the "penetrat[ion of nature's]
law," the "groan" is similar to the "rectifying sigh" that marks the "appearance of the fabric" in the first two "Octaves." *Rvetsia* suggests the emergence of another dimension out of three dimensions. In the last stanza of
"Admiralteistvo" ("The Admiralty"), an affixed form of the verb *rvat'*
appears with reference to the same problem: "I vot razo*rva*ny trekh
izmerenii uzy." The "bonds of three dimensions are sundered," but space is
not eliminated: "I otkryvaiutsia vsemirnye moria" ("And the universal seas
open up").[194] In *Conversation about Dante,* the voice, which remains in
three dimensions, is not eliminated by the conductor's baton but comes to
life beneath it. The conductor's baton coordinating the activity of reading
recalls the "summons" of the medium in *Journey to Armenia,* to which the
growing organism responds: "Thus, the organism for the medium is a
probability, a desirability and an expectation. The medium for the organism is an inviting force. Not so much a covering as a summons."[195] The
poet in the garden does not eradicate the things growing there (cf. Brown's
contrary interpretation of *rvu*),[196] any more than he abandons space in
leaving it, but incorporates them into a new system of values. Constancy
and causality are transformed as the poet picks them, into values charac-

terized by the laws of the "imaginary" geometry of the garden outside of
space.

Ogromnye korni 'enormous roots', in the last line of "And I go out of
space," is further evidence of the new logic of the place outside of space.
The textbook offers "roots" both as an herbal and as a math book. *Korni,*
the last word of the poem, marks the intersection of several themes in the
"Octaves." In the larger context of these poems about cognition and creation, and here, with reference to books and to *uchebnik* 'textbook' in
particular, it suggests the roots of words. In the context of the garden
setting, it suggests the roots of plants (a sense consistent with *tkan'* as
"tissue") and, following *lechebnik* 'herbal', more specifically, medicinal
roots.[197] In the context of *zadachnik* 'problem book' and the mathematical
imagery, it suggests also the roots of numbers, mathematical roots. The
roots are described as "enormous." However, *ogromnye korni* does not
refer to the roots extracted; it refers to the degree of those roots. It is here
that the poet, as reader, undertakes the task that is the reverse of the poet's
project in "The Morning of Acmeism":[198] he must extract the enormous
roots from the work, so as to derive its tiny components. The word *velichina,* like "magnitude," suggests something large (cf. *velikii* 'great',
'big', 'large'). But in the oxymoronic universe outside of space—where
the standard of measurement is the child, considered here a "large"
universe—the quantities invoked are correspondingly small (cf. "The minute appendage of the sixth sense"). The larger the index, the smaller the
result, the actual root, will be.[199]

The problem-book that poses "enormous roots" intends very small
quantities, as is consistent with internal growth; in the garden of infinity,
and consistent with Florenskii's imaginary geometry, these would be infinitesimal ones. The big picture is composed of small quantities ("I mozhno iz
babochek krapa / Risunki slagat' na stenakh" ["And one can compose
pictures / On the walls out of butterflies' specks"]), as Mandelstam implies with reference to Pallas's work, in the passage that the "Octaves"
echo: "Kartina ogromnosti Rossii slagaetsia u Pallasa iz *beskonechno malykh velichin*" ("The picture of Russia's vastness is composed in Pallas of
infinitesimals [infinitely small quantities]"). The small quantities are the
elements that are the matter of the experiment: *lepet, te.*

E is the dominant stressed vowel in the second quatrain of "And I go
out of space": there are five instances, as opposed to zero in the first (there
are four instances of unstressed *e* in the second half, and four in the first).
The prominence of this bright vowel (it is stable, too, in two instances:
uchebnik, lechebnik) reinforces the references to cure (*lechebnik*) and to

the possible solution to a problem (*zadachnik kornei*).[200] In this respect, too, Mandelstam echoes Lermontov's "Vykhozhu odin ia na dorogu" ("I go out alone onto the road"), where *e* appears for the first time as a rhyme vowel in the last stanza, and is the unique rhyme vowel there.[201] In "Schubert on the water," *e* comprises just short of one quarter of the stressed vowels; it appears most conspicuously in combination with *t,* in the future-oriented *te.*

This is the realm the poet enters in going out of space. He penetrates to a future of primitive beginnings, to the rudiments of language—to the "primordial words" ("pervonachal'nye slova") that are, in Gumilev's phrase, the "guarantee of immortality for mortals."

❖ ❖

In going out, the poet follows the fate of Odysseus. The final section of Florenskii's book is devoted to the trajectory of Dante's pilgrimage through the center of the earth, which Florenskii describes in terms of non-Euclidean (Riemannian) space. His controversial discussion[202] supports the possibility of a Dantean connection to the journey "out." While Mandelstam refers to the voyage of Odysseus, and Florenskii to Dante's journey, the two protagonists are very close. Lotman calls them doubles, and sees their likeness not only in the common goal of their different paths— Purgatory—but also in the fact that both of them, unlike all other personages in the *Divine Comedy,* as "voluntary or compulsory exiles, driven by a powerful passion, cross the boundaries separating one realm of the universe from another"; both "constantly cross the borders of forbidden spaces."[203] Florenskii provides the mathematical model for such a transgression.

One version of the hero's journey is the subject of Schiller's fourth epigram: "Endlich trägt das Geschick ihn schlafend an Ithakas Küste, / Er erwacht und erkennt jammernd das Vaterland nicht." Batiushkov reworked Schiller's "Odysseus" as "Sud'ba Odisseia" ("The Fate of Odysseus"): "Kazalos', nebesa karat' ego ustali, / I tikho sonnogo domchali / Do milykh rodiny davnozhelannykh skal. / Prosnulsia on: i chto zh? otchizny ne poznal" ("It seemed the heavens grew tired of punishing him, / And quietly hastened the sleepy one / To the dear, long-desired native crags. / He awoke: and what do you think? he didn't know his fatherland"). This hero, unlike the Odysseus who returns fulfilled in "A stream of golden honey. . . , " awakens from dreams of Ithaca to an alien homeland. The protagonist of the "Octaves," too, comes upon an unfamiliar world.

But, like the voyage of Dante's Ulysses, who does not return, his is a journey of cognition. Sails (*parusa*) are linked to cognition in the "Octaves," as the arcs of their movement trace the "open forms" of speech, and as their architectural counterpart (*kruglye ugly* = **parusa*) defines the cupola associated with the skull and its contents (cf. "Mysl'iu penitsia . . . / Chepchik schast'e—Shekspira otets" ["Froths with thought . . . / Little cap of happiness—Shakespeare's father"]). Mandelstam hails Dante's time as the great age of navigation; sailing was essential to the discovery of new worlds.[204] In *Inferno* 26, "experience" (or "experiment"; cf. Mandelstam's *opyt*) and "knowledge" (cf. cognition as a theme of the "Octaves") are motivations for the expedition: "non vogliate negar *l'esperienza*, / di retro al sol, del mondo sanza gente. / Considerate la vostra semenza: / fatti non foste a viver come bruti, / ma per seguir virtute e *canoscenza*" (116–20). The poet of the "Octaves" resembles the Odysseus who, in Mandelstam's translation of Dante, proposes to go out into uncharted waters: "tuda, gde mir prodolzhaetsia bez liudei" ("where the world continues without people"); compare the "kingdom of the spirit without man" in "The Word and Culture."[205] Mandelstam echoes *bez liudei* in the last "Octave," describing another final voyage into the uninhabited future. The poet undertakes the journey in the same spirit as Dante's hero. His purpose is the antithesis of the dream of the Lermontovian wayfarer in "*Vykhozhu odin ia* na dorogu," who "go[es] out alone" to confront the universe ("pustynia" ["the wilderness"]; cf. "zapushchennyi sad" ["the neglected garden"]) and, sensing a heavenly music, prefers the quietude of the sleep it inspires to the travail of the road.[206] Mandelstam's poet seeks not oblivion but a heightened awareness; participation, not in an eternal harmony, but in a cosmic flow of time. The plot of "And I go out of space" reveals parallels with that of "The Slate Ode," as Ronen describes it: "the plot . . . develops around *the central event of enlightenment,* the transition from a state of obliviousness, through recollection, to a state of superconscious creative ecstasy, and culminates in *the discovery of a secret book of life and a magic curative act.*"[207] The place outside of space, where the poet reads a book that offers medicinal roots, is a state of intensified consciousness, of pure thought.

❖ ❖

For the poet who journeys to the place "without people," the "Octaves," and the final "Octave" in particular, represent an end. The poet has gone out of space; there is no place left to go. The last stanza of "Mistress of guilty glances" confirms the poet's impossible position: "Ty, Mariia—gibnushchim podmoga. / Nado smert' predupredit', usnut'. / Ia stoiu u tverdogo poroga. / Ukhodi, uidi, eshche pobud' " ("You, Maria, are succor to those who are perishing. / One must anticipate death, fall asleep. / I

stand at a firm threshold. / Go away, go, stay a little longer"). The poet
asks for companionship in his mortal hour in the tone of a child going to
sleep.[208] In February 1934, having written the Belyi "Requiem" and "Mistress . . . , " Mandelstam stopped writing again.

He returned to the "Octaves" in July 1935, in Voronezh. These final
poems intersect with the end of the *First Voronezh Notebook*—the first
poetry since February 1934. When the "impulse" appears again in December 1936, Mandelstam describes the future locus of the poet's work in
terms much like those broached in the "Octaves." The landscape of the
future in the poem "Not I, not you—they have" is the brain; its material is
the same anonymous third person plural that appears in "Schubert on the
water" (and in the Belyi cycle) as "those." In "Not I, not you . . . , " the
"futures" are identified simply as "they," and whereas *te* saturates those
other poems, the dominant sound cluster in "Not I, not you . . . " is *ikh.*
This realization of the future life of the poet's work occurs in Voronezh,
after the journey out of space, after the "Octaves"—those tiny quantities
that swell with "inner excess." It occurs because the unexpected appearance of the Voronezh poems, by the poet who, as he says, has already "died
twice," confirms the direction of the one who, completing his journey in the
fall of 1933 and writing his requiem two months later, departed from the
circle, covering his face with his hands.

4

✹ Rod = Род

After Mandelstam's "last" poems in the winter of 1933–34, the Voronezh verse that began to appear more than a year later might be considered his "posthumous" work. Nadezhda Mandelstam called the Voronezh reprieve "one extra day," and Mandelstam, in a letter to Pasternak of April 1936, referred to his "second life." Yet Mandelstam's health was precarious, as he noted in the letter to Pasternak: his heart trouble was complicated by increasing respiratory problems.[1] He wrote to his wife's mother in early 1937: "over the last years I've developed an asthmatic condition. *My breathing is always labored.*"[2] In a letter to his father dated December 12, 1936, he wrote: "Our situation is simply awful. My health is so bad that at 45 I see signs of age 85. I'm a very hearty old man. I can still go a little way from the house with a cane and my wife."[3] Nadezhda Mandelstam, describing Mandelstam's desperate state, echoes the contrary, life-affirming words of the Voronezh verse: "V poslednii voronezhskii god on uzhe ne mog *vykhodit' odin.* I doma byval *spokoen* tol'ko *pri mne*" ("In the last Voronezh year he could no longer go out alone. Even at home he was calm only when I was there");[4] Mandelstam wrote in January: "Eshche ne umer ty, eshche ty ne *odin,* / Pokuda *s nishchenkoi-podrugoi . . .*"; "V roskoshnoi bednosti, v moguchei nishchete / Zhivi *spokoen* i uteshen . . ." ("You have not yet died, you are not yet alone, / While, with a beggar-woman friend . . ."; "In luxurious poverty, in mighty indigence / Live calm and comforted"). (Cf. *vykhodit' odin,* with its connotations of death, and *vykhozhu . . . odin* in the last "Octave.") The presence of a second person confirms the persistence of poetry. The poet has "not yet died" when there is an addressee. Thus, in the December letter to his father, Mandelstam referred to the return of poetry in terms of the return of health: "Now, too, I can't contain myself: in the first place, I'm writing verse. Very persistently. Strongly and well [*Sil' no i zdorovo*].[5] I know its value without asking anyone; in the second place, I've learned to read Spanish."[6]

❖ ❖

In Voronezh, the references to air and breathing that had been constant in Mandelstam's work from the beginning acquire a new urgency. Images of breathing appear frequently in the January poems of the *Second Voronezh Notebook,* and the theme is evident already in the five poems of the opening cycle, the verse that he mentions in the letter to his father.[7] In that cycle, too, there is evidence of Mandelstam's study of Spanish, which is itself linked, as the letter suggests, to the problem of the poet's posthumous life.

Mandelstam's theme of breathing has been the subject of considerable critical attention.[8] Taranovsky, who catalogues relevant examples, observes a shift in tonality in the early 1920s, when air becomes dark, and breathing difficult.[9] In poems of the early 1920s such as "Sisters—heaviness and tenderness . . ." and "Nashedshii podkovu" ("The Finder of a Horseshoe"), air is dense, heavy, reflecting the weighty matter that had been Mandelstam's material since his earliest association of the word with stone; hence the promise of *Stone:* "iz tiazhesti nedobroi . . . prekrasnoe sozdam" ("out of unpropitious weight . . . I will create something beautiful").[10] The recovery of the word, conceived as an act of breathing or imbibing—"Slovno temnuiu vodu ia p'iu pomutivshiisia vozdukh" ("As if it were dark water I drink the turbid air"), is more difficult than lifting a stone: "Legche kamen' podniat', chem imia tvoe povtorit' " ("It is harder to lift a stone than to repeat your name"). Air is heavier than stone, since breathing "turbid air" is equivalent to repeating the word, than which lifting a stone is easier.

In 1923, the year Ronen has called a "turning point in [his] literary biography,"[11] Mandelstam addresses Pasternak in his critical writings for the first time, as the poet who offers a cure for difficult breathing. In "Notes on Poetry," he derives the theme of breathing—his own constant, characteristic metonymy for poetry—from Pasternak, echoing that leitmotif of the recently published *My Sister Life,* respiratory disease:[12]

> Стихи Пастернака почитать—горло прочистить, дыхание укрепить, обновить легкие: такие стихи должны быть целебны для туберкулеза. У нас сейчас нет более здоровой поэзии. Это—кумыс после американского молока.
>
> Книга Пастернака «Сестра моя—жизнь» представляется мне сборником прекрасных упражнений дыханья: каждый раз голос становится по-новому, каждый раз иначе регулируется мощный дыхательный аппарат.[13]

> (Reading Pasternak's verse is clearing the throat, fortifying the breathing, renewing the lungs: such verse must be a cure for tuberculosis. We have no healthier poetry right now. It is *kumys* after American milk.
>
> Pasternak's book *My Sister Life* appears to me a collection of wonderful breathing exercises: each time the voice takes up a new position, each time the powerful breathing apparatus is regulated differently.)

Describing the phonetics of Pasternak's verse in the second part of the essay, published originally as "Boris Pasternak," Mandelstam pursues an important theme of the first part of the essay, published originally as "Vulgata": the function of the consonant as the "seed and guarantee of the posterity of the language" ("Soglasnye—semia i zalog potomstva iazyka").[14] In "Buria i natisk" ("Storm and Stress"), another essay of 1923, Mandelstam compares poetic syntax to the circulatory system, referring to Pasternak's ability to renew the force of the worn-out sentence. With their perpetually startling constructions, these poems require the reader to "breathe" in unexpected places.[15] The poems are a cure—for sclerosis, in Mandelstam's metaphor, or tuberculosis, in Pasternak's;[16] both are diseases associated with respiration, with the blood vessels and the lungs:[17]

> До сих пор логический строй предложения изживался вместе с самим стихотворением, то есть был лишь кратчайшим способом выражения поэтической мысли. Привычный логический ход от частого поэтического употребления стирается и становится незаметным как таковой. Синтаксис, то есть система кровеносных сосудов стиха, поражается склерозом. Тогда приходит поэт, воскрешающий девственную силу логического строя предложения. Именно этому удивлялся в Батюшкове Пушкин, и своего Пушкина ждет Пастернак.[18]

> (Up to now the logical structure of the sentence was becoming obsolete along with the poem itself, that is, it was just the briefest way of expressing a poetic thought. From frequent poetic use, the customary logical sequence fades and becomes unnoticeable as such. Syntax—that is, the system of blood vessels of the verse—is stricken with sclerosis. Then comes a poet who resurrects the virginal force of the logical structure of the sentence. Just this was what amazed Pushkin in Batiushkov, and Pasternak awaits his Pushkin.)

The essays date to the period for which Taranovsky notes the shift in Mandelstam's images of air and breathing, which occurred after the composition of *My Sister Life,* but before its appearance as a book (in large part the poems were written in 1917 and 1918; the book was first published in June 1922). The extent and the importance of the theme of breathing in Pasternak's latest poems may not have been apparent until then (for example, the Povolzh'e poems of chapters 4 and 5, where the theme is concentrated, appeared for the first time only in the book). In Levin's comparative lexical analysis of *My Sister Life* and *Stone,* there are thirty lexical items in the semantic field of illness in *My Sister Life* (including *astma* 'asthma', *vospalenie* 'inflammation', *chakhotka* 'consumption', *batsilla* 'bacillus', and *stafilokokk* 'staphylococcus'), but only six in *Stone.*[19] Levin is comparing Pasternak's 1922 volume with the third edition of Mandelstam's first book, published in 1923, but Mandelstam's are poems written no later than 1916. The single exception is the 1923 "Finder of a Horseshoe," that prime instance of the new thematics of dense air and difficult breathing. Thus the

theme of breathing common to Mandelstam and Pasternak in the early
1920s seems to be a case of convergence rather than influence. The appearance of *My Sister Life* must have made Mandelstam feel that he had been
"called by name."

❖ ❖

Mandelstam repeatedly returned to Pasternak in Voronezh.[20] He sent
his new verse to Pasternak in early 1937—and not just the odd poem he
included in letters to literary acquaintances. When Nadezhda Mandelstam
brought Pasternak a copy of the poems that became the *Second Voronezh
Notebook* (she took down Pasternak's response in notes to be elaborated on
her return to Voronezh), Pasternak, who in a 1924 letter to Mandelstam
confessed that he had only recently read *Stone* with attention for the first
time, recalled the "miracle of the becoming of a book" ("chudo stan-
ovleniia knigi") that he had known with *My Sister Life*.[21] But Pasternak's
response may be no more unexpected than the fact that Mandelstam sent
the poems to him. The *Second Voronezh Notebook* was written with Pasternak in mind, *My Sister Life* in particular.

Pasternak's summer book is the story of a journey between Moscow
and the Povolzh'e (literally the central setting of *My Sister Life,* as the
setting of its central chapters); Mandelstam's winter book is the story of a
stay in that same part of the country and its speculative juxtaposition to the
Russian capitals ("I vy, chasov kremlevskie boi . . ." ["And you, chimes of
the Kremlin clock . . ."];[22] "Slyshu, slyshu rannii led / Shelestiashchii pod
mostami" ["I hear, I hear the early ice / Rustling under the bridges"]). In
the Voronezh verse, toponyms as well as references to physical features of
the region testify not to an abstract geography but to a concrete landscape.
In "Eta oblast' v temnovod'e" ("This region's covered with dark waters"),[23] which represents a kind of map of the area ("Ia liubliu ee
risunok— / On na Afriku pokhozh" ["I love its outline— / It looks like
Africa"]), local place-names recur, and Mandelstam makes a point of this:
"—Anna, Rossosh' i Gremiach'e,— / Ia tverzhu ikh imena" ("—Anna,
Rossosh' and Gremiach'e— / I repeat their names over and over"). While
Mandelstam is referring to a part of the country associated, since the
nineteenth century, with Kol'tsov and Nikitin,[24] the toponyms recall Pasternak's earlier verse, the poetry of the war years in the Urals (cf. "Ural
vpervye" ["The Urals for the first time"])[25] and of 1917, when he wrote
about Balashov and Romanovka, Rzhaksa and Muchkap, those stations
along the railroad line through the Volga lands. In the title poem, Pasternak
implies that place-names will organize his narrative: "Chto v mae, kogda
poezdov raspisan'e / Kamyshinskoi vetkoi chitaesh' v kupe, / Ono gran-

dioznei sviatogo pisan'ia, / I chernykh ot pyli i bur' kanape" ("That in May, when you read the train schedule / In the carriage on the Kamyshinsk line, / It is grander than the Holy Writ / And the seats black with dust and storms"). Mandelstam's place of exile borders on past Pasternakian places: "Chto zh mne pod golovu drugoi pesok podlozhen? / Ty—gorlovoi Ural, plechistoe Povolzh'e / Il' etot rovnyi krai—vot vse moi prava,— / I polnoi grud'iu ikh vdykhat' eshche ia dolzhen" ("Why has another sand been placed beneath my head? / You—throaty Urals, broad-shouldered Povolzh'e, / Or this flat land—here are all my rights— / And I must breathe them all still with a full breast").[26] The land itself is the poet's vital substance, the element he breathes: "I v golose moem posle udush'ia / Zvuchit zemlia—poslednee oruzh'e— / Sukhaia vlazhnost' chernozemnykh ga!" ("And in my voice after asphyxia / The earth sounds—the last weapon— / The dry moistness of the black-earth hectares!").[27] The image of the land as a dense, dark element inhaled recalls the sultry air of the Volga towns in *My Sister Life*. The poems of the *Second Voronezh Notebook* invoke the places and names that, as Mandelstam implies in his essays of the early 1920s, Pasternak associated with difficult breathing, and with its cure.

Mandelstam's associations with Pasternak become increasingly ambivalent over the decade and a half between "Notes on Poetry" and the *Second Voronezh Notebook*. In the fall of 1933, as Mandelstam countered Pasternak's congratulations on his new apartment with the caustic "Apartment," Pasternak, in almost precisely the antithetical mode, called the Stalin epigram suicidal.[28] The stakes might appear to be higher in the case of the epigram, but for Mandelstam the apartment is a manifestation of the same problem. The composition and recitation of "We live, not sensing the country beneath us" is an example of what the mocked writer of "The Apartment" would not do, while the apartment itself implicates its tenant in the business of the state, from its ration-books to its executioners; in the business of fear, and not inspiration.

According to Emma Gershtein, Mandelstam criticized the recently published *Vtoroe rozhdenie* (*Second Birth*) for overburdened writing; he called it "Soviet baroque."[29] His comments reflect a sense that Pasternak had betrayed his mission—the clarifying freshness of lexicon and syntax that Mandelstam wrote about in 1923. Yet Gershtein reports that Mandelstam recited the last stanzas of "Leto" ("Summer"), from that same volume, with great emotion, pronouncing them "verses of genius."[30] Mandelstam's frequent references to Pasternak in his poems of spring and summer 1932 testify to his deep interest, confirming Gershtein's account of her conversations with him in 1932–33. Mandelstam felt Pasternak to be an enormous phenomenon, an inevitable and overwhelming presence.[31] Perhaps the most accurate and comprehensive description of Mandelstam's relation to Pasternak in the 1930s is also the briefest: his Voronezh friend Natasha Shtempel' reports that Mandelstam told his wife he thought so much about Pasternak he became exhausted.[32]

In Voronezh, when breathing both figurative and literal became a crucial issue, Mandelstam looked to Pasternak, whose poetry he had described as "breathing exercises" and a cure for sclerosis or tuberculosis, in an attempt to revitalize the "circulatory system" of the verse. In the poems of winter 1936–37, where references to difficult breathing indicate the urgency of the problem, the precariousness of the poet's word, Mandelstam calls on Pasternak to renew the mission he had foreseen for him nearly fifteen years earlier.

In *Conversation about Dante,* Mandelstam equates respiration with the "metabolism of the planet," linking ocean water and blood ("Obmen veshchestv samoi planety osushchestvliaetsia v krovi").[33] He implies that the poetic impulse, through the relation of the foot to the step, and the step to inhalation and exhalation, is located in the blood: "The step, yoked to breathing and permeated with thought, is what Dante understands as the principle of prosody. . . . The foot of the verse—inhalation and exhalation—is the step"; "The principle of the journey is located in the system of blood vessels."[34] Mandelstam returns to the association of the microcosmic and the macrocosmic respiration with the poetic impulse in the opening cycle of the *Second Voronezh Notebook.*

References to air and breathing occur in each of the five poems of the cycle. In a poem that Pasternak particularly praised,[35] the poem that gives the cycle its name, "Iz-za domov, iz-za lesov" ("From beyond the houses, from beyond the forests"), called, domestically, "Gudok" ("The Whistle"), such references include "Gudok sovetskikh gorodov" ("The whistle of the Soviet cities") and the exhortation "Gudi, starik, dyshi sladko" ("Whistle, old man, breathe sweetly"). In "Moi shchegol, ia golovu zakinu" ("My goldfinch, I'll throw my head back"), the poet asks, concerning the goldfinch, "Chto za vozdukh u nego v nadlob'e?" ("What kind of air does it have in its forehead?"); cf. the companion poem "Kogda shchegol v vozdushnoi sdobe" ("When the goldfinch in the airy pastry"). In the other poems of the cycle, breathing appears as an aspect of respiration in the broader sense: *okeanskoe bezvlast'e* 'oceanic anarchy' and *Ulitki rta naplyv i priblizhen'e* 'The influx and approach of the helix of the mouth' in "The Birth of a Smile"; *sna prilivy i otlivy* 'the ebb and flow of sleep' in "Vnutri gory bezdeistvuet kumir" ("Inside the mountain the idol idles"); and *v prilivakh i otlivakh* 'in the ebb and flow' (see also *dyshashchuiu*

tiazhest' 'breathing heaviness') in "Not I, not you—they have. . . ."[36] In
this last poem, respiration, on the microcosmic and macrocosmic levels,
constitutes the primary frame of reference.[37] The poet urges the addressee
to undertake a journey into the convolutions of the human organism:

Не у меня, не у тебя—у них
Вся сила окончаний родовых:
Их воздухом поющ тростник и скважист,
И с благодарностью улитки губ людских
Потянут на себя их дышащую тяжесть.

Нет имени у них. Войди в их хрящ—
И будешь ты наследником их княжеств.

И для людей, для их сердец живых,
Блуждая в их извилинах, развивах,
Изобразишь и наслажденья их,
И то, что мучит их,—в приливах и отливах.

(Not I, not you—they have
All the power of generic endings:
The reed is singing and porous with their air,
And gratefully the helices of people's lips
Draw on themselves their breathing heaviness.

They have no name. Enter their cartilage—
And you will be the heir of their kingdoms.

And for people, for their living hearts,
Wandering in their convolutions, bifurcations,
You will depict their delights
And what torments them in the ebb and flow.)

"Organic" and "oceanic" images intersect: *prilivy i otlivy* 'ebb and flow'
(literally, 'flow and ebb'), which refers to tides, suggests also, in the context of *serdtsa* 'hearts' and *dyshashchaia tiazhest'* 'breathing heaviness',
the circulation of the blood. *Trostnik* 'reeds' or 'reed (pipe)', *khriashch*
'gravel' or 'cartilage', and *ulitki* 'snails' or 'helices (of lips)' continue the
imagery of the sea with the first set of meanings, while pointing to the
human sphere with the second. Consistent with the association between
respiration and the poetic impulse, *trostnik* 'reed' and *guby* 'lips' point to
the metapoetic plot of this extremely abstract poem about respiration.

So does the verb *izobrazish'* 'you will depict'. Yet the addressee of
"Not I, not you . . ." is charged with a task not typical, it seems, of Mandelstam's poet. In another poem of the *Second Voronezh Notebook*, Mandelstam announces "I ne risuiu ia" ("And I don't draw"),[38] setting himself

apart from such nonverbal representation. I. Mess-Baehr discusses the uncharacteristic mode of representation proposed in the contemporaneous "Verses about Stalin," which has been called the "mother" of the poems of the *Second Voronezh Notebook;*[39] here the poet himself turns to "drawing": "Kogda b ia ugol' vzial dlia vysshei pokhvaly . . ." ("If I took up the charcoal for highest praise . . ."). Nadezhda Mandelstam describes the uncharacteristic process of the composition of that "Ode": Mandelstam sat at the table, while his usual way was to work "by voice" and to compose while walking (poetry is always "on the go" [*na khodu*]).[40] In one of his conversations with Gershtein, Mandelstam distinguished himself in this respect from Pasternak, who, he said, could not write except seated at a desk.[41] The activity of *izobrazit'* 'to depict, portray, represent' is closer to writing as a physical act than to Mandelstam's less graphic mode.

In two other instances, Mandelstam associates *izobrazhenie* 'representation', which appears rarely in his verse, with Pasternak. In "The Apartment," he refers to the despised and slavish versifier as "Kakoi-nibud' izobrazitel'" ("Some dauber").[42] In "Impressionizm," a poem dated May 23, 1932, he attributes the activity of the verb *izobrazit'* to a Pasternakian artist:

ИМПРЕССИОНИЗМ

Художник[43] нам изобразил
Глубокий обморок сирени
И красок звучные ступени
На холст, как струпья, положил.

Он понял масла густоту—
Его запекшееся лето
Лиловым мозгом разогрето,
Расширенное в духоту.

А тень-то, тень все лиловей,
Свисток иль хлыст, как спичка, тухнет,—
Ты скажешь: повара на кухне
Готовят жирных голубей.

Угадывается качель,
Недомалеваны вуали,
И в этом солнечном развале
Уже хозяйничает шмель.

(IMPRESSIONISM

The artist portrayed for us
A deep swoon of lilac

And put sonorous steps of paint
On the canvas like scabs.

He understood the richness of oils—
His parched summer,
Dilated into sultriness,
Is warmed by a lilac brain.

But the shade, the shade turns still deeper lilac,
A whistle or a whip, like a match, is extinguished—
You'd say: cooks in the kitchen
Are preparing fat doves.

You can just make out the swing,
The veils are not quite explicit
And in this sunny disarray
The bumblebee is already master.)

Mandelstam had reason to link painterly representation, and impression-ism in particular, with Pasternak. Leonid Pasternak, the poet's father, has been associated with impressionism.[44] Pasternak, consistent not only with his reverence for his parents and his sense of the derivation of his poetry from his father's painting,[45] but perhaps even with the tendencies of early Futurism, defined his own purpose, in the 1916 essay "Chernyi bokal" ("The Black Goblet"), as the "impressionism of the eternal" ("impres-sionizm vechnogo").[46] Pasternak's introduction to the literary world came as a kind of combination of his father's painting with his mother's music: according to his own later account in the *Autobiographical Sketch,* he gave impressions, on the piano, of the people entering the artistic society Serdar-da.[47] Pasternak uses a form of the verb *izobrazit'* (*izobrazhat'*): "Sam ia vstupil v 'Serdardu' na starykh pravakh *muzykanta,* improvizatsiiami *na fortepiano izobrazhaia* kazhdogo vkhodiashchego v nachale vechera, poka sobiralis' " ("I myself joined 'Serdarda' on the strength of my standing as a musician, portraying, with improvisations on the piano, each person who came in at the beginning of the evening, while they were gathering").[48] In his much-cited response to a 1927 inquiry in "Na literaturnom postu," Pasternak describes Pushkin's early importance for him with reference to both key terms, *izobrazit'* and *impressionizm:*

> In my work I feel the influence of Pushkin. The Pushkinian aesthetic is so broad and elastic that it permits different interpretations at different ages. Pushkin's impulsive pictorialness [*poryvistaia izobrazitel'nost'*] allows us to understand him also impressionistically [*impressionisticheski*], as I under-stood him fifteen years ago in accordance with my own tastes and the ruling currents in literature. Now my understanding of him has broadened, and ele-ments of a moral nature have entered it.[49]

Tomas Venclova, with reference to a passage about Pushkin in *Doctor Zhivago,* suggests that Pasternak is describing himself: "Pasternak in many respects identifies with Pushkin, has a sense of himself as his double."[50] Critics have noted the appropriateness of the phrase *poryvystaia izobrazitel'nost'* 'impulsive pictorialness' to Pasternak's own work.[51]

Mandelstam's "Impressionism" might be a portrait of Pasternak's poetry.[52] The subject of the painting and its treatment—"Glubokii obmorok sireni" ("A deep swoon of lilac")—recall various pictures from *My Sister Life.* The color scheme of the poem is characteristic: "Ego zapeksheesia leto[53] / *Lilovym* mozgom razogreto, / Rasshirennoe v dukhotu. //A ten'-to, ten' vse *lilovei* . . ." ("His parched summer, / Dilated into sultriness, / Is warmed by a lilac brain. // But the shade, the shade turns still deeper lilac . . ."). Lilac—the color (*lilovyi*) and the flower (*sirenevyi, siren'*)—is a recurrent motif in *My Sister Life;* it appears also in the volume *Themes and Variations* (and the lilac color remains characteristic of Pasternak as late as *Doctor Zhivago*).[54] Lilac is a subject in the programmatic "Tak nachinaiut. Goda v dva" ("So they begin. At about age two"), a poem about the birth of poetry and the poet: "Chto delat' strashnoi krasote / Prisevshei na *skam'e sireni* . . ." ("What is the terrible beauty to do, / The lilac resting on the bench . . ."). Both "Impressionism" and "So they begin . . ." are in iambic tetrameter with alternating masculine and feminine rhymes; in each poem, *siren'* 'lilac' appears as a rhyme word in the genitive singular. "Lilac" is the color of Pasternak's world during a storm, which is the world taken over by poetry: "Chto v grozu lilovy glaza i gazony . . ." ("That during a storm eyes and lawns are lilac . . .") ("Sestra moia—zhizn' i segodnia v razlive . . ." ["My sister life today too in the downpour . . ."]).[55] In Akhmatova's "Poet," her 1936 poem about Pasternak, the whole world is so colored: "V lilovoi mgle pokoiatsia zadvorki, / Platformy, brevna, list'ia, oblaka" ("In the lilac haze rest the back yards, / Platforms, logs, leaves, clouds"). That state of the world is associated with illness in Pasternak's work (see, for example, *Lilovyi otek* 'lilac edema' in "Spasskoe").[56] Mandelstam's "Glubokii obmorok sireni" ("A deep swoon of lilac") echoes Pasternak's nearly identical representation of another flower, in "Dushnaia noch'" ("A Sultry Night"): "Byl mak kak *obmorok glubok*" ("The poppies were deep as a swoon"), and "deep swoon" and the other allusions to illness in "Impressionism" recall the medical terms in *My Sister Life,* where Pasternak refers frequently to respiratory disease. Like *obmorok* 'swoon', *dukhota* 'sultriness' or 'stuffiness' is a key Pasternakian motif, linked to the theme of difficult breathing and, more generally, to the appearance of poetry.[57]

❖ ❖

The composition of "Impressionism" must be seen in the context of Mandelstam's intense interest in Pasternak during the spring and summer of 1932. Less than a month after that poem, Mandelstam wrote "Batiushkov," a portrait that alludes to the poet of the 1923 essays—where he had associated Pasternak with Batiushkov:[58]

БАТЮШКОВ

Словно гуляка с волшебною тростью,
Батюшков нежный со мною живет.
Он тополями шагает в Замостье,
Нюхает розу и Дафну поет.

Ни на минуту не веря в разлуку,
Кажется, я поклонился ему.
В светлой перчатке холодную руку
Я с лихорадочной завистью жму.

Он усмехнулся. Я молвил: спасибо.
И не нашел от смущения слов:
—Ни у кого—этих звуков изгибы . . .
—И никогда—этот говор валов . . .

Наше мученье и наше богатство,
Косноязычный, с собой он принес—
Шум стихотворства и колокол братства
И гармонический проливень слез.

И отвечал мне оплакавший Тасса:
—Я к величаньям еще не привык;
Только стихов виноградное мясо
Мне освежило случайно язык . . .

Что ж! Поднимай удивленные брови
Ты, горожанин и друг горожан,
Вечные сны, как образчики крови,
Переливай из стакана в стакан . . .

(BATIUSHKOV

Like a loafer with a magic wand,
Tender Batiushkov lives with me.
He strides along by the poplars in Zamost'e,
Sniffs a rose and sings of Dafna.

Not for a moment believing in separation,
I bowed to him, it seems:

The cold hand in the bright glove
I grasp with feverish envy.

He grinned. I muttered: thanks.
And I couldn't find words from embarrassment.
—Nobody has these windings of sounds,
And never—this murmur of waves. . . .

Our torment and our riches,
Tongue-tied, he brought with him—
The noise of versifying and the bell of brotherhood,
And the harmonious downpour of tears.

And the one who mourned Tasso answered me:
—I'm not yet used to celebration;
It's just that the grape meat of verse
Has accidentally refreshed my tongue. . . .

So! Raise astonished brows,
You, city-dweller and city-dwellers' friend,
Eternal dreams, like blood samples,
Transfuse from glass to glass. . . .)

In "Storm and Stress," Mandelstam granted Pasternak's poetry the crucial power, which he attributes also to Batiushkov's verse, to "revive the virginal force of the logical construction of the proposition"; to cure the sclerotic vessels of the language ("Syntax, that is, the system of blood vessels of the verse, is stricken with sclerosis").[59] Thus Ronen, quoting "Tol'ko stikhov vinogradnoe miaso / Mne *osvezhilo* sluchaino iazyk" ("It's just that the grape meat of verse / Has accidentally refreshed my tongue"), writes that Batiushkov and Pasternak "represent innovation and freshness, a cure for the 'dry blood'" for Mandelstam.[60] In "Batiushkov," a decade later, Mandelstam returns to the comparison of verse and circulation with the final image of poetry as transfused blood.

Along with the decanted dreams (*perelivai*), the liquid imagery in "Batiushkov" includes the Pasternakian *garmonicheskii proliven' slez* 'harmonious downpour of tears'. The last two words echo Pasternak's signature motif of downpour, which accompanies and allows the making of poetry,[61] and of which tears are a typical manifestation. The first word is linked to Pasternak through a passage in "Storm and Stress," where, comparing Pasternak to Batiushkov, Mandelstam calls Pasternak's "new harmony" the future material of Russian poetry: "So vremen Batiushkova v russkoi poezii ne zvuchalo stol' novoi i zreloi garmonii. . . . Etoi novoi garmoniei mozhno vyskazat' vse, chto ugodno,—eiu budut pol'zovat'sia

vse, khotiat oni togo ili ne khotiat, potomu chto otnyne ona—obshchee
dostoianie vsekh russkikh poetov" ("Such a new and mature harmony has
not sounded in Russian poetry since Batiushkov's time. . . . With this new
harmony anything at all can be said—everyone will use it, whether they
want to or not, because from now on it is the common property of all
Russian poets").[62] The "accidental" nature of poetry ("Mne osvezhilo
sluchaino iazyk" ["Has accidentally refreshed my tongue"]), as I have
noted, is also typically Pasternakian (cf. "I chem sluchainei, tem vernee /
Slagaiutsia stikhi navzryd" ["And the more accidentally, the more truly /
Verses are composed in a sob"]). The characterization of the poet as "city-
dweller and city-dwellers' friend," too, points to Pasternak.[63] Mandelstam's Pasternak is a poet of the city. Mandelstam commented to Gershtein
that Pasternak would be "inconceivable outside of Moscow."[64] Nadezhda
Mandelstam writes: "Pasternak is a domestic, familiar, Moscow phenomenon"; "Moscow belonged to Pasternak from birth."[65] "Batiushkov" is a
Moscow poem. It appears in the *Moscow Notebooks,* titled, like the *Voronezh Notebooks,* after their place of composition. Mandelstam eliminated
the word *topolia* 'poplars' from the third line when told (erroneously,
according to Nadezhda Mandelstam) that Moscow had no poplars;[66] he
seems to have been concerned not to suggest a city that could not be
Moscow. The protagonist of "Batiushkov" is the poet of "U sebia doma"
("At Home"), with its "heat on seven hills," as well as the poet of "Progulka
po Moskve" ("A Stroll around Moscow").

Lexical and thematic keys link "Batiushkov" with "Not I, not you—
they have." Taranovsky cites "Vechnye sny, kak obrazchiki krovi, / Perelivai iz stakana v stakan" ("Eternal dreams, like blood samples, / Transfuse from glass to glass . . .") as a reiteration of the theme of "I haven't
heard Ossian's tales";[67] cf. "Ia poluchil blazhennoe nasledstvo, / Chuzhikh
pevtsovbluzhdaiushchie sny" ("I've received a blessed inheritance, /
Other singers' wandering dreams"). In "Not I, not you," in turn, Mandelstam echoes those lines from "Ossian": "I budesh' ty naslednikom ikh
kniazhestv. // I dlia liudei, dlia ikh serdets zhivykh, / Bluzhdaia v ikh
izvilinakh, razvivakh, / Izobrazish' i naslazhden'ia ikh, / I to, chto muchit
ikh" ("And you will be the heir of their kingdoms. // And for people, for
their living hearts, / Wandering in their convolutions, bifurcations, / You
will depict both their delights / And what torments them"). The word
bluzhdat' occurs in the essays of the early 1920s with the same range of
meanings that it has in the 1914 and 1936 poems. It appears in "Notes on
Poetry" with reference to the Russian language: "Poetic speech is given life
by a wandering [*bluzhdaiushchii*], polysemic root"; and in "On the

Nature of the Word" with reference to Russian culture in general: "Our culture to this day wanders [*bluzhdaet*] and cannot find its walls." In "The Word and Culture," the word itself "wanders": "The living word does not designate objects, but freely chooses, as if for lodging, one or anther material significance, thingness, dear body. And around the thing the word freely wanders [*bluzhdaet*], like a soul around an abandoned but not forgotten body."[68] In each of its appearances, *bluzhdat'* suggests the unconstrained relation between the word and its store of meanings, which allows the poet to "transfuse eternal dreams from glass to glass." The wandering poet, like the wandering word, is open to the future.

In "Batiushkov," Mandelstam alludes to Batiushkov's "Est' *naslazhdenie* i v dikosti lesov" ("There is delight in the wildness of the forests"): cf. "Ni u kogo etikh zvukov izgiby, / I nikogda etot govor valov" ("Nobody has these windings of sounds, / And never—this murmur of waves") with "I est' garmoniia v sem govore valov" ("And there is harmony in this murmur of waves").[69] *Naslazhdenie* 'delight' does not appear in "Batiushkov," but it appears in "Not I, not you," in lines that recall "Nashe *muchen'e* i nashe *bogatstvo,* / Kosnoiazychnyi, s soboi on prines" ("Our torment and our riches, / Tongue-tied, he brought with him"); cf. "Izobrazish' i *naslazhden'ia* ikh, / I to, chto *muchit* ikh v prilivakh i otlivakh" ("You will depict their delights / And what torments them in the ebb and flow").[70] Along with the pair *naslazhdenie* 'delight' and *muchenie* 'torment', *kosnoiazychie* 'tongue-tie', the poet's attribute in "Batiushkov," is essential to the business of the poet in "Not I, not you," who will enter an unarticulated embryonic material: "Net imeni u nikh. Voidi v ikh khriashch . . . I . . . Izobrazish' . . ." ("They have no name. Enter their cartilage . . . And . . . You will depict . . ."). This attribute of the poet, too, is Pasternakian. Gifford writes of Pasternak: "He was indeed celebrated for his impatient, confused utterance [*kosnoiazychie*], the drawback which he acknowledges in a letter to the Georgian poet, his close friend Paolo Yashvili. There he speaks of 'an everlasting inability to express the essence alone of what is felt, without complicating details.' "[71] Savely Senderovich links Zhivago's dream of a simple style with Pasternak's own ("Like the author of the novel, he [Zhivago] dreams of achieving simplicity in his poetry"). The desired speech, as Pasternak describes it, is the antithesis of "tongue-tie": it is "restrained, uninsistent," "unnoticeable . . . , not attracting anyone's attention"; "the reader and listener master the content without noticing how they assimilate it."[72] Yet the poet's "inability," the presence of "complicating details," is the quality that Mandelstam values in Pasternak, as in Batiushkov. Calling it "kosnoiazychie," Mandelstam gives the mode of indirection highest praise. That mode can be associated with the "convolutions" of the medium he proposes that the poet enter in "Not I, not you."

A crucial link between "Batiushkov" and "Not I, not you" is the response to the poet's gift—gratitude: "Ia molvil: spasibo" ("I muttered: thanks"); "I s blagodarnost'iu ulitki gub liudskikh / Potianut na sebia ikh dyshashchuiu tiazhest'" ("And gratefully the helices of people's lips / Draw on themselves their breathing heaviness").[73] Yet in "Not I, not you," attributing "lips," the poet's prime implement, to the grateful people, Mandelstam indicates that this is not just a relation between the audience and the poet. The prototype of the anonymous plural (*ikh* 'them') in "Not I, not you" is the "terrible dictors" of *Conversation about Dante;* that authority par excellence provides the copious material that fills the copier with gratitude: "He is replete with a feeling of ineffable gratitude [*blagodarnost'*] for that voluminous wealth that falls into his hands."[74] Compare "Primi zh ladoniami svoimi / Peresypaemyi pesok" ("So take with your palms / The sand that has been poured back and forth") in "Ne veria voskresen'ia chudu" ("Not believing in the miracle of resurrection"), which is echoed, in turn, in "Vechnye sny . . . / Perelivai iz stakana v stakan" ("Eternal dreams . . . / Transfuse from glass to glass"). In "Batiushkov," too, the poet expresses his gratitude, in this case to another poet, thus appearing in the role of reader.

Mandelstam reveals the importance of gratitude in "Vypad" ("A Lunge," published in 1924), where he mentions Pasternak among other Russian poets for the ages ("not for yesterday, not for today, but for always") who are objects of readers' ingratitude.[75] Gratitude remains typical of the ideal reader in the 1930s. The people may have need of the poet's gift, as in "Ia nynche v pautine svetovoi" ("Now I'm in a web of light"), a January poem of the *Second Voronezh Notebook:* "Narodu nuzhen svet i vozdukh goluboi . . . // Narodu nuzhen stikh tainstvenno-rodnoi" ("The people need light and blue air . . . // The people need verse that is mysteriously kindred"). Or they may resemble the uncomprehending contemporaries of Baratynskii's "Na posev lesa" ("On Sowing a Forest"): the "generation agitated by the bellows of dusk" (Ronen's translation)[76] is "embarrassed" by the poet's treasure ("Kak svetoteni muchenik Rembrandt" ["Like Rembrandt, martyr of chiaroscuro"]). Mandelstam recalls Baratynskii's hard-hearted crowd ("Ia dni izvel, stuchas' k liudskim serdtsam" ["I wasted days, knocking at people's hearts"]) in the line "I dlia *liudei,* dlia ikh *serdets* zhivykh" ("And for people, for their living hearts").[77] In "Not I, not you," unlike "On Sowing a Forest," the people are grateful for the material offered (the people's gratitude for "their breathing heaviness," explicit in the first part of "Not I, not you," is the anticipated response to the proposed activity of the addressee in the second part), but

the structure remains the same: the poet's verse must go out to people—
whether they appreciate it or not. Thus at the end of "On the Nature of the
Word," Mandelstam makes "hostility" and "compassion" equally significant responses to the work.[78] Thus, too, describing ingratitude towards
Pasternak and others in "A Lunge," Mandelstam preserves the essential
relation of gratitude between reader and poet.

The theme of gratitude is itself characteristic of Mandelstam's relation
to Pasternak (Mandelstam is the reader to Pasternak's poet). In the letter of
April 1936, Mandelstam thanks Pasternak for having "given voice" to
concerns about him. In a letter dated January 2, 1937, six days after the
completion of "Not I, not you," he expresses gratitude for Pasternak's
work, its past and its future:

2/1/37
    С новым годом!
    Дорогой Борис Леонидович.
Когда вспоминаешь весь великий объем вашей жизненной работы,
весь ее несравненный жизненный охват—*для благодарности не най-
дешь слов.*
    Я хочу, чтоб ваша поэзия, которой мы все избалованы и неза-
служенно задарены—рвалась дальше, к миру, к народу, к детям. . .
    Хоть раз в жизни позвольте сказать вам: спасибо за все и за то, что
это «все»—еще не «все».
    Простите, что я пишу вам, как будто юбилей. Я сам знаю, что
совсем не юбилей: просто вы нянчите жизнь и в ней меня, недостой-
ного вас, бесконечно вас любящего.

                                             О. Мандельштам[79]

(January 2, 1937
    Happy New Year!
    Dear Boris Leonidovich.
When one recollects the whole enormous volume of your life's work, its whole
incomparable vital scope—one can't find words to express one's gratitude.
    I want your poetry—which has spoiled us all and has been showered on us
undeservedly—to venture further, to the world, to the people, to children. . . .
    Just once in my life let me say to you: thank you for everything and for the
fact that this "everything" is still "not everything."
    Forgive me for writing to you as if it were an anniversary. I myself know that
it's not at all an anniversary: it's simply that you nurture life and in it, me,
unworthy of you, loving you endlessly.

                                             O. Mandelstam)

The same combination of gratitude and embarrassment (cf. the English
expression "an embarrassment of riches") occurs in "Batiushkov": "On
usmekhnulsia. Ia molvil: *spasibo, / I ne nashel ot smushcheniia slov*" ("He

grinned. I muttered: thanks. / And I couldn't find words from embarrassment"). Again, the attitude is characteristic of the reader's relation to the
poet—and of Mandelstam's relation to Pasternak.

In a poem dated January 2, 1937, Mandelstam pursues the other theme
of the letter to Pasternak written the same day, the theme, also, of "Not I,
not you": the poet's posthumous existence; the future life of the artist in his
"native land," which he had associated with Pasternak in "Storm and Stress"
(cf. the theme of the Stalin "Ode": the future life of the protagonist—both
the revered leader and the poet—among people):

Твой зрачок в небесной корке,
Обращенный вдаль и ниц,
Защищают оговорки
Слабых, чующих ресниц.

Будет он обожествленный
Долго жить в родной стране—
Омут ока удивленный,—
Кинь его вдогонку мне.

Он глядит уже охотно
В мимолетные века—
Светлый, радужный, бесплотный,
Умоляющий пока.[80]

(Your pupil in the heavenly coating,[81]
Turned to the distance and down,
Is defended by the reservations
Of the weak, perceptive lashes.

Worshipped, it will live
Long in its native land.
Astonished deep pool of the eye,
Cast it after me.

It is already looking eagerly
Into the fleeting ages—
Luminous, iridescent, incorporeal,
Still supplicating.)[82]

The poem was dedicated to Nadezhda Mandelstam,[83] while the eye in
question apparently belonged to the Mandelstams' cat (cf. "Kashchei,"
supposedly inspired by a cat belonging to Natasha Shtempel'); Nadezhda
Mandelstam registers her discomfort with this bit of realia.[84] But neither
detail provides for a satisfactory interpretation. Ronen, looking in a different direction, notes that the "fact that the poem was addressed or dedicated

to N. Ja. Mandel'tam . . . does not preclude the possibility of a double reference."[85] In fact, the subject of the poem resembles the addressee of the letter of January 2.

The pupil is a Pasternakian protagonist. Pasternak compares himself to a horse's eye in *Themes and Variations:* "Kak konskii glaz, s podushek, zharkii, iskosa, / Gliazhu, strashas' bessonnitsy ogromnoi" ("Like a horse's eye, from the pillows, hot, aslant, / I watch, terrified of vast insomnia"),[86] and Akhmatova responds in "The Poet": "On, sam sebia sravnivshii s konskim glazom . . ." ("He, comparing himself to a horse's eye . . ."); Tsvetaeva, taking up the equine comparison, uses the archaic *oko* 'eye', which appears also in "Your pupil . . . ," in her essay on Pasternak, "Svetovoi liven'" ("A Downpour of Light").[87] Mandelstam's pupil has the large luminousness of Pasternak's eyes,[88] while its "speech" (cf. the communication of the tiny creatures in "The minute appendage of the sixth sense") suggests Pasternak's typical indirection[89] and apparent passivity:[90] "Tvoi zrachok . . . / Zashchishchaiut ogovorki / Slabykh, chuiushchikh resnits" ("Your pupil . . . / Is defended by the reservations / Of the weak, perceptive lashes).[91]

The lexicon and imagery of the poem is Pasternakian, echoing poems associated with Pasternak as well as Pasternak's own poems. Akhmatova refers to *korka* ("khrust arbuznoi korki" ["the crunch of watermelon rind"]) in her poem about Pasternak. "Astonished" brows appear in the portrait of the poet in "Batiushkov," with its Pasternakian subject: cf. "Omut oka udivlennyi" with "Chto zh! Podnimai udivlennye brovi" ("Astonished deeps of the eye" and "So! Raise astonished brows" both suggest amazement at an enormous vision: "the fleeting ages," "eternal dreams").[92] The reference to "your pupil" recalls the poet's attribute in Pasternak's programmatic poem about the childhood origins of poetry: "Tak, nochi letnye, nichkom / Upav v ovsy s mol'boi: ispoln'sia, / Groziat zare *tvoim zrachkom*" ("So, summer nights, falling prone / In the oats with the entreaty: Come true, / Threaten the dawn with your pupil").[93] As in Mandelstam's poem, in "So they begin . . . ," too, "your pupil," instigator of poetry, acquires attributes of the sky. Mandelstam's *nits* '[face] down' echoes Pasternak's synonymous **nichkom,** which refers grammatically to **nochi** *letnye* 'summer nights' but has been transferred from its direct referent, the poet-addressee, possessor of the pupil that challenges the dawn. *Dal'* 'the distance' is a crucial Pasternakian category, early and later ("Gde dal' pugaetsia"; "Ty riadom, dal' sotsializma"; see also "Okno s mechtoi smiatennoiu azalii" ["Where the distance is frightened"; "You're nearby, distance of socialism"; "The window with the confused dream of azaleas"]).[94]

The position, present and future, of the subject of "Your pupil" is comparable to the position urged on the addressee of the January 2 letter: cf. "Obrashchennyi vdal' i nits" ("Turned to the distance and down") and "Budet on . . . / Dolgo zhit' v rodnoi strane" (". . . it will live / Long in its native land")[95] with "Ia khochu, chtob vasha poeziia . . . rvalas' dal'she, k miru, k narodu, k detiam" ("I want your poetry . . . to venture further, to the world, to the people, to children"); cf. also "Ukhodiat vdal' liudskikh golov bugry" ("Mounds of people's heads disappear into the distance") in the Stalin "Ode." In each case the future hypostasis of the subject has not yet been realized: "Umoliaiushchii poka" ("Still supplicating"); ". . . eto 'vse' poka 'ne vse'" ("this 'everything' is still 'not everything'"). Ronen describes the pupil as the "future object of national adoration";[96] the same can be said about the addressee of the letter. The perspective of the pupil is the perspective of Mandelstam's ideal observer: the eye of the naturalist who discovers the poet's protoform, the eye that sees broadly (*vdal'*) and deeply (*nits*).

The ideal observer is not Mandelstam's only picture of Pasternak at this period. Boris Gasparov attributes to Mandelstam in 1932 a view of Pasternak antithetical to his conception in 1923, writing that the later Mandelstam associated Pasternak with "'greasiness,' friability, diseased breathing, as symptoms of servility and the loss of the 'righteous voice.'"[97] Yet the shift in features that Gasparov observes—the emphasis on difficult breathing rather than cure, for example—suggests not necessarily the failure of the poet but the heightened terms of the problem. Just as Mandelstam expressed doubts, during the period of "Impressionism" and "Batiushkov," about the excesses of *Second Birth,* so the letter to Pasternak, for all the fulsome praise, for all the inexpressible gratitude offered, is indeed hardly a whole-hearted endorsement. The elaborate tone is indicative.[98] The abundant superlatives and reiterated *ves'* 'all', 'the whole', 'everything', which appears six times in three short paragraphs, link the letter with the "Ode." Like that poem, the letter is a portrait of the great man, the artist, who labors for people and children ("k miru, k narodu, k detiam"; cf. ". . . emu narod rodnoi— / Narod-Gomer khvalu utroit," "No v knigakh laskovykh i v igrakh detvory, / Voskresnu ia skazat', chto solntse svetit" [". . . to the world, to the people, to children"; cf. "the native people, / The people, a Homer, will treble their praise of him," "But in loving books and in children's games, / I will rise again to say the sun is shining"]), and whose work must continue into an indefinite future ("rvalas' dal'she"; cf. "Ukhodiat vdal'" ["venture further"; cf. "disappear into the distance"]). The present writer is unworthy of his subject ("nedodostoinogo vas"; "Pust' nedostoin ia eshche imet' druzei" ["unworthy of you"; "Even if I am

still unworthy of having friends"]), and therefore cannot thank him enough
("Spasibo za vse, i za to, chto eto 'vse'—eshche 'ne vse' "; "I ia khochu
blagodarit' kholmy / Chto etu kost' i etu kist' razvili" ["Thank you for
everything and for the fact that this 'everything' is still 'not everything' ";
"And I want to thank the hills / That developed this bone and this hand"]).
Gregory Freidin traces the appearance of *ves'*, in the letter, to Pasternak's
"New Year's epigram" of January 1936, "Ia ponial: *vse* zhivo" ("I understand: everything's alive"), one of two portraits of Stalin he wrote at
Bukharin's request (the other is "Khudozhnik" ["The Artist"], where Pasternak juxtaposes the poet and the leader as artists).[99] Mandelstam echoes,
too, Pasternak's *zhivo* 'alive': "ves' velikii ob"em vashei *zhiznennoi*
raboty, ves' ee nesravnennyi *zhiznennyi* oxvat"; "vy nianchite *zhizn'* ";
"Khot' raz v *zhizni* pozvol'te skazat' vam . . ." ("the whole enormous
volume of your life's work, its whole incomparable vital scope"; "you
nurture life"; "Just once in my life let me say to you . . ."). And with
"spasibo za vse i za to, chto eto 'vse'—eshche 'ne vse' " ("thank you for
everything and for the fact that this 'everything' is still 'not everything' "),
he refers to the second and third stanzas of Pasternak's Stalin poem: "Spasibo, spasibo / Trem tysiacham let, / V trudakh bez razgiba / Ostavivshim
svet. // Spasibo predtecham, / Spasibo vozhdiam. / Ne tem zhe, tak ne-
chem / Otplachivat' nam" ("Thanks, thanks / To three thousand years, /
Leaving light behind / In labors without let-up. // Thanks to the forebears, / Thanks to the leaders. / If not with the same, then there's nothing /
We can repay them with").[100] Mandelstam, writing to Pasternak just a year
after the publication of Pasternak's New Year's poems, commented, in the
final paragraph, on the tone of his own letter, which approaches that of the
"Ode": "Prostite, chto ia pishu vam, kak budto iubilei. Ia sam znaiu, chto
sovsem ne iubilei" ("Forgive me for writing to you as if it were an anniversary. I myself know that it's not at all an anniversary"). Here he speaks
directly for the first time, minus the flourishes of an anniversary
greeting.[101]

The invocation of "people" in "Not I, not you" must be seen in light
of Mandelstam's polemic with Pasternak in the 1930s concerning the
relation between the poet and the people. Fleishman quotes Mandelstam's letter of January 2 as a response to yet another of Pasternak's 1936
poems:

Счастлив, кто целиком,
Без тени чужеродья,
Всем детством—с бедняком,
Всей кровию—в народе.

Я в ряд их не попал,
Но и не ради форса
С шеренгой прихлебал
В родню чужую втерся.

Отчизна с малых лет
Влекла к такому гимну,
Что небу дела нет—
Была ль любовь взаимна.

Народ, как дом без кром,
И мы не замечаем,
Что этот свод шатром,
Как воздух, нескончаем.

Он—чащи глубина,
Где кем-то в детстве раннем
Давались имена
Событьям и созданьям.

Ты без него ничто.
Он, как свое изделье,
Кладет под долото
Твои мечты и цели.[102]

(Fortunate is the one who entirely,
Without the shadow of alien birth,
By virtue of his whole childhood is with the poor,
By virtue of all his blood is with the people.

I didn't end up in their rank,
But—not in order to show off—
I supped with the column,
I worked my way into an alien kin.

The fatherland drew [me]
From a young age to such a hymn,
That heaven doesn't care
Whether the love was mutual.

The people is like a boundless home,
And we don't notice
That this vault, like the air,
Is an endless tent.

It is the depth of a grove,
Where, in early childhood,
Someone gave names
To events and creations.

Without it you are nothing.
It places beneath the chisel,
As its own handiwork,
Your dreams and goals.)

Since the appearance of the poem in the October issue of *Novyi mir,*
Pasternak had been subjected by the literary establishment to repeated
charges of slander (*kleveta*) against the Soviet people.[103] Mandelstam's
letter may be, as Fleishman suggests, an attempt to support Pasternak in his
time of trouble.[104] At the same time, in the letter as in "Not I, not you,"
finished a few days earlier, Mandelstam pursues the polemic of which "The
Apartment" and the discussion of the Stalin epigram are earlier instances.
Arising in the period when Mandelstam insisted on the need for civic verse,
this polemic involves the role of the poet as citizen. Mandelstam disputes
Pasternak's conception of the relation between the poet and the people,
though on different grounds from those of Pasternak's official critics.

As Mandelstam's response indicates, Pasternak's "Fortunate is the
one . . . ," for all the critical uproar, is far from politics. The poem records
the poet's attempt to place himself within the "boundless home" that the
people constitute, where, apparently, he does not belong. He is not the
lucky one, "without the shadow [without a trace] of alien birth" ("Ia v riad
ikh ne popal" ["I didn't end up in their rank"]). The speaker is the poet who
felt, as late as 1949 (and probably to the end of his life), that his Jewish
origins remained an obstacle to his participation in Russian poetry.[105]
Hence, at least in part, the urgent embrace of the "people," as the source of
the poet's language and the instrument that crafts it.

The theme of *narod* 'the people',[106] Fleishman notes, first appeared in
Pasternak's work, and in Soviet literature, in 1936.[107] But the problem of
the poet's relation to the people is incipient in 1931, in *Second Birth,* where
Pasternak considers the need for a new poetic voice and a new audience.[108]
Pasternak pronounced his famous lines about "simplicity" in the opening
cycle, "Volny" ("Waves"): "Est' v opyte bol'shikh poetov / Cherty es-
testvennosti toi, / Chto nevozmozhno, ikh izvedav, / Ne konchit' polnoi
nemotoi. // *V rodstve so vsem, chto est', uverias',* / I znais' s budushchim
v bytu, / Nel'zia ne vpast' k kontsu, *kak v eres',* / V neslykhannuiu *pros-
totu*" ("There are, in the experience of great poets, / Features of that
naturalness / That make it impossible, when one comes to know them, /
Not to end in complete muteness. // Assuring oneself of kinship with
everything that exists, / And associating with the future in everyday life, /
One can't help but fall, as into a heresy, / Into an unheard-of simplicity").
As the convoluted syntax of Pasternak's lines indicates, this is more than a

question of writing, as William Carlos Williams put it, something his grandmother would understand. The theme of *prostota* 'simplicity' recurs throughout the 1931 poems of *Second Birth,* accompanied by two other features that define the artist and his relation to his audience: **priamizna* 'straightness' and *pravota* 'rightness'.[109] Each of these three words implies or entails the others in Pasternak's exploration of the new poetic voice.

While Pasternak makes "simplicity" a corollary of the "kinship [*rodstvo*] with everything that is," he indicates elsewhere in *Second Birth* that the kinship is not to be taken for granted (*uverias'* 'assuring oneself,' in any case, is not a finite verbal form). He proposes to achieve simplicity despite origins that are not "straight": "O, esli b ia priamei voznik, / No pust' i tak—ne kak brodiaga, / Rodnym voidu v rodnoi iazyk" ("Oh, if only I had started out straighter, / But even so—not as a vagrant, / I will enter the native language as a native").[110] Hence the importance of the poet's choice of audience. That audience had a concrete exemplar in Pasternak's recent love, and the woman who would become his second wife, Zinaida Neigauz.[111] Pasternak describes the addressee in "Liubit' inykh—tiazhelyi krest" ("Loving some is a hard cross to bear") as "prekrasna bez izvilin" ("splendid without convolutions")—another reference to the prized "straightness." Rightness is implied throughout this portrait of the beloved: "I prelesti tvoei sekret / Razgadke zhizni ravnosilen. // Vesnoiu slyshen shorokh snov / I shelest novostei i istin. / Ty iz sem'i takikh osnov" ("And the secret of your charm / Is equivalent to the solution to life's riddle. // In spring the rustle of dreams is audible, / And the stirring of tidings and truths. / You belong to the family of such fundamentals"). "Rightness" appears explicitly in "Opiat' Shopen ne ishchet vygod" ("Again Chopin does not seek advantage"), Pasternak's response to Mandelstam's "Roial'" ("The Piano"), a poem of April 1931 for which the inspiration was a concert by the pianist Genrikh Neigauz (the husband of Zinaida Neigauz at the time she became acquainted with Pasternak):[112] "No, okryliaias' na letu, / Odin prokladyvaet vykhod / Iz veroiat'ia v pravotu" ("But, taking wing in flight, / Alone paves the way out / From likelihood to truth");[113] "A vek spustia, v samozashchite / Zadev za belye tsvety, / Razbit' o plity obshchezhitii / Plitu krylatoi pravoty" ("And a century later, in self-defense / Brushing against the white flowers, / [To] break on the stones of the dormitories / The slab of winged truth").[114] In 1929 Pasternak had commented that what he lacked in his striving for Russianness was a relationship with a Russian woman.[115] In the poems to Neigauz, he anticipates the regret for the "shadow of alien birth" ("ten' chuzherod'ia").[116] The desired end, in 1931 as in 1936, is total participation in the Russian language and culture; the poet must be "rhymed" with the new muse, as nature rhymes "summer with Lermontov / And geese and snow with Pushkin" ("Rifmuet s Lermontovym leto / I s Pushkinym gusei i sneg"): "I ia b khotel, chtob posle smerti . . . / Zarifmovali nas vdvoem" ("And I would like us, after death . . . / To be rhymed together").[117] For the poet who was not born "straight," "rightness" must be acquired.

Mandelstam reconsiders Pasternak's triad in the poems on the death of Belyi.[118] He refers to all three terms in the first poem, "Blue eyes and burning frontal bone": "Chasto pishetsia kazn', a chitaetsia *pravil'no*— pesn'. / Mozhet byt', *prostota*—uiazvimaia smert'iu bolezn'? // *Priamizna* nashei rechi ne tol'ko pugach dlia detei, / Ne bumazhnye desti, a vesti spasaiut liudei" ("Often death sentence is written, and song is correctly read. / Maybe simplicity is an illness exacerbated by death? // The straightness of our speech is not just a child's toy gun, / Not paper quires but tidings save people").[119] The lines recall *Vysokaia bolezn'* (*A Sublime Malady,* 1928), where the rhyme *pesn'* 'song' / *bolezn'* 'illness' occurs twice and Pasternak rejects the lyric as inappropriate "in an age of such shadows."[120] In the late 1920s, Pasternak remarked on his new sense of the need for epic: "I consider that the epic is inspired by the time, and thus in the book *1905* I shift from lyric thinking to the epic, although this is very difficult"; "the lyric has almost ceased to sound in our time."[121] Pasternak's regretful parting with the lyric is echoed in Mandelstam's assertion, a few years later, that "now we must write only civic poetry." But Mandelstam never abandons the "elements of a moral nature" associated by Pasternak with the epic as opposed to the lyric; these elements may be found, after all, in the lyric mode. He redefines "song" as a "death sentence," and "simplicity" as a "fatal illness."[122] Simplicity is "direct" ("straight") speech, which is not child's play—it has real consequences.

Thus, in the first poem of the "Requiem," the body of the dead poet must lie, "endlessly straightening" ("beskonechno priamias'"); the figure, we have seen, is a curve. In the second poem, "10 January 1934," quoting Pasternak as well as Belyi with the image of the ice skater,[123] Mandelstam again makes straightness a curve, pursuing the oxymoron that is essential to the non-Euclidean geometry of the "Octaves": "gde *priamizna* rechei, // *Zaputannykh,* kak *chestnye zigzagi* . . .?" ("where is the straightness of the speeches, // Involved, like honest zigzags . . .?"); the interstanzaic enjambment emphasizes the initial adjective and mimics its meaning.

Curves, specifically convolutions, had appeared in Pasternak's 1919 poem "S polu, zvezdami oblitogo" ("From the floor, spilled over with stars"), where *muka* 'torment' and *izviliny* 'convolutions' occur together (as in "Loving some is a hard cross to bear," the latter is a rhyme word in the genitive plural): "Do snegu gnulsia. Podkhvatyval / S polu, ves' mukoi izvilin / Zvezdy i noch'" ("Bent to the snow. Picked up / From the floor, all in the torment of the convolutions, / Stars and night"). The "torment of the convolutions" has concrete referents, both in the actual bare winter branches and in the metaphorical antlers that burden the creature bending to the snow. But it is also the "chaos of the ages," which "was not sawed off the antlered one" ("U sokhatogo / Khaos vekov byl nespilen"), and which the protagonist participates in, joining earth and sky in a gesture.[124] Mandelstam's "torture of ebb and flow" is revealed by the act of "wandering in [the] convolutions, bifurcations"; the link between the torment and the convolutions is the theme of respiration, which, as in Pasternak's example, has manifestations that are both concrete and figurative, and both local and universal: the operations of the human organism or the "metabolism of the planet."[125] Thus the convolutions are the proper response to the complexity of things (to the "depth of events") in the "Requiem," as in the "Octaves."[126] In "Not I, not you," Mandelstam urges a return to these inclinations—to the convolutions that he conceives as fundamental to Pasternak's poetics, and to the method of indirection that he associates with poetry in action.[127] "Wandering in their convolutions," the poet works "for people" (in the *Autobiographical Sketch,* Pasternak calls his writings *bluzhdaniia* 'wanderings'). The poet's path is a convoluted one. In the context of convolutions, Mandelstam's poet achieves straightness and rightness.

Nadezhda Mandelstam writes that to her question about the identity of the third person plural in "Not I, not you," "Kto eto oni? *narod?*" ("So who are they? the people?"), Mandelstam responded, "Nu net. Eto bylo by chereschur *prosto*" ("Well no. That would be too simple"). I have noted that her testimony often reveals his thought, less through her analysis than through her words. In her report, this exchange contains two words— *prosto* and *narod*—that are key in the poets' dialogue. Mandelstam might have been responding to Pasternak, who makes "simplicity" (*prostota*) a manifestation if not a condition of the poet's essential relation to the people (*narod*). For him, the "power of ancestral endings" does not rest with the people. Thus, Nadezhda Mandelstam concludes, "'they' [*oni*] are something that exists outside the poet, those voices, that harmony that he tries to grasp with the inner hearing 'for people, for their living hearts.'"[128]

Attributing that power to an anonymous and abstract principle rather than to Pasternak's concrete, local, and nameable "people," Mandelstam recalls a poem Pasternak published in *Znamia* in April 1936 and apparently addressed, in part, to him.[129] With the lines "Ne u menia, ne u tebia—u nikh / *Vsia sila okonchanii rodovykh*" ("Not I, not you—they have / All

the power of generic endings"),[130] Mandelstam rejects Pasternak's com-
plaint about the exhaustion of language: *"Vse naklonen'ia i zalogi /
Izzhevany do odnogo"* ("All verbal moods and voices / Have been chewed
up to the last one"); he refutes, however, not the immediate fact but the
implied premise. The verbal categories belong to an impersonal authority.
These are forms of the future; they cannot be "exhausted," because they are
"embryonic."[131] In "All verbal moods and voices," as in "Fortunate is the
one," the people is the source of the poet's material, vital to his existence:
"On dlia tebia voda i vozdukh"; "On—chashchi glubina" ("It [the people]
is water and air for you"; "It is the depth of a thicket"); compare "Ty bez
nego nichto" ("You are nothing without it"); in "Fortunate is the one," the
people is also the instrument that crafts the material: "On, kak svoe
izdel'ia, / Kladet pod doloto / Tvoi mechty i tseli" ("It places beneath the
chisel, / As its own handiwork, / Your dreams and goals"). Pasternak
suggests the renewal of the poet's speech through a new relation to the
people, comparable to the poet's earlier relation to nature ("On—prezhnii
liutik lugovoi" ["It is the former meadow buttercup"]), to life as subject and
author of his verse.[132] Mandelstam insists on a different relation; just as he
rejects Pasternak's doubts as to the efficacy of language, so he rejects his
solution. The third person plural form *ikh* refers in "Not I, not you" both to
the unnamed third person plural (**oni*) and to people (*liudi*), but Mandelstam distinguishes these two categories. "They" are linked with the people
through their respective relations to the poet, whether "I" or "you." The
relationship goes not from the people to the poet but from the poet to people
("I dlia liudei . . . Izobrazish' . . ." ["And for people . . . You will
depict . . ."])—and from "them" to the poet ("Ikh vozdukhom poiushch
trostnik i skvazhist" ["The reed is singing and porous with their air"]).

Nadezhda Mandelstam contrasts Pasternak with Mandelstam as a "legitimate heir," in social and literary terms (she calls Moscow Pasternak's
birthright).[133] In "Not I, not you," Mandelstam urges the addressee to take
another path, which ensures another kind of inheritance.

❖ ❖

For Mandelstam, the poet's material is not a primordial and timeless
Russian language, as Pasternak suggests in "Fortunate is the one . . ." ("On
[*narod*]—chashchi glubina, / Gde kem-to v detstve rannem / Davalis'
imena / Sobyt'iam i sozdan'iam" ["It is the depth of a grove, / Where, in
early childhood, / Someone gave names / To events and creations"]). In
The Noise of Time, Mandelstam describes the acquisition of language as a
move from childhood babble to articulate speech, accomplished through
the perception of time, of historical process ("and only listening to the

swelling noise of the age . . . did we acquire a language").[134] In the
"Whistle" cycle he explores the appearance of poetry (cf. "the appearance
of the fabric," the theme of the "Octaves") with reference to the ages of
man, which Nadezhda Mandelstam, mentioning that cycle in particular,
identifies as a "structural conception" in his thinking.[135] The cycle spans
the stages from infancy through maturity, but it incorporates, too, the
possibility of the spiritual death of the idol.[136]

"The Goldfinch" and the other goldfinch poems are related to "The
Smile" ("Kogda zaulybaetsia ditia" ["When a child begins to smile"])
through the motif of the child (Nadezhda Mandelstam notes that both
"The Smile" and "The Goldfinch" split off from the contemporaneous
"Detskii rot zhuet svoiu miakinu" ["The childish mouth chews its
chaff"]).[137] In the last lines of "When the goldfinch in the airy pastry,"
Mandelstam speaks in the half-condescending, half-warning tone of an
adult addressing a child:

Когда щегол в воздушной сдобе
Вдруг затрясется, сердцевит,—
Ученый плащик перчит злоба,
А чепчик—черным красовит.

Клевещет жердочка и планка,
Клевещет клетка сотней спиц,
И все на свете наизнанку,
И есть лесная Саламанка
Для непослушных умных птиц!

(When the goldfinch in the airy pastry
Suddenly, heartfully begins to tremble,
The scholarly cloak is peppered with spite,
And the skullcap is blackened.

The little pole and board spread slander,
So does the cage with its hundred spokes,
And everything in the world is inside out
And there is a forest Salamanca
For disobedient, clever birds!)

Writing at the time of the attacks on Pasternak for slander, Mandelstam
recalls Pasternak's "Klevetnikam" ("To the Slanderers"), from *Themes and
Variations*. In that poem, "slander," as a hypocritical stance antithetical to
poetry, is juxtaposed to childhood, the true measure of things. Indeed, one
of Pasternak's definitions of slander is the rejection of age as a meaningful
category: "O detstvo! Kovsh dushevnoi glubi! / O vsekh lesov aborigen"

("O childhood! Dipper of the soul's depth! / O aboriginal of all forests");
"Pravdopodob'e bed kleveshchet, / Sosedstvo bogachei, / Khoziaistvo za
dver'mi kleveshchet, / Veselyi zvon kliuchei. // Rukopozhat'e lzhi
kleveshchet, / Manishek aromat, / Iziashchestvo darenoi veshchi, /
Kleveshchet khiromant. // Nichtozhnost' vozrastov kleveshchet . . ."
("The plausibility of misfortunes slanders, / So do the neighboring rich
folk, / The housekeeping behind the door slanders, / So does the merry
ring of keys. // The handclasp of falsehood slanders, / So does the aroma
of shirtfronts, / The elegance of a gift slanders, / So does the chiro-
mancer. // The insignificance of age slanders . . .").[138] The rhythmical
outline and lexicon of "To the Slanderers" are echoed in "When the goldfinch in the airy pastry. . . ." Mandelstam's tetrameters, in the lines beginning with the word *kleveshchet,* combine Pasternak's tetrameter lines,
which end with that word, and the trimeter line that begins with it.[139]
Pasternak's door and keys have been transformed into Mandelstam's cage
and its appurtenances (*kleveshchet* is reinforced by Mandelstam's *kletka*
'cage' as it is by Pasternak's *kliuchi* 'keys').[140] For Mandelstam's goldfinch, "slander" now describes the entire world ("And everything in the
world is inside out"). In response, therefore, the poet offers not a Pasternakian "child that has known no injury" ("*obid* ne znavshee ditia"),[141] with
its primordial childhood ("the aborigine of all forests"), but the rambunc-
tious goldfinch, closer to the offended child of "Oh, how we love to dissemble" than to the serene infant of the "Octaves" or "The Smile."

Nadezhda Mandelstam identifies the realia behind Mandelstam's
goldfinch and the child associated with it: Mandelstam gave a goldfinch to
a neighbor boy who caught and traded in birds.[142] But the association has
older sources. The image of the goldfinch in the cage is traditional in
Western European iconography beginning in the Middle Ages: goldfinches
were household pets, and were represented, in paintings and in poetry, as
captive birds. In numerous depictions the goldfinch was attached to a string
held by a child. In devotional paintings, the goldfinch often accompanied
images of the Christ Child. The goldfinch poem that entered the cycle as
"The Goldfinch" is linked to this tradition. The situation and behavior of
the bird in "The Goldfinch" can be understood accordingly:[143]

Мой щегол, я голову закину—
Поглядим на мир вдвоем:
Зимний день, колючий, как мякина,
Так ли жестк в зрачке твоем?[144]

Хвостик лодкой, перья черно-желты,
Ниже клюва в краску влит,

Сознаешь ли—до чего щегол ты,
До чего ты щегловит?

Что за воздух у него в надлобье—
Черн и красен, желт и бел!
В обе стороны он в оба смотрит—в обе!—
Не посмотрит—улетел.

(My goldfinch, I'll throw my head back—
Let's look at the world together:
Is the winter day, prickly, like chaff,
Just as hard in your pupil?

Little tail's like a boat, the feathers are black and yellow,
Below the beak it's infused with color,
Are you aware to what degree you're a goldfinch,
To what degree you're foppish?

What kind of air does it have in its forehead—
Black and red, yellow and white!
It's looking in both directions—both!—keeping both [eyes] open—
Stops looking—flies away!)

In the first stanza, the poet asks whether the goldfinch, with which he proposes to "look at the world together," sees the world the way he does: "Is the winter day, prickly, like chaff, / Just as harsh in your pupil?" The goldfinch, associated with Christ's martyrdom, was said to have acquired the red spot on its breast as it was pierced by a thorn it removed from Christ's brow.[145] Mandelstam emphasizes the red breast in one variant of "The Goldfinch": "I nagrudnik krasnym shit" ("And the bib is sewn with red").[146] Hence, too, the epithet *koliuchii* 'prickly' with reference to the troubling surroundings. The significance of the question about the winter day, and the answer to it, appears only at the end of the poem, as the goldfinch looks cautiously "in both directions." Playing on the expression *smotret' v oba* 'to keep a careful lookout', Mandelstam refers to the representation of the goldfinch in its capacity as harbinger of illness: the bird is said to look at the sick child who will recover, and away from the child who will not.[147] Another poem linked to the "Whistle" cycle, "Nynche den' kakoi-to zheltorotyi" ("It's a kind of yellow-mouthed day today"), recalls the "yellow plover" that was supposed to draw jaundice out of the sick person.[148] Nadezhda Mandelstam refers to that first line as "an avian comparison";[149] and Mandelstam's "yellow-mouthed" (or perhaps "yellow-beaked") day looks at him, as the bird might look at the patient: "I

gliadiat primorskie vorota / V iakoriakh, v tumanakh na menia" ("And,
full of anchors and fogs, / The sea gates look at me"). Moreover, "Ne mogu
ego poniat'" ("I can't understand it") might be a reference to the poet's
expectation of the bird-day: will it heal? will it turn away? Mandelstam's
goldfinch is looking not at a person but at the "world"; but the winter
landscape is not only the poet's illness, it is his equal. The association of the
ailing poet with the landscape and its own illness is constant throughout the
Second Voronezh Notebook.[150] The goldfinch cannot guarantee the recovery of the winter day or the poet.[151]

The "Whistle" cycle itself promises no certain outcome. The end of
speech, as in "On *ulybaetsia* svoim *tishaisim* rtom" ("It smiles with its very
quiet mouth") ("The Idol"), contrasts with its beginnings, as in "Rozhdenie
ulybki" ("The Birth of a Smile"). "The Idol" and "The Smile" comprise an
antithetical pair.[152] Both invoke limitless space, emotion, thought: in the
first case, "v pokoiakh bezbrezhnykh" ("in boundless chambers"); in the
second, "okeanskoe bezvlast'e" ("an oceanic anarchy"), "nepobedimo
khorosho" ("invincibly good"), "beskonechnoe poznan'e" ("endless cognition"); both associate iridescence, linked elsewhere in Mandelstam's
work to acuity of visual perception (e.g., *raduzhnyi* 'iridescent' in "Your
pupil"),[153] with the child's lips: "Ego indiiskoi *radugoi* kormili" ("He was
fed on an Indic rainbow") and "I *raduzhnyi* uzhe strochitsia shov" ("And an
iridescent seam is already being stitched"). In "The Idol," however, the
chambers are "boundless" ("bezbrezhnykh") but also "guarded" ("berezhnykh"); the rainbow is the object of a verb in the past tense. Youth is
irretrievably gone: the present is not the pregnant silence of the child (cf.
"Rebenok molchan'ia khranit" ["The child keeps silent"]) but the "Bud-
dhist" calm that Mandelstam rejects in the essay "The Nineteenth Century":
"Vnutri gory bezdeistvuet kumir / V pokoiakh berezhnykh, bezbrezhnykh
i schastlivykh, / A s shei kaplet ozherelii zhir, / Oberegaia sna prilivy i
otlivy" ("Inside the mountain the idol idles / In guarded, boundless, and
happy chambers, / And from its neck necklaces' fat drips, / Guarding the
ebb and flow of sleep"); "Kost' usyplennaia zaviazana uzlom" ("The drowsy
bone is tied up in a knot"). "The Smile" is about birth, about the infinite
creative or cognitive moment; "The Idol" is about a state like death, about
sterility and stagnation.

The idol "inside the mountain," like Mandelstam's Kashchei in "Ottogo vse neudachi" ("The cause of all failures"), has been compared to
Stalin.[154] But Mandelstam is referring, characteristically, to Stalin's literary counterpart, the Kremlin recluse of Pasternak's "Artist":[155] "A v te zhe
dni na rasstoian'i, / Za drevnei kamennoi stenoi,[156] / Zhivet ne
chelovek—deian'e, / Postupok rostom v shar zemnoi" ("While at the

same time, at a distance, / Behind the ancient stone wall, / Lives not a man—an act, / A deed of the magnitude of the earthly sphere"). Mandelstam's idol, however, is not more but less than human, having betrayed his boyhood promise ("Kogda on mal'chik byl . . ." ["When he was a boy . . ."]).

In this respect, the portrait of the idol is illuminated by Nadezhda Mandelstam's sketch of Nikolai Tikhonov, to whom Mandelstam sent "Kashchei" on December 31. Nadezhda Mandelstam discusses the accompanying letter and Mandelstam's vain hopes for an answer; she refers, specifically, to a "material" response, in exchange for the "gold" and "precious stones" of the poem.[157] Mandelstam sent the poem as such treasure: "In this work, by very modest means, with the help of the letter *shcha* and a little something else I have made a (material) piece of gold,"[158] as if *Ko*lia *Ti*khonov were Kashchei (cf. "U nego [Kashcheia] / *Kot* zhivet . . ." ["A cat lives / With him (Kashchei) . . ."]): "Shchiplet zoloto gvozdei" ("He pinches the gold of nails").[159] Mandelstam was initially fascinated by Tikhonov, Nadezhda Mandelstam writes: "Nonetheless O. M. too fell under the spell of Kolia Tikhonov, but that did not last long." Tikhonov was only a few years younger than Mandelstam and others in his circle, but he was considered a "boy" ("and O. M. liked both youths: 'See what a son Chukovskii has—a nice guy'"; "[Tikhonov and others] remained boys for very a long time [*ochen' dolgo khodili v mal'chikakh*]"). Some inexplicable change occurred in the "young Kolia": "Many to this day are under the spell of this former Kolia Tikhonov, although they don't understand what happened to him afterwards." The idol, too, has undergone a transformation from the compelling boy he had been ("Kogda on *mal'chik* byl i s nim igral pavlin, / Ego indiiskoi radugoi kormili" ["When he was a boy and the peacock played with him / He was fed on an Indic rainbow"]). *Tiho*nov resembles the idol "with its very quiet mouth"— "svoim *tishaishim* rtom," while his name prevails over his manner of speech as the model for the idol's language: "Nikolai Tikhonov, a poet, always spoke with conviction, loudly, expressively." Both descriptions are consistent with the speech of one who does not, after all, say much of anything: "A papier-mâché container never contains anything truly valuable."[160] Like a living being turned into a "papier-mâché figurine," the idol embodies the dangers of the descent to lower forms; his is the fate of the one who fails to preserve the capacity for speech in the underworld. With his distorted perceptions, he is bewildered by his fall; his attempt to recover his former features is doomed: "On myslit kostiiu i chuvstvuet chelom, / I vspomnit' silitsia svoi oblik chelovechii" ("It thinks with its bone and feels with its brow, / And struggles to recall its human aspect"). Not his power over others but his retreat from language into silence and sleep makes the idol threatening.

The characterization of Tikhonov recalls Nadezhda Mandelstam's account of Mandelstam's biologist acquaintance Kuzin, who, in later years, "hardened" and "set" ("zastyval," "zastyl"), realizing tendencies present, she suggests, even in the early 1930s. Mandelstam himself, she writes, became aware of Kuzin's limitations: his inability to admit change, to accept anything new (including new poems).[161] Yet for a time Kuzin played a different role. The Kuzin of *Journey to Armenia,* where growth is a leitmotif, "did science on the go," and his investigations involved the collection of cochineal,[162] with which the idol was associated in youth: "Davali moloka iz rozovatykh glin / I ne zhaleli koshenili" ("They administered milk from rose-colored clays / And didn't spare the cochineal"). This is the friend who "awakened" Mandelstam, as he indicates in the poem dedicated to Kuzin: "Kogda ia spal bez oblika i sklada, / Ia druzhboi byl, kak vystrelom, razbuzhen" ("When I was sleeping without face or form, / I was awakened by friendship, as by a shot").[163]

In "Notes on Poetry," Mandelstam calls the Pasternakian poet's work wakeful: "So, gesticulating, muttering, poetry makes its way, staggering, dizzying, blissfully crazy and yet the only sober, the only wakeful [*prosnuvshaiasia*] thing in the world."[164] Pasternak continues in the tradition of Fet, whose "Shepot, robkoe dykhan'e" ("Whisper, timid breathing"), cited by Mandelstam in the same essay, contains a sequence of events characterized by increasing arousal: "When Fet appeared, Russian poetry was agitated by the 'silver and quiver of the sleepy brook'" ("Kogda iavilsia Fet, russkuiu poeziiu *vzbudorazhilo* 'serebro i kolykhan'e sonnogo ruch'ia'"). In "On the Nature of the Word," the poet himself keeps vigil ("Vse spali, kogda Annenskii bodrstvoval" ["Everyone slept, while Annenskii stayed awake"]). The apprentice poet must "awaken the beast of literature [*razbudit' zveria literatury*]" as Mandelstam writes concerning his boyhood visits to his teacher V. V. Gippius in *The Noise of Time.*[165] Similar imagery recurs in the 1914 poem "O vremenakh prostykh i grubykh" ("[Tales] of times simple and crude"), where this plot and its consequences are acted out: the Pushkinian "caretakers in heavy fur coats / Sleep on wooden benches" ("I dvorniki v tiazhelykh shubakh / Na derevianykh lavkakh spiat"),[166] and the rousing of the gatekeeper opens the way into the ancient past. In *Conversation about Dante,* Mandelstam distinguishes poetry from ordinary ("automatic") speech: the latter we experience as if in sleep, while poetry "arouses [*budit*] us and shakes us up in mid-word" (hence Annenskii's vigilance).[167] In "Now I'm in a web of light," dated January 19 of the last Veronezh winter, poetry is summoned to keep people awake.[168]

Poetry, equated with fate, keeps the protagonist awake in Pushkin's insomniac lines: Ronen refers to Mandelstam's "[use of] Pushkin's sleepless quest for meaning, 'Stixi, sočinennye noč'ju vo vremja bessonnicy,' to overcome Lermontov's yearning for oblivion in 'Vyxožu odin ja na dorogu.'"[169] Mandelstam revises Lermontov's last stanza in the last stanza of "Now I'm in a web of light": "*Chtob* vsiu noch', ves' den' moi slukh leleia, / Pro liubov' mne sladkii golos pel, / Nado mnoi *chtob, vechno* zeleneia, / Temnyi dub sklonialsia i shumel" ("[So] that all night, all day, caressing my hearing, / A sweet voice will sing to me of love, / [So] that above me, showing eternally green, / A dark oak will bend and rustle"); cf. "Narodu nuzhen stikh tainstvenno-rodnoi, / *Chtob* ot nego on *vechno* prosypalsia" ("The people need verse that is mysteriously their own, / So that they will eternally awaken from it").[170] Mandelstam had already countered Lermontov's dream in "And I go out of space," where, "go[ing] out" (*vykhozhu*), the solitary protagonist (*odin*) engages in just such a quest for meaning: "I tvoi, beskonechnost' [cf. *pustynia*], uchebnik, / Chitaiu . . . / Zadachnik ogromnykh kornei" ("And your textbook, infinity, / I read . . . / Problem book of enormous roots").

Mandelstam implies the same function of poetry in the "Whistle" cycle, where, Mess-Baehr points out, the task of the poet, as Sadko or as the factory whistle, is to "arouse" or "awaken" the people ("*budit* narrod").[171] The "torture of ebb and flow" in "Not I, not you" is opposed to the "ebb and flow of sleep" in "The Idol"; the idol's torpor is the antithesis of poetry. Corresponding to that opposition is the one between cartilage and bone, the petrified protagonist's somnolent substance: "Kost' usyplennaia zaviazana uzlom" ("The drowsy bone is tied up in a knot"). The embryonic medium that the poet is urged to explore in "Not I, not you" precedes the birth of the infant and is the alternative to the idol as the unworked material of the future. As opposed to the silence of the idol, the embryonic medium is full of sound.

The opposition is supported on the level of sound texture. Velars are prominent in both poems, but the stop recurs throughout "The Idol," while the spirant is characteristic of "Not I, not you." In the first poem, *k* (as in *kost'*) appears thirteen times, and *g* five times, a total of eighteen velar stops in thirteen lines;[172] *kh* appears four times, in the line that resembles "Not I, not you" syntactically and contrasts with it thematically: "V *pokoiakh* berezhnykh, bezbrezhnykh i schastlivykh." In "Not I, not you," *k* appears seven times and *g* twice, a total of nine times in eleven lines; *kh* (as in *khriashch*) appears nineteen times. The contrast between the stop and the spirant corresponds to the opposition between bone and cartilage, silence and sound. The spirant, with its characteristic disturbance of the air flow, as opposed to the cessation of the air flow in the stop, suggests the charged embryonic medium, the "breathing heaviness" that is the poet's material, handed down by the anonymous plural "them" (*ikh*).

The spirant is associated with the plural subject itself: of its nineteen appearances, *kh* appears thirteen times in combination with the phoneme *i*. The unit *ikh,* characteristic of the embryonic medium, saturates the poem. *Khriashch,* which designates that medium, is the key word, the last word in the central (sixth out of eleven) and uniquely unrhymed line (as a rhyme-word, *khriashch* is a hybrid, incorporating the supporting consonant and masculine ictus of the rhymes in *ikh* with the stressed vowel of the rhymes in *a*-). Dentals, too, are prominent, as Mandelstam recognized when he described the orchestration of "Not I, not you" in terms of *iz* along with *ikh*.[173] In "Vulgata," the essay later joined with "Boris Pasternak" as "Notes on Poetry," Mandelstam emphasizes the productivity of the consonant in Russian word formation, calling it the "multiplier of the root" ("mnozhitel' kornia") as well as the "seed and guarantee of the posterity of the language."[174] Ronen refers to the "Baratynskian syntax" of "Not I, not you";[175] Baratynskii provides, also, the image of *khriashch,* which, as "gravel," is planted with trees in "On Sowing a Forest": "Zarodyshi elei, dubov i sosen" ("Embryos of firs, oaks, and pines").[176] Mandelstam makes the "seed" of the verse the first consonant of the word that names the medium.

Mandelstam's doubts about Pasternak increased in the period of *Second Birth,* with reference to which V. V. Trenin and N. I. Khardzhiev, in their 1932 essay "O Borise Pasternake" ("On Boris Pasternak"), comment on the predominantly vocalic texture of Pasternak's latest poetry, as opposed to his earlier work.[177] In "Notes on Poetry," Mandelstam calls "monastic speech" a "litany of vowels" and mentions Pasternak as one who worked towards the healthy "secularization" of the language. He implies the insistent consonantal orchestration of Pasternak's verse:

> Да, поэзия Пастернака прямое токованье (глухарь на току, соловей по весне), прямое следствие особого физиологического устройства горла, такая же родовая примета, как оперенье, как птичий хохолок.
>
> Это—круто налившийся свист,
> Это—щелканье сдавленных льдинок,
> Это—ночь, леденящая лист,
> Это—двух соловьев поединок.[178]

(Yes, Pasternak's poetry is a real mating call [a woodgrouse on the mate, a nightingale in the spring], a direct consequence of the peculiar physiological construction of the throat, a generic marker just like plumage, or a bird's tuft.

It's a thoroughly saturated whistle,
It's the clicking of compressed ice,
It's night icing a leaf,
It's the duel of two nightingales.)

The passage, culminating in the quotation from "Definition of Poetry," is full of the velars and dentals that permeate "Not I, not you."

Four days after completing "Not I, not you," Mandelstam returns to the problem of consonantal orchestration in the letter to Tikhonov accompanying "The cause of all failures." In emphasizing the crucial role of *shch* in that poem, Mandelstam returns, in particular, to another consonant he had considered in his prose of the 1920s. The year after "Notes on Poetry," in the last chapter of *The Noise of Time*, "In a Fur Coat above One's Station," Mandelstam discussed the sounds beloved of his literature teacher, V. V. Gippius:[179]

> Между тем вся сила его личности заключалась в энергии и артикуляции его речи. У него было бессознательное влечение к шипящим и свистящим звукам и «т» в оконченьи слов. Выражаясь по-ученому, пристрастие к дентальным и небным.
>
> С легкой руки В. В. и поныне я мыслю ранний символизм как густые заросли этих «щ». «Надо мной орлы, орлы говорящие». Итак, мой учитель отдавал предпочтенье патриархальным и воинственным согласным звукам боли и нападенья, обиды и самозащиты. Впервые я почувствовал радость внешнего неблагоразумия русской речи, когда В. В. вздумалось прочесть детям «Жар-птицу» Фета—«На суку извилистом и чудном»: словно змеи повисли над партами, целый лес шелестящих змей.[180]

(But the entire force of his personality consisted in the energy and articulation of his speech. He had an unconscious attraction to hushing and hissing sounds and to *t* in the word ending. In scholarly terms, a predilection for dentals and palatals.

Since V. V. set things going, to this day I conceive of early Symbolism as dense thickets of these *shch*'s. Thus, my teacher gave preference to the patriarchal and militant sounds of pain and attack, injury and self-defense. I felt the joy of the external imprudence of Russian speech for the first time when V. V. took it into his head to read the children Fet's "Firebird"—"On a sinuous and strange branch": as if snakes hung over the desks, an entire rustling forest of snakes.)

The harsh and prickly language of Mandelstam's teacher is characterized by "militant" velars as well as "militant" palatals and dentals: "Iz gortani rvutsia shipiashchie, klokochushchie zvuki: voinstvennye 'shch,' 'i,' 'g'" ("From the larynx burst hissing, gurgling sounds: militant *shch, i, g*").[181] Gippius might be pronouncing the first syllable of *shchegol* (with its reduced vowel). The language of the goldfinch is characterized by the same sounds as Gippius's speech: **shchego**l **kleveshchet** (cf. sh*ipi*ashch*ie*, klok*och*ushch*ie* zv*u*ki)—by the "sounds of pain and attack, injury and self-defense." The theme associated with the goldfinch is the same as the theme of Mandelstam's teacher, who "instead of literature taught a much more interesting subject—literary spite [*literaturnuiu zlost'*]."[182] Literary spite is the key to the poetry of the past century:

> Ты приправа к пресному хлебу понимания, ты веселое сознанье неправоты, ты заговорщицкая соль, с ехидным поклоном передаваемая из десятилетия в десятилетие, в граненой солонке, с полотенцем! Вот почему мне так любо гасить жар литературы морозом и колючими звездами. Захрустит ли снегом? Развеселится ли на морозной некрасовской улице? Если настоящая—то да.[183]

> (You are the seasoning for the unleavened bread of understanding, you are the cheerful consciousness of injustice, you are the conspiratorial salt passed down with a venomous reverence from decade to decade in a cut-glass saltcellar, with a serving cloth! That's why it's so pleasant to extinguish the heat of literature with frost and prickly stars. Does the snow crunch? Is there cheer in the frosty Nekrasovian street? If it's real—then yes.)

"Spite" or "malice"—Lermontov's *zlost'*, Nekrasov's *zloba*—had been a "secret motive" of the civic tradition of Russian verse.[184] In the "Whistle" cycle, Mandelstam hears "spite" in the speech of the aggrieved goldfinch: "Kogda shchegol v vozdushnoi sdobe / Vdrug zatriasetsia, serdtsevit" ("When the goldfinch in the airy pastry / Suddenly, heartfully begins to tremble"). The "prickly" winter day of "The Goldfinch" is the weather of the nineteenth century. The poet responds to that weather with "literary spite," invoking the language of nineteenth-century Russian literature.

In the 1922 theater sketch "'Grotesk'" ("The 'Grotesque'"), pursuing the association between salt and stars that appears also in the contemporaneous poems "Umyvalsia noch'iu na dvore" ("I washed at night in the yard") and "To some winter is arrack and blue-eyed punch,"[185] Mandelstam links the "salt" of the anecdote with the stars' un-Lermontov-like signaling: "ostroumnichaiut, ekhidstvuiut, mertsaiut s podmigivan'em" ("they wisecrack, they spread venom, they glimmer, winking").[186] He quotes Akhmatova's 1917 reminiscence of the prewar cabaret life, "Da, ia liubila ikh, te sborishcha nochnye" ("Yes, I loved them, those nocturnal assemblages"), including the key line "Veselost' edkaia [*sic*] literaturnoi shutki" ("The caustic cheer of the literary joke"). G. A. Levinton, referring to Mandelstam's use of that poem, points out the basic similarity between the comprehension of a joke and the deciphering of a quotation or allusion (both require "recognition"): "we are speaking not of particular, marginal cases, but of one of the general, fundamental features of poetry."[187] Akhmatova makes *veselost'* 'cheer' a characteristic of the poet in the 1913 "Ne budem pit' iz odnogo stakana," a poem about the eternal connection through verse as opposed to the impossible temporal connection. Her *veselaia podruga* 'cheerful [female] friend,' rather more pointed than it might appear (*veselyi* 'cheerful' is equated, in this context, with *vernyi* 'faithful' and *nezhnyi* 'tender'), distances the speaker from the addressee in the present as it links them in the ages. Mandelstam's 1914 "Ossian" is a counterpart to Akhmatova's poem. The first two lines are an instance of what Sergei Bobrov called "assimilation according to rhythm and sound" (1922): compare "Ia ne slykhal rasskazov Ossiana, / Ne proboval starinnogo vina" ("I haven't heard Ossian's tales, / I haven't tried ancient wine") with "Ne budem pit' iz odnogo stakana / Ni vodu my, ni krasnogo vina" ("We will not drink, from the same glass, / Water or red wine"). Mandelstam's poem is a typically historical-cultural version of the problem of literary dialogue across time, which Akhmatova treats in her own typically "intimate" terms.

Levinton's classification of the joke might be extended to its close relative, "literary spite." Mandelstam associates both not only with stars and salt, but also with the motif of cheer, which appears not only in Akhmatova's poems but also in Mandelstam's prose ("ty veseloe soznan'e nepravoty"; "Razveselitsia li na moroznoi nekrasovskoi ulitse?" ["you are the cheerful consciousness of injustice"; "Is there cheer in the frosty Nekrasovian street?"]). When there is no more malice in the stars and mockery in the snow, something crucial has been lost; thus ends the "Petersburg period" of Russian literature ("Davno otshumel blestiashchii peterburgskii ⟨1⟩913 god" ["The sound of the splendid Petersburg year of 1913 has long since died away"]).[188] Ronen finds that in the Voronezh verse, with its "spirit of humble defiance," Mandelstam "repudiated the Lermontovian temptation of answering the iron compulsion of the era with 'an iron verse steeped in bitterness and malice.'"[189] But "literary spite" is not a partial, limited emotion.[190] Like the joke, like the "trifles" Mandelstam mixes with what is "important," literary spite is of the essence. It does not disappear, but remains an undercurrent without which the lyric voice could not persist. Thus Mandelstam mourns the passing of the Petersburg of the Civil War years in the lyrical digressions of "Shuba" ("The Fur Coat"),[191] as he does the prewar Petersburg in the sharper notes of the contemporaneous "'Grotesque,'" where the cold and the "salt" of the night have been replaced by "accidental warmth" and by "nice, amusing" entertainment.[192] So, too, in "To some winter is arrack" the intimate inner stanzas (2–3) are framed by the micro-epic of the outer stanzas (1, 5–6), the yearning for warmth juxtaposed to the recognition and acceptance of the cold.[193] Echoes of this theme can be heard in the *Voronezh Notebooks;* the "Whistle" cycle includes the goldfinch poems along with "Not I, not you—they have."

Mandelstam returns to the language of literary spite in the extraordinary conditions of the third Voronezh winter, of which Nadezhda Mandelstam writes: "We knew that this miserable winter was our last breathing-space, and we took from it all that it could give. . . . That's why the most serene and life-affirming notebook appeared just at this period."[194] In the Ovid passage in Pushkin's *Gypsies,* consecutive quatrains of which Mandelstam quotes in "The Word and Culture" and "On the Nature of the Word," the "alien people" swathe the exiled Roman poet in furs to protect him from the Russian snows. The absurd luxury of the "fur coat beyond one's station" appears at the most terrible time, the time of "authority and cold"; just as the harsh conditions of the age fur the beast of literature, so a different winter furs the Voronezh exile.[195] "Literary spite," like the fur of the beast of literature, like Akakii Akak'evich's overcoat, is a response to wintry conditions.[196] Winter demands a prickly, hoarse speech. It accounts for the versification and lexicon of the Voronezh poems: the imprecise rhymes, the nonstandard verse forms and "unpoetic" vocabulary.[197] So the poet avoids the fate of the idol, with its "very quiet mouth"; so, in "Eshche ne umer ty, eshche ty ne odin" ("You have not yet died, you are not yet alone"), he can rejoice in the cold and hunger that make the "sinless labor" possible. That poem is linked to "V litso morozu ia gliazhu odin" ("Alone, I look the frost in the face") by rhyme and theme; the two poems share the mood of "calm and comfort[. . .]" derived from the harsh winter landscape and the poet's sense of moral independence from his surroundings, maintained with effort (cf. the contrasting pictures of the plains in the third and fourth lines of the two poems). It is this sense that distinguishes "Alone, I look the frost in the face" from "To some winter is arrack"; the final lines echo each other, but the snow, in the second poem, is no longer a source of pain: "A belyi, belyi sneg do boli ochi est" ("But the white, white snow devours the eyes painfully"); "I sneg khrustit v glazakh, kak chistyi khleb, bezgreshen" ("And the snow crunches in the eyes, sinless, like pure bread"). Nadezhda Mandelstam writes that the "struggle for the poet's dignity in society, his right to speak, and his position is perhaps the fundamental tendency defining Mandelstam's life and work." She hears in the *Second Voronezh Notebook,* beginning with the "Whistle" cycle, the "theme of the poet's self-affirmation in poetry."[198] The recollections of the first "wintry period" of his work recur as Mandelstam reasserts the poet's sense of rightness in the face of the frost.

❖ ❖

The goldfinch reappears in the last stanza of "This region's covered with dark waters," written towards the end of Mandelstam's work on the "Whistle" cycle: "Gde ia? Chto so mnoi durnogo? / Step' bezzimniaia gola. / Eto machekha Kol'tsova? / Shutish'—*rodina shchegla*" ("Where am I? What's wrong with me? / The winterless steppe is bare. / Is this Kol'tsov's stepmother? / You're joking—it's the homeland of the gold-finch"). The juxtaposition of *rodina* 'homeland' and *machekha* 'step-mother' hints at the complicated relations between the poet and his birth-place,[199] which is not, as Pasternak would have it, the "boundless home" that cherishes the poet "without the shadow of alien birth." In these lines— among those Pasternak singled out with the comment "dizzying in authen-ticity and expression"[200]—Mandelstam echoes Pasternak's "Opredelenie dushi" ("Definition of the Soul"), from *My Sister Life:* "Nashu *rodinu* buria sozhgla. / Uznaesh' li gnezdo svoe, ptenchik? / O moi list, ty puglivei *shchegla!*" ("A storm has burned up our homeland. / Do you recognize your nest, fledgling? / O my leaf, you're more fearful than a gold-finch").[201] Mandelstam had responded to "Definition of the Soul" already, just after the appearance of Pasternak's book. Ronen has pointed out ech-oes of that and other poems from *My Sister Life* in the "Hayloft" poems of 1922.[202] Viach. Vs. Ivanov comments on the connection between "Defini-tion of the Soul" and "Ia polesenke pristavnoi" ("On a step ladder I [climbed]"). Referring to the lines "Iz gnezda upavshikh shcheglov / Ko-sari prinosiat nazad. / Iz goriashchikh vyrvus' riadov / I vernus' v rodnoi zvukoriad" ("The mowers are bringing back / The [small] goldfinches that have fallen from their nests. / I shall get out of the burning rows / And I shall return to the sound row which is my original homeland" [Ivanov's translation]), he writes: "In both poems the small goldfinch is out of his nest, which is a symbol of a spiritual homeland."[203] Following Pasternak's "Uznaesh' li gnezdo svoe, ptenchik? . . . ," *rodina shchegla* is a place where the poet is not quite at home. This is a new and strange homeland, where the freight trains speak not Russian, but Ukrainian: "V gushche vozdukha stepnogo / Pereklichka poezdov / Da ukrainskaia mova / Ikh rastianutykh gudkov" ("In the thick of the steppe air / The trains calling to each other, / And the Ukrainian talk / Of their extended whistles"); it is this interchange that the poet would join, as he urges the addressee in the opening poem of the "Whistle" cycle: "Dlinnei tovarnykh poezdov, / Gudi . . ." ("Longer than freight trains, / Whistle . . .").

Nor is the spiteful language of the goldfinch characteristic of the Russian writer alone. Mandelstam's description, in "Notes on Poetry," of the consonant as the "multiplier of the root" in Russian could apply to Hebrew, where the root is constructed entirely of consonants.[204] The consonantal harmony of "Not I, not you" is a "generic marker," like the "clicking" and "jugging" in Mandelstam's 1923 version of Pasternak's verse (cf. his quotation from "Definition of Poetry," full of the same types of sounds), like a bird's plumage and tuft—like the "black and yellow feathers" of the goldfinch, which has the same colors as Mandelstam's Judaism.[205] As Mandelstam recalls the language of the nineteenth century in the "Whistle" cycle, the non-Russianness of his speech is as important as its Russianness. Tynianov describes Mandelstam's work as "almost that of a foreigner on the literary language."[206] Uspenskii, referring to Mandelstam's distanced relationship to his native language,[207] cites as evidence his "grammatical theme," where the Russian verbal paradigms become a subject of the verse. He points to the line "Ne u menia, ne u tebia—u nikh," with its alternation of genitive pronominal forms, as one example.[208]

The grammatical theme is evident throughout "Not I, not you," where the unit *ikh* recurs at least once in each line, whether as a pronoun or as an inflected ending. Giving the pronoun without an antecedent ("they have no name," and they exist only in a Baratynskian embryonic form),[209] Mandelstam calls attention to its grammatical status. Bloomfield comments on the purely grammatical definition of the "substitute," in this case, the pronoun: "The substitute differ from an ordinary linguistic form, such as *thing, person, object,* by the fact that its domain is grammatically definable. Whether an ordinary form, even of the most inclusive meaning, such as *thing,* can be used of this or that practical situation, is a practical question of meaning; the equivalence of a substitute, on the other hand, is grammatically determined."[210] The grammatical theme accounts for the abstractness of "Not I, not you," which is appropriate to the embryonic nature of the poet's material. Thus, as he does throughout his work, Mandelstam tells everything he knows, though what he knows, here, is located in an abstract dimension, has not yet come into being ("A tam, gde tsepilis' biriul'ki, / Rebenok molchan'ia khranit" ["While, where the jackstraws are joined, / The child keeps silent"]). Verbs appear to refer to concrete and familiar actions, but in the context of the poem they prove to have no such referents (the one possible exception is the figurative *potianut,* which might be understood in context as "inhale").[211]

The sound texture of "Not I, not you," which exploits and emphasizes grammatical forms, further distances it from paraphrase, brings it close to babble, or to an incomprehensible "foreign" tongue.[212] Mandelstam himself conceived of the material of the poem in terms of another language. He heard in the repeated *ikh* and *iz* the "influence of Spanish phonetics" (though Nadezhda Mandelstam notes that "Mandelstam's Spanish was absolutely fantastical").[213] The case of his Spanish is not the same as that of the other voices (German, Italian, French, Armenian) that, as Ronen writes, Mandelstam differentiates in his work in these years.[214] The language of the "Whistle" cycle is a hybrid, as if, having confirmed the possibility of the "true Russian voice,"[215] Mandelstam now acknowledges its other aspect.

Mandelstam was studying Spanish in Voronezh, as he informed his father in his letter of December 12; he was also reading the biography of a Spanish poet of Jewish origins; and he adopted a Sephardic ancestor, a victim of the Inquisition,[216] along the lines of Pasternak's forebear Isaac Abravanel.[217] He could have learned of Pasternak's Sephardic heritage from Valentin Parnakh's 1926 article about contemporary Russian poets, among them Mandelstam as well as Pasternak.[218] Parnakh discussed the Abravanel family in his 1934 *Ispanskie i portugal'skie poety, zhertvy inkvizitsii* (*Spanish and Portugese Poets, Victims of the Inquisition*), a book that inspired Mandelstam to read the Spanish poets.[219] Taranovsky finds no evidence of Mandelstam's "ancestor" in Parnakh's book, and Nadezhda Mandelstam does not identify him, but the details of his supposedly apocryphal story coincide with Parnakh's account of the life of Luis de León.[220]

That sixteenth-century poet and scholar, represented in Parnakh's *Spanish and Portugese Poets* by a brief biographical sketch and by one of his lyrics in Parnakh's translation, was a professor at the Salamanca university. Hence *uchenyi plashchik* 'scholarly cloak' and *chepchik* 'skullcap' in the goldfinch poems, where the reference to Salamanca is further evidence of the Spanish motif associated with the "Whistle" cycle.[221] De León was incarcerated by the Inquisition for five years for heretical interpretation of the Bible, for translating the Song of Songs into Spanish, for offending the Catholic Church, for his Jewish origins. While in prison, he composed a sonnet a day in his head. He was released, then rearrested. These facts are reflected in Nadezhda Mandelstam's paraphrase of Mandelstam's words to the Voronezh commandant: "O. M. answered that . . . he was studying the Spanish language and literature, in particular one poet, a Jew by nationality, who spent many years in the dungeons of the Inquisition and every day composed a sonnet. After he was freed, he wrote down his sonnets, but soon he was arrested again and put in chains. It's not known whether he continued his poetic activity even then."[222]

The poet's story is reflected, too, in the last lines of "When the goldfinch in the airy pastry," where *lesnaia Salamanka* is hardly the "forest paradise" Nadezhda Mandelstam describes.[223] Mandelstam refers to the confining forest in the letter to Tikhonov of December 31: "I am gravely ill, abandoned by everyone and destitute. . . . Here, in Voronezh, I live as if in a forest [*kak v lesu*], people, trees—there's no difference. I am literally physically perishing."[224] The sense of confinement is a leitmotif of the *Second Voronezh Notebook:* "Ne sravnivai: zhivushchii nesravnim. / S kakim-to laskovym ispugom / Ia soglashalsia s ravenstvom ravnin, / I neba krug mne byl nedugom" ("Don't compare: a living person's incomparable. / With a kind of tender fright / I tried to agree with the equality of the plains, / And the circle of the sky was my ailment"); "Kuda mne det'sia v etom ianvare? / Otkrytyi gorod sumasbrodno tsepok . . . / Ot zamknutykh ia, chto li, p'ian dverei?— / I khochetsia mychat' ot vsekh zamkov i skrepok" ("What am I to do with myself this January? / The open city is wildly tenacious . . . / Am I drunk from closed doors?— / And I want to bellow from all the locks and fasteners"). The oppressiveness of the open landscape culminates in the lines about the "deadness of the plains": "I ne polzet li medlenno po nim / Tot, o kotorom my vo sne krichim,— / Narodov budushchikh Iuda?" ("And isn't he crawling slowing through them, / The one we scream about in sleep, / The Judas of future nations"?).[225] Yet another poem links the poet's plains with the goldfinch's forest: "O, etot medlennyi, odyshlivyi prostor!— / Ia im presyshchen do otkaza,— / I otdyshavshiisia raspakhnut krugozor— / Poviazku by na oba glaza!" ("Oh, this slow, winded expanse!— / I'm sated with it to revulsion,— / And the horizon, catching its breath, is opened out— / I need a bandage on both eyes!"). The phrase *Poviazku by na oba glaza* echoes the thrice-repeated *v oba* [*obe*] in "The Goldfinch": "V obe storony on v oba smotrit—v obe!" ("It's looking in both directions—both!— keeping both [eyes] open"), to which *glaza* 'eyes' is the understood complement. In medieval Flanders, finches were blinded so that they would sing undistracted in competitions.[226] In the world where "everything is inside out,"[227] the forest, like the Voronezh plains, is another cage; a "bandage on both eyes" would free the poet of the sight of his plein-air prison. The tradition of the captive goldfinch links the fractious bird with the slandered Sephardic poet.[228]

The poem by de León included in Parnakh's anthology is linked thematically to the goldfinch poems and to Mandelstam's verse of the *Second Voronezh Notebook* more generally. Called, in Parnakh's translation, "Tiur'ma" ("Prison"),[229] it concerns the poet unjustly confined: "Zdes' lozh' i zavist' piat' let / Derzhat menia v zatochen'i" ("Here falsehood and envy have held me / Five years in confinement").[230] The theme of the poem is spiritual freedom in straitened circumstances: "No est' otrada v smiren'i / Tomu, kto pokinul svet, / Uidia ot zlogo volnen'ia. // I v etom dome ubogom, / Kak v pole blazhenstva, on / Ravniaetsia tol'ko s bogom / I myslit v pokoe strogom, / Ne prel'shchaia, ne prel'shchen" ("But there is joy in humility / For the one who has left the world behind, / Escaping from vicious agitation. // And in this poor home, / As in fields of bliss, he / Can be compared only to God, / And reflects in austere retirement, / Not tempting, not tempted"). That theme appears in the Voronezh verse in January 1937: "V roskoshnoi bednosti, v moguchei nishchete / Zhivi spokoen i uteshen. / Blagoslovenny dni i nochi te, / I sladkoglasnyi trud bezgreshen. // Neschastliv tot, kogo, kak ten' ego, / Pugaet lai i veter kosit, / I beden tot, kto sam poluzhivoi / U teni milostyniu prosit" ("In luxurious poverty, in mighty indigence / Live calm and comforted. / Blessed are those days and nights, / And the sweet-voiced labor is sinless. // Unhappy is the one whom, like his shadow, / Barking frightens and the wind mows down, / And poor is the one who, himself half alive, / Begs alms of a shadow").[231]

Nadezhda Mandelstam, referring to Mandelstam's Spanish genealogy, describes his ancestral memory as "idiosyncratic."[232] But the foreign lineage of the Russian poet, whether inherited or invented, is itself a theme of Russian poetry,[233] and the Spanish connection is one recurrent instance. As Taranovsky and Ronen, among others, have noted, Mandelstam's black and yellow are the colors not only of Judaism but also of the imperial Petersburg.[234] The "Sephardic" goldfinch speaks the spiteful language of Mandelstam's nineteenth-century Russia.[235] Commenting on Blok's transformation of certain themes of the nineteenth century into myth, Mandelstam mentions in particular the (Spanish) themes of Carmen and Don Juan.[236] V. N. Turbin discusses the problem of "bilingualism":[237]

Both Pushkin and Lermontov carried throughout their lives an image, hazily outlined in their consciousness, of some other, foreign land, whence each of them traced his origins [rod]. For Lermontov such a land was the mysterious Scotland (however, echoes of those reminiscences stopped in the poet's youth). Pushkin never ceased to remember his African roots.[238]

Mandelstam refers to Tiutchev's as well as to Lermontov's Scotland (cf. "Arfa skal'da" ["The Harp of the Skald"] and "Zhelanie" ["A Wish"], respectively) in "I haven't heard Ossian's tales," the first time he turns to the problem of the "foreign word."[239] Lermontov's other, probably apocryphal ancestral homeland was Spain.[240]

Pasternak makes *rodnoe* 'kindred' or 'native' the test of the poet's relation to the language and people ("No pust' i tak—ne kak brodiaga, / Rodnym voidu v rodnoi iazyk" ["But even so—not as a vagrant, / I will enter the native language as a native"]). Mandelstam's *rodnoe* is an attachment that transcends biological kinship (cf. Nesbet on the Goethean "elective affinities").[241] In his elaboration of a poetic voice, Mandelstam does not, as Pasternak does, seek assimilation to the people, any more than he seeks simplicity and straightness. Lidiia Ginzburg connects the desire to "be like everyone" with the striving for simplicity in Pasternak's verse. She finds the same desire in Mandelstam, but, she writes, "in his verse he did not admit concessions, his poetry was soundly guarded."[242]

Mandelstam distinguishes between *rodnoe* and *rodovoe,* with their common root and overlapping meaning. Both words can mean a relation of blood kinship; they may be as close as *prirozhdennyi* 'innate' and *vrozhdennyi* 'inborn' in Mandelstam's 1914 "Avtoportret" ("Self-Portrait"), which refer respectively to the "awkwardness" of the man and the poet's "rhythm" that must overcome it. But *rodnoe* suggests, further, the individual and personal, *rodovoe*—the collective and impersonal (cf. *rodovoi* as 'generic,' as opposed to *vidovoi* 'specific'). Mandelstam modifies and extends these meanings: *rodnoe* is alienable ("elective"), though kindred; *rodovoe* is inalienable, even if alien. Levin writes that the opposition *rodnoe* 'kindred' / *chuzhdoe* 'alien' is fundamental and definitive in Mandelstam's work.[243] *Rodovoe* participates in both members of the opposition.

Pushkin's Africa is again an instructive example. Brown cites *Eugene Onegin* 1.50 as a subtext of Mandelstam's (almost trans-sense) lines "V Peterburge my soidemsia snova, / Slovno solntse my pokhoronili v nem" ("We will meet again in Petersburg / As if we had buried the sun there"): "I sred' poludennykh zybei, / Pod nebom Afriki moei, / Vzdykhat' o sumrachnoi Rossii, / Gde ia stradal, gde ia liubil, / Gde serdtse ia pokhoronil."[244] Africa belongs to the poet (*moia* 'mine'), but "dusky Russia" is the land from which he has been exiled, the place "where [he] buried his heart." The difference parallels Mandelstam's distinction between *rodovoe,* which refers to the poet's own, like it or not, and *rodnoe,* which refers to spiritual but not physical kinship.

In "Fleity grecheskoi teta i iota" ("The Greek flute's theta and iota"), the protagonist creates what is native, as Mandelstam learns his native Russian: "Chto kogda-to on more *rodnoe* / Iz sirenevykh *vylepil* glin" ("That once he fashioned a kindred sea / Out of lilac clay"). In "Drozhzhi mira dorogie" ("The dear yeast of the world"), *rodnoe* is alienated: "Skuchno mne—moe rodnoe / Delo taratorit vkos'" ("I feel bad—my kindred / Business jabbers on aslant"). In "The Bookcase," *rod* refers to the inalienable paternal (Jewish) element; *chuzhoi* refers to the maternal (Russian): "This strange little library, like stratification, was deposited, not by accident, over decades. The paternal and the maternal in it did not mix, but existed separately, and, in its cross-section, this little bookcase was the history of the spiritual exertion of an entire clan [*rod*] and its inoculation with alien blood [*chuzhaia krov'*]."[245] In "Ossian," the alien (*"Chuzhikh pevtsov bluzhdaiushchie sny"* ["Other singers' wandering dreams"]) was assimilated ("I snova skal'd *chuzhuiu* pesniu slozhit, / I *kak svoiu* ee proizneset" ["And again the bard will compose another's song / And pronounce it as his own"]), as the familiar was rejected ("Svoe *rodstvo* i skuchnoe sosedstvo / My prezirat' zavedomo vol'ny" ["We are perfectly free to despise / Our origins and tedious neighborhood"]). In "Not I, not you," the ancestral source (*okonchaniia rodovye*) is acknowledged as the poet's inheritance. Mandelstam echoes the final lines of Tiutchev's "Sviataia noch' na nebosklon vzoshla" ("Holy night has risen onto the horizon"), the poem that, with its imagery of the "covering cast over the abyss," modeled the opposition between the "mirage of well-proportioned Petersburg" and the "Judaic chaos" in *The Noise of Time*. Man is isolated and alone, "thrown back on himself . . . / And there is no buttress or boundary from without" ("Na samogo sebia pokinut on— / . . . I net izvne opory, ni predela . . ."). The implicit **rodnoe* ("I chuditsia davno minuvshim snom / Emu teper' vse svetloe, zhivoe" ["And now everything bright and alive / Seems to him a long past dream"]) contrasts with the explicit *rodovoe:* "I v chuzhdom, nerazgadannom, nochnom, / On uznaet *nasled'e rodovoe"* ("And in the alien, the undeciphered, the nocturnal, / He recognizes the *ancestral inheritance"*); cf. "Vsia sila okonchanii *rodovykh"*; "I budesh' ty *naslednikom* ikh kniazhestv" ("All the power of *ancestral* endings"; and "And you will be the *heir* of their princedoms"). Thus, in "Not I, not you," Mandelstam recognizes *rodovoe, not rodnoe,* however dear (cf., for example, "golubka Evridika" ["darling Eurydice"] in "Chut' mertsaet prizrachnaia stsena" ["The spectral stage barely glimmers"], a poem about the poet's beloved and vulnerable Russian language),[246] as the poet's birthright, and as the reader's obligatory object.

Mandelstam invokes the ancestral inheritance with the Spanish motif of the "Whistle" cycle. The formal identity between the *ikh* of pronouns and the *ikh* of endings in "Not I, not you" supports the proposition that Uspenskii leaves unspoken: *rodovoe,* which refers to generic— grammatical—endings, refers also to generic, "ancestral" endings. The play with grammatical categories, associated with the poet's sense of distance from the Russian language, implies the problem of origins.[247] The phrase "okonchaniia rodovye," in its second sense, reinforces this reference (the very endings that are evidence of Mandelstam's distanced relation to Russian are "Spanish"). The prevalence of forms in the genitive case suggests "generation" (the pronoun **oni* is given first, and in nine out of ten instances, in the genitive; the single exception, the accusative in line 11, is formally identical to the genitive).

The total context of Mandelstam's work supports the interpretation of *rodovoe* as "generic" in the sense of "ancestral." In "A Lunge," Mandelstam considers the emergence of the individual literary phenomenon ("osob'") out of the genus, the source, which he calls "rodovaia poeziia" ("generic poetry"). He is referring to Symbolism, but the principle is a general one; thus Ronen, in his discussion of "The Slate Ode," describes the "creative tension of the many, which corresponds phylogenetically ('rodovaja poezija' . . .) to the subliminal initial stage of the individual, personal act of creation."[248] Symbolism has "innate authoritativeness, patriarchal weightiness, legislative gravity" ("vrozhdennaia avtoritetnost', patriarkhal'naia veskost', zakonodatel'naia tiazhest'").[249] The poetry of "generic endings," embodied in the anonymous plural of "Not I, not you," has a similar authority—the same authority as the pronouncements of the dictors in *Conversation about Dante,* which the "so-called poet" gratefully copies.

Just as the scribe's work is not a mechanical business, so the poet's relation to "authority or, more precisely, authoritativeness," as Mandelstam puts it in *Conversation about Dante,* has nothing to do with correctness ("insurance against mistakes") and everything to do with confidence ("that grandiose music of trustfulness, of trust, the subtlest—like an Alpine rainbow—nuances of probability and conviction"). His is the confidence that informs the certainty of the future reader's existence, without which the poet cannot be sure of his own (the corollary to his sense of rightness). "Dante's colloquy with the authorities," which Mandelstam explicates in terms of experimental science, and calls "the form and method of his cognition," is like the experience of the museum-goer among the impressionists in *Journey to Armenia:* an exchange, a "diplomatic treaty"; a gradual, Goethean, accustoming of the eye—"the preparation of the eye for the apperception of new things" (*Conversation about Dante*). The viewer in "The French," moreover, is not to "enter [the museum] as if entering a chapel," but to "stroll right through, as if along a boulevard!"[250] There is no false piety here.[251]

Following the discussion of authority in *Conversation about Dante* is the description of reading as a departure into another dimension. Reading, the poet's activity, entails an accommodation to the authority of the text ("with all your might and with complete conviction"). The comments on reading in *Journey to Armenia* complement the discussion of authority. As Mandelstam writes in the associated notes called "Chitaia Pallasa" ("Reading Pallas"), the reader seeking "generic features" in the book seeks the authoritativeness that Dante looked for in his "experiments." The "physiol-ogy of reading" is a process of recollection (*pripomnit'*) rather than com-mitting to memory (*zapomnit'*): "Buduchi *vsetselo* okhvacheny de-iatel'nost'iu chteniia, my bol'she vsego liubuemsia svoimi *rodovymi* svoistvami. Ispytyvaem kak by vostorg klassifikatsii svoikh vozrastov" ("When we are *entirely* gripped by the activity of reading, we admire first of all our *generic* characteristics. We experience a kind of ecstasy at the classification of our ages").[252] The book does not appeal to the imagina-tion: "the ancients did not seek illusion. Aristotle read dispassionately. The best of the ancient writers were geographers"; nor does it appeal to the individual memory: "my memory is hostile to everything personal" ("Ko-missarzhevskaia"); Mandelstam refers by contrast to the "much-abused" demand that "modern literature . . . has made on the writer . . . : don't dare to describe anything in which the inner state of your soul isn't reflected in one way or another." In "A Lunge," Mandelstam rejects "criticism as the arbitrary interpretation of poetry" and calls for "objective scientific investi-gation, a science of poetry."[253] In the essay on Blok's death he sets forth the task of the critic in similar terms: "Ustanovlenie literaturnogo genezisa poeta, ego literaturnykh istochnikov, ego *rodstva* i proiskhozhdeniia srazu vyvodit nas na tverduiu pochvu. Na vopros, chto khotel skazat' poet, kritik mozhet i ne otvetit', no na vopros, otkuda on prishel, otvechat' obiazan" ("The establishment of the poet's literary genesis, his literary sources, his *ancestry* and origins immediately brings us onto firm ground. The critic need not answer the question of what the poet wanted to say, but he is obliged to respond to the question of where he has come from").[254] Like the emphasis on *rodovoi* 'ancestral', 'generic' in the Pallas drafts, the emphasis on *rodstvo* 'ancestry' is Mandelstam's. V. V. Gippius taught this kind of reading, treating Russian literature "not as a temple but as a clan [*rod*]."[255] Mandelstam teaches it in "Not I, not you," telling the poet to enter the material of the "generic endings."

In his 1910 essay "Zhizn' stikha" ("The Life of Verse"), Gumilev had commented on reading as a physiological process. Verse lives through poetic "gesture": the concrete features of the poem (word order, sound orchestration, rhythm) ensure "that the reader . . . strikes the pose of its hero, copies his facial expressions and movements and, thanks to the suggestion of his own body, experiences what the poet himself did." Gum-ilev's representation of the relation between the physical and the emotional experience seems to echo William James's theory of emotion as following, and resulting from, physical change rather than preceding and causing it.[256] Mandelstam's discussion of the native, "generic" features that come into play in reading recalls Gumilev: the "joy, the sorrow, the despair the reader feels are only *his own* [*svoi*]" (Gumilev's emphasis), while his "physiological" model of the process of reading is consistent with Gumilev's Jamesian conception.

That conception may be reflected, too, in Mandelstam's discussion of "performance." Ronen comments on the two manifestations of the "voice of instruction" that guides the poet: it is the "dogmatic, canonical spiritual authority, on the one hand, and the 'voiceless' poetic 'matter' . . . which produces the necessary impetus . . . and exists only in the 'performance,' on the other."[257] As an example of the latter he quotes Mandelstam's early poem "I glagol'nykh *okonchanii* kolokol" ("And the bell of verbal endings . . ."); compare "Vsia sila *okonchanii* rodovykh." The anonymous plural that possesses "all the power of ancestral endings" is associated, through that "power" and their "princedoms," with the dictors; through the "endings" and their "cartilage," with the abstract, embryonic material of poetry.

In this case, as in the case of Mandelstam's Greek, the poet takes as embryonic material a "foreign" language, close to trans-sense (thus Greek, like Hebrew, was the rare language among those he attempted that Mandelstam "never mastered").[258] But during the quarter century between the two poems, the source changes: it is no longer the Greek of Mandelstam's Mediterranean culture but the "Spanish" of his Sephardic origins.

The word *rod*, suggesting "genus" as well as "family," "stock," "origin," is equivalent to the Mandelstamian *Stamm* (which, as we have seen, might also be translated "rod," as in "rod of almond"). The poet's word, based on *Mandelstam*, is not a personal (given) but a generic (family) name. The *-stam* in *Mandelstam* is literally a generic ending, **rodovoe okonchanie.**[259] Mandelstam's consideration of *Mandelstam* represents the "etymologization of a foreign word or name," as Levinton describes the phenomenon that is the opposite of the revelation of the foreign etymology of a Russian word.[260] In the process, Mandelstam makes the poet's strange and "cursed" name the proper, "generic" matter of poetry.

Trostnik 'the reed' is another version of the "stem" or "stalk" that is the Mandelstamian *Stamm*. It recalls the pipe of Pushkin's "Muse" ("Po zvonkim *skvazhinam* pustogo *trostnika*" ["Upon the ringing holes of the empty reed": cf. "Ikh vozdukhom poiushch *trostnik i skvazhist*"]) and Tiutchev's "thinking reed" ("mysliashchii *trostnik*," in "Pevuchest' est' v morskikh volnakh" ["There is melodiousness in the sea waves"]). It is associated also with the poet's non-Russian ancestry, and has antecedents in Mandelstam's earlier verse. Ronen calls the reed the subject of Mandelstam's "personal myth" of "birth out of chaos and . . . death into cosmos."[261] He compares the opening lines of "Not I, not you" to the first stanza of one of the Jewish poems of 1910: "Iz omuta zlogo i viazkogo / Ia vyros trostinkoi, shursha,— / I strastno, i tomno, i laskovo, / Zapretnoiu zhizn'iu dysha" ("From an evil and viscous pool / I grew rustling, like a thin reed, / And passionately, langorously, tenderly / Breathing a forbidden life"). In "Inexorable words," a related poem of that year, the body of the subject is a "stem" ("stebel'") that drowns in the "native pool" ("rodimyi omut"). Described as "thin and alien" ("tonkii i chuzhoi"), the stem is a link to the Jewish element.[262]

Tiazhest' 'heaviness' is what brings the poet to the ancestral place: "To—vseiu tiazhest'iu ono [serdtse] idet ko dnu, / Soskuchivshis' po milom ile" ("Now with all its weight it [the heart] sinks to the bottom, / Missing the dear silt"); "I, s kazhdym migom tiazheleia, / Ego ponikla golova" ("And, growing heavier by the moment, / His head drooped").[263] *Tiazhest'* is characteristic also of the prophet's speech, as the words of Moses reveal: "ia tiazhelo govoriu i kosnoiazychen" ("I *am* slow of speech [literally: I speak heavily], and of a slow tongue") (Exod. 4:10). *Tiazhest'* is the locus of poetry. While in the programmatic poem that closed the first edition of *Stone,* heaviness is the material out of which the poet will build ("iz *tiazhesti* nedobroi" ["from unpropitious weight"]), in "Sisters—heaviness and tenderness . . . ," heaviness coexists with tenderness as an essential feature of the poet's material. "Dyshashchaia tiazhest'," where the "inspiration" (breath) that is a feature of "heaviness" becomes its explicit attribute,[264] appears a function of what Ronen describes as the elimination of the opposition between the turbid "Jewish" water and the lucid "Christian" air.[265] The reed that had once "breath[ed] a forbidden life" beyond the Jewish pool now sounds not with the Christian air, but with the Jewish poet's Russian, the hybrid language of the child of Mandelstam's parents: "Rech' otsa i rech' materi—ne *sliianiem* li etikh dvukh pitaetsia vsiu dolguiu zhizn' nash iazyk, ne oni li slagaiut ego kharakter?" ("Our father's speech and our mother's speech—isn't our language nourished all its long life on the confluence of these two, don't they compose its character?").[266]

That hybrid language, the "breathing heaviness" of the "generic endings," is the speech of the goldfinch. Mandelstam calls the goldfinch *shcheglovit* 'foppish', playing on the near homonymity of *shchegol* 'goldfinch' and *shchëgol'* 'dandy' or 'fop'. The pun is justified not only by the striking coloration of the bird but also by the sounds associated with it. Ronen writes, with reference to the sound texture of Mandelstam's "Kashchei": "In addition to saturating the text with stridents, Mandel'štam cultivates the opposition grave/acute, consistently in the same sequence," and he lists a number of examples from "The cause of all failures."[267] The word *shche-*

gol itself is an example of such sound texture, with its strident and acute *shch* and grave *g,* both sounds that Mandelstam singles out in his description of Gippius's speech; *kleveshchet* is constructed similarly. Yet another example is the "Spanish" Mandelstam identifies in "Not I, not you," where the acute *z* alternates with the grave *kh;* the same alternation of features persists in at least one word per line, on the average, including the key word *khriashch,* which combines *kh* with *shch.*

Returning to these types of sounds in his discussion of *Inferno* 32,[268] Mandelstam suggests that the model for the language of the canto is "defective" speech: "It seems to me that Dante attentively studied all the speech defects, paid attention to stammerers, lispers, people who speak with a twang and who don't articulate their letters, and learned a lot from them."[269] The "language of dandies" (*iazyk shchëgolei*) is improper speech; it is, in particular, the incorrect Russian of the aristocratic women of Pushkin's time, who were brought up on French.[270] Pushkin praised this speech for its mistakes and mispronunciations: "Kak ust rumianykh bez ulybki, / Bez grammaticheskoi oshibki / Ia russkoi rechi ne liubliu" ("Like ruddy lips without a smile, / I don't like Russian speech / Without a grammatical error") (*Eugene Onegin* 3.28); "Nepravil'nyi, nebrezhnyi lepet, / Netochnyi vygovor rechei / Po-prezhnemu serdechnyi trepet / Proizvedut v grudi moei" ("Incorrect, careless babble, / Imprecise enunciation, / Produce, as before, / A heartfelt thrill in my breast") (3.29). Pushkin noted that the lack of a simple Russian prose language (neither the common speech nor the high ecclesiastical style) compels the writer to invent turns of phrase.[271] But this is precisely the situation that leads to linguistic invention. The poet's speech defect is the counterpart to the composer's deafness or the naturalist's blindness.[272] "Defective" speech is the life of language; it is least conducive to sleep. Thus Pasternak's verse, with its startling consonantal orchestration, is the common property of Russian poets—the future of Russian poetry.

In the letter to Tynianov of January 21, 1937, Mandelstam envisions the future of his own verse: "Vot uzhe chetvert' veka, kak ia, meshaia vazhnoe s pustiakami, naplyvaiu na russkuiu poeziiu; no vskore stikhi moi *sol'iutsia* s nei, koe-chto izmeniv v ee stroenii i sostave" ("Here it is already a quarter century that I, mixing what's important with trifles, have been floating towards Russian poetry; but soon my verse will commingle with it, changing something in its construction and composition").[273] The verb *sol'iutsia* 'will confluence' echoes the description of the poet's language as a commingling (*sliianie*) of two elements, the paternal and the maternal speech, and it has a similar force.[274] In "Not I, not you—they have," Mandelstam tells the poet, not to disappear in the "people," but to enter the future material of the work, for people's sake. He seeks not the transformation of the poet, not his "straightening," but the transformation of the medium. Thus in 1937, as his poetry flows into the sea of the Russian tradition, Mandelstam turns to the poet who had cured the sclerotic circulatory system of the verse, its difficult breathing. Through a return to "ancestral endings," the poet with the "shadow of alien birth" becomes a part of Russian poetry—"changing something in its construction and composition." In entering the vital embryonic medium the poet avoids the fate of the idol, "avoid[s] sleep and death."[275] Poetry remains conscious, awake, alive.

Notes

Note: Osip Mandelstam is cited in the notes as OM; Nadezhda Mandelstam as NM; and Boris Pasternak as BP. Osip Mandelstam's *Sochineniia* (Works [1990]) are cited as *S,* and his *Sobranie sochinenii* (Collected Works [1967, 1971, 1969, 1981]) are cited as *Ss.*

CHAPTER I. THE READER AND THE WRITER

1. For an excellent and profound survey of Mandelstam's life and work, see Ronen 1990.

2. See Ronen 1983, 1; *S* 1:502.

3. Gasparov 1990, 336.

4. An increasing number of articles treat Mandelstam's work of the 1930s, notably Levin 1978 on versification, lexicon, and thematics and Gasparov 1990 on metrics; Glazova 1984 on Dante in Mandelstam's work of the period and Mess-Baehr 1991 on its cryptic language.

5. See NM 1987, 169–70; *S* 2:501.

6. Gifford 1977, 241–43; NM 1970, 157–62; Epstein 1991.

7. Struve 1982; Cavanagh 1988. See also Przybylski 1987. Alice Stone Nakhimovsky writes: "Poetry, for Mandelstam, is Christian in origin and in practice" (1992, 24–25).

8. Baines 1976, 34.

9. Ronen notes, for example, about "Gde noch' brosaet iakoria" ("Where night casts its anchors"): "N. Ia. 's interpretations of this forgotten poem . . . suffer from the same literal reading of metaphors and pronounced neo-Orthodox bias as some of her other comments on M.'s religious imagery" (1983, 32 n. 20).

10. NM, personal communication, Moscow, December 1976.

11. Ronen 1973b; Taranovsky 1976. Taranovsky writes: "the poet feels that he has no inherent right to become an equal participant in Russian life" (1976, 52). These poems have been discussed also by Cavanagh (1988).

12. Thus for a time Marxism, too, appealed to Mandelstam. Ronen cites "the evolutionary theories of Goethe and Darwin" as further examples of Mandelstam's "search for an 'integral world view' and an 'internal sense of rightness' without which he found writing poetry unthinkable" (1973b, 295–96).

13. Isenberg 1986, 15.

14. Alter 1978, 42.

15. *S* 2:96. In *Fourth Prose,* too, Mandelstam describes being completely "riddled" and "*stam*ped" with his own name ("ia ves' izreshechen i pro*shtem*pelevan sobstvennoi familiei") (*S* 2:98).

16. Ronen writes: "Before *GO* ["Grifel'naia oda" ("The Slate Ode")], M.'s stable associations were between poetry and architecture, not 'wild stone'" (1983,

76 n. 19). Thus by 1923, the beginnings of the shift in Mandelstam's conception of order are already evident. That year he wrote much of *The Noise of Time,* including, apparently, the earlier chapters, where the image of the chaos of the poet's origins first appears (see *S* 2:379).

17. Ronen refers to "Mandelshtam's realization that the Jewish predicament cannot be escaped by turning to alien cultures and religions" (1973b, 296; see also Ronen 1990, 1643). Isenberg calls "Return to the incestuous bosom" a "rueful and ambiguous acceptance of the predominance of the Jewish over the Hellenic strain in Mandelstam's art" (1986, 30).

18. Taranovsky 1976, 66–67.

19. NM 1970a, 169.

20. See Taranovsky 1976 and Ronen 1973a and 1983 for discussion and application of the subtextual approach. Their work has given rise to some of the most fruitful studies of Mandelstam.

21. Ronen 1983, XV.

22. Ronen 1973a, 371.

23. "No, mozhet byt', poeziia sama— / Odna velikolepnaia tsitata" (Akhmatova, "Ne povtoriai—dusha tvoia bogata" ["Don't repeat—your soul is rich"], 1956).

24. *S* 2:41. In his translation of this passage, Ronen glosses *raznochinets* as a reference to "those educated people who were not of inherited or personal nobility but no longer belonged to the civil estate from which they originated" (1990, 1621); thus, like Mandelstam's poet, the *raznochinets* stands outside the social hierarchy.

25. *S* 2:121, 366.

26. Cf. the new orientation, observed by Ronen in Mandelstam's work of the 1930s, towards the voice of the addressee (1983, 186–87).

27. *S* 2:187–88.

28. Vladimir Vasil'evich Gippius (1876–1941) (see Brown 1965, 196).

29. *S* 2:48.

30. *S* 2:150.

31. *S* 2:14.

32. "Rebiacheskii imperializm" ("Childish Imperialism") (*S* 2:8–11).

33. *S* 2:14. Cf., in "Bunty i frantsuzhenki" ("Rebellions and Frenchwomen"), the third chapter of *The Noise of Time:* "The Judaic chaos penetrated all the cracks of the stone Petersburg apartment, in the threat of destruction, in the cap in the room of the guest from the provinces, in the hooked script of the unread books of 'Genesis,' cast into the dust on the lower shelf of the bookcase, beneath Goethe and Schiller, and in the fragments of the black and yellow ritual" (*S* 2:13).

34. *S* 2:14–15.

35. Cf. Anne Nesbet's somewhat different view of the childhood bookcase; she suggests that the Judaica, while it cannot be "disinherit[ed]," is "repressed" or "suppressed" beneath the Germans, while these latter are to be emphasized (1988, 109–10).

36. Cf. Arthur A. Cohen's account of an early conversation, in 1909 or 1910,

in which Mandelstam professed a lack of interest in his kin (1974, 29). As Mandelstam's writings attest, this perspective changed in the 1920s and the 1930s. Thus, for example, Isenberg notes: "In the twenties the Jewish theme is displaced to the prose, where it will undergo a substantial evolution" (1986, 30). Towards the end of my work on this chapter I came across the extensive examination of Mandelstam's "genealogy" in Cavanagh's unpublished dissertation (1988, esp. chs. 4 and 5), which overlaps with my discussion in some instances (though her ultimate concerns, and some of her conclusions, are not the same).

37. NM 1972, 577–78.

38. Ibid., 577.

39. S 2:19–20. Cavanagh writes: "His mother's Russian is 'pure,' but 'impoverished' and lifeless" (1988, 194); cf. Cohen 1974, 29–30.

40. Mandelstam confirms his bookish origins in the 1932 poem "K nemetskoi rechi" ("To the German Speech"): "I mnogo prezhde, chem ia smel rodit'sia, / Ia bukvoi byl, byl vinogradnoi strochkoi, / Ia knigoi byl, kotoraia vam snitsia" ("And long before I dared be born, / I was a letter, I was a grape line, / I was the book you dream about").

41. In the ancient conception, the Torah was God's blueprint for the universe (see Steinsaltz 1976, 7). Barry Holtz writes: "The rabbis throughout Jewish history were essentially *readers*. . . . We tend usually to think of reading as a passive occupation, but for the Jewish textual tradition, it was anything but that. Reading was a passionate and active grappling with God's living word" (1984, 16).

42. Epstein 1991, 201. I was pleased to discover Epstein's compelling, confirming study of Mandelstam and Pasternak as representatives, respectively, of Talmudic and Hasidic Judaism. My characterization of the two as "reader" and "writer" is based on a similar treatment of similar material, which I presented as a paper called "Pasternak and Mandel'štam: The Writer and the Reader" at the meeting of the American Association of Teachers of Slavic and East European Languages in New York in December 1986. I, too, have come to the conclusion that Mandelstam's "poetics of the addressee," in Ronen's term (1983, 186), reveals parallels with the principles of Talmudic Judaism. I do not examine Pasternak as a "Hasid," though Epstein's consideration of Pasternak in these terms is a useful foil to the discussion of Mandelstam's poetics.

Ronen describes *The Noise of Time* as the account of a period when "an entire generation of the Jews made a supreme spiritual effort 'to graft alien blood' . . . to its ancient interpretive preoccupation with the sacred text: the Talmudic tradition of the ghetto, which had subliminally affected the poet's own attitude to the word and to the entire body of world poetry" (1990, 1623).

43. S 2:14.

44. S 2:169.

45. With reference to this characterization of Bergson, Isenberg notes that Mandelstam is "explicit about the Jewish element in [his] Hellenism" (1986, 45).

46. S 2:173.

47. Holtz 1984, 35.

48. Cf. Mandelstam's diatribe against official literature in *Fourth Prose:* "I have no manuscripts, no notebooks, no archive. I alone in Russia work by ear, while all around absolute scum writes. What the hell kind of writer am I!" (*S* 2:92).

49. Stephen Jay Gould clarifies the meaning of this most misunderstood and misapplied of proverbs. Only when "proves" means "tests," in the sense of the Latin *probare,* does the exception have probative value (1982, 71–72; cf. Bloomfield, 1933, 438).

50. *S* 1:587.

51. Describing the scene, with the table, pencils, and paper, Nadezhda Mandelstam observes, "a writer like any other" (NM 1970a, 217).

52. See also NM 1972, 534–35; cf. *Conversation about Dante* (*S* 2:248–49).

53. Steiner 1985, 16–17.

54. Ibid., 13.

55. *S* 2:248–49.

56. Cf. Gershom Scholem on the "awe of the text" (1971, 290).

57. See the minor tractate of the Mishnah *Sefer Torah,* which concerns not only the document itself but the process of writing, and the conduct of the scribe as he writes. The Talmud warns in particular against improperly setting down God's name, which was thought to be present in every stroke of the Torah.

58. Scholem refers to the "authority of commentary over author," and he writes: "The 'chain of tradition' is never broken; it is the translation of the inexhaustible word of God into the human and attainable sphere; it is the transcription of the voice sounding from Sinai in an unending richness of sound" (1971, 291, 297). Cf. Epstein: "The writer for Mandelstam is not so much an original creator, which would hardly be compatible with the traditional Judaic view of the Lord as the First Creator of everything, but rather a translator and interpreter of some primary text" (1991, 201).

59. Holtz 1984, 16.

60. R. D. B. Thomson suggests that the status of the Mandelstamian poet undergoes a shift from the early stance of the "poet-listener" to the active builder of the architecture poems (1991, 503, 510). Yet the two hypostases of the poet are not incompatible with each other, and the poet-listener remains Mandelstam's protagonist to the end. The builder is, as Thomson himself notes, a craftsman, and the poet's construction is always a response to the material and not creation ex nihilo.

61. With reference to the nonexistence of Dante's manuscripts, Mandelstam writes that "drafts are never destroyed," for the text preserves the traces of its origins (*S* 2:231).

62. *S* 2:248.

63. NM 1987, 60.

64. "Za to, chto ia ruki tvoi ne sumel uderzhat'" ("Because I could not hold on to your hands" [1920]); "Sokhrani moiu rech' navsegda, za privkus neshchast'ia i dyma" ("Preserve my speech forever, for an aftertaste of misfortune and smoke" [1931]).

65. NM 1972, 363.

66. Alter 1978, 43.

67. *S* 2:250. Mandelstam's calligraphy has the same implications as the "wreaths" or "crowns" that, according to one story, God added to the letters of the Torah, telling Moses that they were to be explicated generations later by Rabbi Akiba: "he will expound heaps and heaps of laws upon every tittle" (recounted from Menahoth 29b in Scholem 1971, 283).

68. Clarence Brown writes: "The entire tone of the story is thoroughly Semitic. Parnok [the protagonist of *The Egyptian Stamp*] is a Jew" (1965, 51).

69. *S* 2:86.

70. See, e.g., Steinsaltz 1989, 48–59. Scholem writes: "Not system but *commentary* is the legitimate form through which truth is approached. . . . Commentary thus became the characteristic expression of Jewish thinking about truth, which is another way of describing the rabbinic genius" (1971, 289–90). Epstein says of Mandelstam's work: "Every poem is an inscription in the margins of the Book, a kind of commentary" (1991, 201).

71. *S* 2:218.

72. Fleishman 1981, 205 and n. 28. Cf. the version of Pasternak's creative biography in *Safe Conduct:* "A fifteen-year abstinence from the word, which had been sacrificed to sound, doomed [me] to originality, as a different crippling dooms [one] to acrobatics" (BP [1931] 1982, 202). In quoting this passage, Fleishman refers to Pasternak's own lameness, the result of the childhood injury described in the second chapter of *Safe Conduct* (Fleishman 1981, 206; cf. BP [1931] 1982, 193).

73. BP [1931] 1982, 212, 211.

74. BP 1981, 13–14.

75. Cf. Victor Erlich's observations about the participation of Pasternak's poet as another object in the landscape of his verse (1964, 136 and passim).

76. A. D. Siniavskii describes Pasternak's "transfer of the author's rights to the landscape" in the interests of "authenticity" (BP 1965, 23).

77. BP [1931] 1982, 273. See also Pasternak's account of that same summer in the drafts of a chapter called "My Sister Life," not included in the final version of *Liudi i polozheniia* (*People and Situations,* known in English as the *Essay in Autobiography,* or *Autobiographical Sketch* [1956]):

The infectious universality of their [people's] enthusiasm eliminated the boundary between man and nature. In this remarkable summer of 1917 in the interval between two revolutionary periods, it seemed that, along with people, roads, trees, and stars held mass meetings and orated. The air from end to end was gripped by a hot thousand-mile inspiration and appeared a person with a name, appeared clairvoyant and animated. (BP [1931] 1982, 491)

78. Tynianov 1929, 566–67. Cf. "I chem sluchainei, tem vernee / Slagaiutsia stikhi navzryd" ("And the more accidentally, the more truly / Verse is composed in sobs"), the conclusion of the first poem of Pasternak's first book in its 1929 revision ("Fevral'. Dostat' chernil i plakat'" ["February. Get ink and cry"]).

79. At one point Pasternak makes his autobiography an accidental feature of someone else's life: "I am not writing my autobiography. I refer to it when another's [autobiography] demands it" (BP [1931] 1982, 201–2).

80. Indeed, similar perceptions were a typical response to Pasternak's lyrics (see Lotman 1977, 224–25).

81. BP [1931] 1982, 231.

82. Ibid., 231.

83. In "Marburg," and in the corresponding chapters of *Safe Conduct*, the protagonist learns that love is one possible manifestation of the more general passion, and, like every particular, can be replaced by a different one (BP [1931] 1982, 230–31). Similarly, in the Scriabin chapter of *Safe Conduct*, Fleishman writes, "it is a question, in fact, not of [Scriabin] himself, but of 'feeling'" (1981, 206). Images, things are interchangeable, hence "nonobligatory": the "sole symbol [of art] is in the clarity and nonobligatoriness [*neobiazatel'nost'*] of the images characteristic of it *as a whole*" (BP [1931] 1982, 231; emphasis in original).

84. Lotman 1970, 38–43.

85. As I suggested in "Pasternak and Mandel'štam: The Writer and the Reader," Tolstoy, Pasternak's model of the author as authority (the authorial perspective pervades Tolstoy's universe, where the author is, arguably, the only authority), has a similar relation to details as random and essential (cf. Elliott Mossman's discussion of the importance of Tolstoy for Pasternak [1972]). Epstein emphasizes Pasternak's conception of detail as typical of the Hasidic worldview, where a tiny spark may contain the sacred (1991, 196–97).

Pasternak invokes a similar conception with reference to the author himself in his description of Tolstoy in death, in the *Autobiographical Sketch*. Tolstoy is an enormous presence that takes up all of space, and in terms of which other things are defined as partial manifestations. The relation of Sof'ia Andreevna to her husband is characteristic: "In the room lay a mountain, something like Elbrus, and she was its large separate crag. The room was occupied by a storm cloud the size of half the sky, and she was its separate lightning" (BP [1931] 1982, 440). (The procedure and the intonation of the description recall the prayer "Anu Ammekha," part of the Yom Kippur liturgy, where God and man are linked by a series of, for the most part, metonymic pairs that describe, metaphorically, their relation.) Cf. Lermontov's "Nochevala tuchka zolotaia / Na grudi utesa velikana" ("A little gold cloud spent the night / On the breast of a cliff-giant"), the epigraph to "Devochka" ("The Little Girl"), a poem where the detail takes over, and is perceived to be as large as, the entire scene: "Rodnaia, gromadnaia, s sad, a kharakterom— / Sestra! Vtoroe triumo!" ("Kindred, enormous, garden-sized, and by nature— / A sister! A second pier glass!").

86. See Barnes 1989, ch. 1.

87. To Jacqueline de Proyart, May 2, 1959 (Proyart 1964, 40–41; see also Stora 1968, 354). Pasternak apparently imagined his baptism. Cf. Fleishman on the "grain of truth" in this myth, with reference to the history of the Sephardic Abravanel family, the Pasternak ancestors (1990, 18–20).

88. Lotman 1970, 38–43.

89. "What does an honest person do when he speaks *only* the truth? While he is speaking the truth time passes; during this time life goes on. His truth remains behind, it deceives"; "In Russian 'to tell lies' [*vrat'*] means rather to talk excessively than to deceive. It is in that sense that art lies [*vret*]" (BP [1931] 1982, 223).

90. *S* 2:363.

91. *S* 2:93.

92. *S* 2:126–127.

CHAPTER 2. MANDELSTAM'S *MANDEL'SHTEIN*

Mandelstam's name is pronounced "Mandel'shtam"; it sounds like *mandel'shtein.*

1. See NM 1972, 524. See also Grigor'ev and Petrova 1977, 181.

2. For "expansion of borders" and "confinement" in *Journey to Armenia,* see Avins 1983, 152–53. Iu. I. Levin discusses a similar opposition in the *New Verse* (1978, 120–21).

3. Levin 1972, 184; see also Pinskii 1989, 367.

4. Mandelstam quotes Dante's opening lines in *Fourth Prose,* written within a year before the journey, in response to accusations of plagiarism. He returns to the same Dantean figure as late as 1936: "Ia v serdtse veka—put' neiasen" ("I am in the heart of the age—the way is unclear").

5. Ronen 1983, 186–87.

6. "Kuda mne det'sia v etom ianvare?" ("What am I to do with myself this January?").

7. "Puteshestvie s razgovorami" (*Ss* 3:185).

8. On Kuzin in the role of Mandelstam's guide, see NM 1970a, 245–46.

9. *S* 2:114.

10. *S* 2:114.

11. "The conversation turned on the 'embryonic field theory' proposed by Professor Gurwitsch" (*S* 2:114). On Mandelstam's interest in Gurwitsch (1874–1954), see Harris 1986, 6 n. 14. See also Haraway 1976, 54, 57f., 177.

12. See Bergson 1908, ch. 1.

13. On Mandelstam and Bergson's *élan vital,* see Levin 1972, 186.

14. See Bertalanffy 1933, 46–50.

15. The semiotic approach to the text has been a strong strain in Mandelstam studies (see Steiner 1976; Levin et al. 1974).

16. In some earlier publications, the third chapter of *Journey to Armenia* was called "Zamoskvorech'e," with reference to that part of Moscow just south of the river where the Mandelstams were living in the summer of 1931 (see *S* 2:427).

17. The "metaphors of organicism," which include "fibers, spheres, helices, and the tissues woven from them" (Haraway 1976, 48), became an important part of Mandelstam's vocabulary in the early 1930s. Those four figures are central to the biological investigation of the origins of the word that is a theme of the "Octaves." (Haraway's book, *Crystals, Fabrics, and Fields,* with its Mandelstamian title, might

be a study of *Conversation about Dante,* where, as in Mandelstam's verse of the 1930s, crystals, fabrics, and fields are prominent.)

18. *S* 2:114.

19. In "Admiralteistvo" ("The Admiralty"), man's work (here, an architectural construction) is seen to exist in more than three dimensions and to compose a fifth element. Cf. the "sixth sense" of the "Octaves" and *Journey to Armenia,* the third in the sequence of extraordinary characteristics defining the creative enterprise.

20. *S* 2:115.

21. Cf. Viach. Vs. Ivanov 1991a, 26. See also Haraway 1976, 57, 177.

22. Mandelstam refers to *Wilhelm Meisters Wanderjahre* in the third chapter of *Journey to Armenia* (*S* 2:113–14); in 1935 he prepared the radio broadcast "Iunost' Gete" ("Goethe's Youth"), the title of which reflects his association of Goethe with "the land where the lemon trees bloom": *Iug* (*ЮГ*) 'the south.' For discussions of Goethe in Mandelstam's *Journey,* cf. Pollak 1983, 114–63, and Nesbet 1988.

23. *S* 2:364.

24. *Ss* 3:169.

25. A similar aid to vision appears in "Sukhum": "From the balcony, one can easily see with field glasses [*voennyi binokl'*] the racetrack and the stand on the swampy parade ground, which is the color of a billiard table" (*S* 2:117). The scene recalls the open view of the bright green meadow with its pagan thinkers and heroes in *Inferno* 4 (115–20ff.). So does the image of field glasses, which, in "Canzone," have a "usurious power of vision" ("S rostovshchicheskoiu siloi zren'ia"). Usury is one of the Dantean themes Mandelstam considers in *Conversation about Dante.* See Ronen on usurious vision as poetic vision (1968, 259–61).

26. Goethe [1810] 1949, 20. "The eye may be said to owe its existence to light, which calls forth, as it were, a sense that is akin to itself; the eye, in short, is formed with reference to light, to be fit for the action of light; the light it contains corresponding with the light without. . . . This immediate affinity between light and the eye will be denied by none; to consider them as identical in substance is less easy to comprehend" (Goethe [1810] 1970, liii).

27. Goethe's *originality* is close not to Pasternak's own, but to Mandelstam's *tradition.*

28. Goethe [1816–17] 1950, 291 (*Italienische Reise,* 2: Sicily 1787, 17 April).

29. [1810] 1949, 428–49 (*Italienische Reise,* 3: Rome 1787, 28 August).

30. *S* 2:362.

31. *S* 2:185. The formulation dates to 1922 ("On the Nature of the Word"), but the conception of an organic poetics is evident in "Utro akmeizma" ("The Morning of Acmeism") and might be traced in the works of the minor Acmeists (Mikhail Zenkevich's *Dikaia porfira* [*Wild Porphyry*], Vladimir Narbut's *Alliluiia* [*Hallelujah*]).

32. "Ne gorod Rim zhivet sredi vekov, / A mesto cheloveka vo vselennoi" ("It's not the city of Rome that lives amid the ages, / But man's place in the universe") ("Pust' imena tsvetushchikh gorodov" ["Let the names of the blossoming cities"]).

33. This training is the subject of the fifth chapter of *Journey to Armenia,* "Frantsuzy" ("The French"), which is presented as a lesson in looking at impressionist paintings.

34. This "Vokrug naturalistov" appeared in *Za kommunisticheskoe prosveshchenie* (Moscow), April 19, 1932.

35. *S* 2:369. Daphne West discusses Mandelstam's writings "on the naturalists" as a key to his poetics (1981, 30).

36. *S* 2:121.

37. *S* 2:370.

38. *S* 2:365.

39. Pallas's counterpart is the Goethe, for example, of Baratynskii's elegy: "Pogas! no nichto ne ostavleno im / Pod solntsem zhivykh bez priveta" ("Expired! but nothing alive on earth / Was left by him unacknowledged") ("Na smert' Gete" ["On the Death of Goethe"]).

40. *Ss* 3:164.

41. *S* 2:364–65.

42. *S* 2:120.

43. Pallas's eye must be compared with the eye of Gogol, whom Mandelstam imagines as Pallas's companion on the journey (*S* 2:364) (see, e.g., Stilman 1974). His eye must be compared, too, with Belyi's, the "hard blue eye" of the "Octaves" (see Pollak 1983, 237–43).

44. Ronen 1968, 259–60.

45. Mandelstam is apparently referring to the Siberian "steppe cat" *Felis manul,* in popular usage, "the Pallas's cat." *Felis manul* is known for its short, low-set ears; hence, perhaps, its "deafness." The cat is known also for the peculiar placement of its eyes, high in its broad head, an adaptation, it has been suggested, that allows the cat to "peer . . . over rocky ledges . . . [while exposing] only a small part of itself to its prey" (*New Encyclopedia Britannica,* 15th ed., Micropaedia, s. v. "Pallas's cat"). The eye of *Felis manul* confirms the metonymic vision of the cat's eye: it is a metonymy, as the visible manifestation of the whole of the animal. Pallas mentions seeing one remarkable cat on the way from Petersburg to Tsaritsyn (Pallas 1812, 1:48–49). *Felis manul* appears in an appendix to Pallas 1793, vol. 5.

46. The epithet *glukhoi* in what I have called Mandelstam's "first" poem (Pollak 1988) testifies to the enormous potential of the object, here, the sound: "Zvuk ostorozhnyi i glukhoi / Ploda, sorvavshegosia s dreva" ("The sound, discreet and muted, / Of a fruit torn from a tree").

47. *S* 2:365.

48. *Ss* 3:161. L. S. Vygotskii refers to Beethoven as an example of "overcompensation" where the "path to accomplishment lies through the overcoming of obstacles, the hindering of a function is the stimulus for its heightening" (1983, 36). Oliver Sacks, in his study of deafness, singles out Vygotskii's insistence that the achievements of the blind or deaf child come "'*in another way, by another course, by other means*'" (Sacks 1990, 50–51 n. 55; Sacks's emphasis).

49. Cf. V. N. Toporov's comments on the possibility of the view that "the text

creates the author." Among his examples, appropriately in this instance, is Jung's proposition that "Goethe did not create Faust; rather, the spiritual component of Faust created the personality of Goethe" (Toporov 1991, 7–8).

50. *S* 2:364.

51. *S* 2:121.

52. I am grateful to Wallace Sherlock for pointing this out. Cf. *belyi grib* (*boletus edulus*) with "*Belymi* rukami . . . sobiraet rossiiskie *griby*."

53. "Ariost," "Armeniia."

54. Mandelstam characterizes poetic material as *syr'e* 'raw material' in the drafts to *Conversation about Dante* (*S* 3:181–82).

55. The conjunction of the meteorological and mineralogical spheres is implied by Pallas's major geological contribution. Pallas recognized, primarily on the evidence of the Ural and Altai ranges, a successive deposition of rocks, which revealed the relative age of the layers. The same conjunction is one of Goethe's interests on his journey; from the opening pages of *Italienische Reise,* the Neptunist poet makes detailed observations about the topography, soil, climate of the regions he passes through, and he suggests that the mountains determine their own weather. Ronen notes Goethe's importance for Mandelstam in this regard (1983, 77).

56. *S* 2:250.

57. Pallas 1812, 1:182; 2:230–31.

58. Fersman 1920, 257–79. Ronen identifies Fersman as a source for Mandelstam (1968, 264).

59. See Ronen 1968, 262.

60. "[A vkus u nego byl gor'kii, mindal'nyi. Raz kak-to on skazal: — Betkhoven dlia menia slishkom sladok—i oseksia]" ("[But his taste was a bitter, almond one. Once he said: "Beethoven is too sweet for me—and stopped short]") (*S* 2:360).

61. *S* 2:124–25.

62. Technically, *mindalina* does not refer to the thyroid gland (*shchitovidnaia zheleza*), involved in goiter; but Mandelstam invokes that word by describing the goggle eyes characteristic of goiter as "almond-shaped." The image of glandular disease appears in Mandelstam's December 1930 reminiscence of Petersburg, "Leningrad": "Ia vernulsia v moi gorod, znakomyi do slez, / Do prozhilok, do detskikh pripukhlykh zhelez" ("I returned to my city, familiar to tears, / To veins, to a child's swollen glands"); and it recurs in the 1932 poem "Kogda v dalekuiu Koreiu" ("When to distant Korea"): "Byla pora smeshlivoi bul'by / I shchitovidnoi zhelezy, / Byla pora Tarasa Bul'by / I nastupaiushchei grozy" ("It was a time of laughter's bubble / And of the thyroid gland. / It was the time of Taras Bulba / And of the approaching thunderstorm" [translated by Ronen 1990, 1625]). In each case swollen glands (a salience) are associated with childhood, which, like illness, is characterized by the distorted vision that accompanies the creative state ("Derzha irisku za shchekoi" ["Holding a toffee in my cheek"—Ronen] anticipates the image of swollen glands). The "approaching storm" that rhymes with the "thyroid gland" in the second poem is another sign of poetry: Mandelstam links "storm" with

"event," as a prerequisite of poetry (see "To the German Speech" and "Iz zapisei raznykh let" ["From Notes of Various Years"] [*S* 2:375]).

63. Cf. the "makeweight" (*dovesok*) of the "bread Sophias" (*khlebnye Sofii*) in the 1922 poem "Kak rastet khlebov opara" ("How the bread's leaven grows").

64. *S* 2:170.

65. See Ronen on the significance of the fact that the form Mandelstam quotes is not the passive (*laudanda*) but the future active participle (*laudatura est*) (1990, 1628).

66. *S* 2:102.

67. *S* 2:129; cf. *Purgatorio* 4. 88–90.

68. In this respect the pilgrim is distinguished from the second hypostasis of the hero that appears in Mandelstam's work: the Odysseus of *Conversation about Dante*, the one who does not return. Lotman comments on the journey of Dante the pilgrim, distinguishing his "spiral" path from Ulysses's horizontal one (1986, 31–33). Cf. the spiral movement in the "Octaves" and in the poems on the death of Belyi.

69. *S* 2:127.

70. See Lamarck [1809] 1984, 350–53.

71. Ibid., 403–4.

72. "Shestogo chuvstva kroshechnyi pridatok" ("The minute appendage of the sixth sense").

73. *S* 2:107.

74. Cf. *ugadyvat'* with *gadat'*, in the 1918 poem "Tristia": as I will show elsewhere, the women who "are fated to die guessing" or "telling fortunes" (*gadaia*) are as much a model for the poet as the men whose "lot is cast only in battle."

75. Cf. Lamarck [1809] 1984, 352.

76. Cf. "Rakovina" ("The Shell"), Mandelstam's 1911 poem, and the planned title poem of Mandelstam's first book (*The Shell* was advertised; *Stone* appeared) (see Ronen 1973a, 368 n. 3). The substitution accomplishes, among other things, a shift of focus from the poet to the material. Levin describes the orientation of Mandelstam's word in his early poetry towards the object (the message or the referent), as opposed to the later orientation towards the addressant, the addressee, and the contact (1978, 137–38). In the account of the Armenian church, stone sings like shells.

77. *S* 2:127.

78. Mandelstam's church has origins in life and in art. The diminutive Karmravor in the village of Ashtarak is indeed tiny, with room for a few rows of seats and a small altar area; but the painted cupola, as Mandelstam notes, gives the traveler an unexpected sense of space. At the same time, the church of "Ashtarak" might be described by an entry in Mandelstam's "Baedeker": it resembles Goethe's Santa Rosalia, hewn out of the rocky face of a cliff (on Monte Pellegrino, another pilgrim's mountain), in *Italienische Reise* ([1816–17] 1950, 259–62 [Sicily 1787, 6 April]).

79. *S* 2:108.

80. *S* 2:363.

81. The study of ancient Armenian is the study of the intricately carved gravestones (*khachkar*) scattered through the Armenian landscape.

82. *S* 2:118.

83. The church, with its extraordinary cupola, is constructed on the same principle as the ancient Armenian language. Viach. Vs. Ivanov gives a similar account of the relation between Mandelstam's two stony media in his discussion of Armenian verse: "Symbols of earth and of the book, of clay as material 'in the library of potter authors' are joined together—buildings have begun to speak in an 'ominous' ancient language" (1985, 455).

84. *S* 2:126.

85. *S* 2:127. Pavel Nerler, the editor of *Sochineniia,* refers to Marr's *Grammatika drevnearmianskogo iazyka: Etimologiia* (Saint Petersburg, 1903) (*S* 2:433). The verb *tverzhu* (cf. *tverdyi* 'hard') confirms the hardness of the object.

86. The title of the second chapter, "*Ashot* Ovanesian," testifies to a connection with the seventh, "*Ash*tarak." (On the "concentric" construction of *Journey to Armenia,* another connection with Dante, see Pollak 1983, 86–104.)

87. *S* 2:106.

88. *S* 2: 106. In the corresponding seventh chapter, Mandelstam writes: "From the sky fell three apples: the first to the one who told, the second to the one who listened, the third to the one who understood. So end the majority of Armenian tales" (*S* 2:128).

89. *S* 2:223.

90. *S* 2:114.

91. Cf. Levin on the "inner psychological space" as one of the aspects of the "syncretic space"—of which another correlate is the underworld—in *Tristia* (1975b, 5–6 and passim).

92. Hence the "archaic" language: the Old Church Slavonic *prisnosushchii* 'everlasting' corresponds to, as it characterizes, the ancient Armenian that Mandelstam refers to in the Ashtarak passage.

93. "Substantial proofs of being," in Isenberg's felicitous rendering. The attraction of the archaic and primitive becomes a prominent theme in Mandelstam's work of the early 1930s. The archaic is a terrible, terrifying power; it threatens the very being of the protagonist, though it may be the poet's salvation. Some commentators suggest that the descent is a protest and a sacrifice; others suggest that it is an attraction to a creative source. Both are correct.

94. *S* 2:123, 122.

95. Berthelot 1932, 52–53; his emphasis.

96. *S* 2:122.

97. *Surovost'* 'rigor' recalls the Lamarckian state Berthelot gives as *immobilité froide* (cf. rigor mortis).

98. *S* 2:128. Cf., in "The Word and Culture": "Ona [vsiakaia poeziia, poskol'ku ona klassichna] vosprinimaetsia kak to, chto dolzhno byt', a ne kak to, chto uzhe bylo" ("It [all poetry, inasmuch as it is classical] is perceived as what must be, not as what already has been") (*S* 2:170).

99. Ernst Mayr points out that the attribution of a theory of volition to Lamarck is erroneous, based on the mistranslation of *besoin* as "want" instead of "need" (Lamarck said nothing about *want*): "Lamarck was not as naive [as] to think that wishful thinking could produce new structures" (1982, 357).

100. 1983, 219.

101. Again Goethe is the guide; in Goethe's *Youth* Mandelstam quotes one of the self-appraisals typical of *Italienische Reise:* "With this journey I want once and for all to sate my soul, which yearns for the beautiful arts. . . . But afterwards, when I return, I return to the crafts. . . . The time for the beautiful is over. Only utility and strict necessity govern our contemporary life" (*Ss* 3:78). Here I would take issue with Jane Gary Harris, whose interpretation of the "Ashtarak" draft passage depends on her translation of *uperet'sia:* "With all the fibers of my being I want to exert pressure against the impossibility of choice, against the total absence of freedom" (1979, 395). Harris implies that choice and volition are invoked as positive values and objects of the poet's pursuit (see 1986, 15, 16), but the situation is more complicated. Gifford observes, concerning the attraction of the mountain: "[Mandelstam] wants to come up against a necessity, and to obey it" (1979, 29).

102. *S* 2:145.

103. *S* 2:363. Cf. Mandelstam's paean to German, written in the summer of 1932: "Zvuk suzilsia, slova shipiat, buntuiut, / No ty zhivesh', i ia s toboi spokoen" ("Sound has narrowed, words hiss, rebel, / But you live, and I am tranquil with you") ("To the German Speech").

104. Cf. Viach. Vs. Ivanov 1991a, 20, 21; 1991b, 6.

105. *S* 2:131.

106. *S* 2:122.

107. Viach. Vs. Ivanov 1991a, 16, 18.

108. Cf. the protagonist of Annenskii's "Staryi kolokol" ("The Old Bell"), a translation of Baudelaire's "La cloche felée": "A on nedvizhno i v soznan'i umiraet." The old bell "dies, immobile and conscious" (this from a poet for whom, at times, "the injury of a doll is more pitiful than one's own injury").

109. *S* 2:122.

110. Here I revise my earlier suggestion that these capacities, among others, define the poet (cf. Pollak 1987, 464).

111. See Bergson 1959, 388–89.

112. *S* 2:124.

113. This same indifference accounts for the neglect of the drawbridge, as if nature does not care whether man crosses over. But it seems that man is saved by not joining the ranks of oblivious creatures.

114. Cf. Baratynskii's comparison of thought to a sword: "No pred toboi, kak pred nagim mechom, / Mysl', ostryi luch! bledneet zhizn' zemnaia" ("But before you, as before a naked sword, / Thought, sharp ray! earthly life pales") ("Vse mysl' da mysl'! Khudozhnik bednyi slova!" ["Nothing but thoughts and thoughts! Poor artist of the word!"]).

115. Cf. Pushkin and Annenskii, where the presence of vegetable life by the

grave suggests the triumph of nature, whether comforting or tormenting for the poet: "I pust' u grobovogo svoda / Mladaia budet zhizn' igrat', / I ravnodushnaia priroda / Krasoiu vechnoiu siiat'" ("And let young life play by the vault of the tomb, / And indifferent nature / Shine with eternal beauty") ("Brozhu li ia vdol' ulits shumnykh" ["Whether I wander along noisy streets"]); "Pust' travy smeniatsia nad kapishchem volnenii / I voskovoi v grobu zabudetsia ruka" ("Let grass give place to grass above the temple of agitation / And the waxen hand be forgotten in the grave") ("Moia Toska" ["My Anguish"]).

116. Mandelstam hears this speech as a Slavic dialect (*S* 2:244; see also *Ss* 3:184).

117. Ronen 1968, 258. Taranovsky comments: "The *'blažennoe, bessmyslennoe slovo'* from 'V Peterburge my sojdemsja snova' (1920) should be interpreted as the 'mladenčeskii lepet,' the 'detskaja zaum',' expressing joy" (1976, 19 n. 29). He compares *lepet* in the "Octaves" to the same passages from *Conversation about Dante* (67 n. 23): "Eshche chto menia porazilo—eto infantil'nost' ital'ianskoi fonetiki, ee prekrasnaia detskost', blizkost' k mladencheskomu lepetu, kakoi-to izvechnyi dadaizm"; "Dant vvodit detskuiu zaum' v svoi . . . slovar'" ("Another thing that struck me was the infantalism of Italian phonetics, its sublime childishness, its closeness to infantile babble, a kind of age-old Dadaism"; "Dante introduces childish trans-sense into his . . . vocabulary").

118. "Ty krasok sebe pozhelala" ("You wished for paints").

119. *S* 2:298.

120. *S* 2:298.

121. *S* 2:297.

122. *S* 2:13–14.

123. "The Judaic Chaos," "Komissarzhevskaia" (*S* 2:20, 41–42).

124. Epstein 1991, 201. See "The Judaic Chaos": "The Russian speech of a Polish Jew? —No. The speech of a German Jew? —No again. Maybe a peculiar Kurlandish accent? —I haven't heard any like that. An entirely abstract, invented language, the ornate and tangled speech of an autodidact, where ordinary words are intertwined with the antique philosophical terms of Herder, Leibniz, and Spinoza, the whimsical syntax of a Talmudist, the artificial, not always finished sentence—it was anything you like, but not a language, whether in Russian or in German" (*S* 2:20).

125. "Bunty i frantsuzhenki" ("Rebellions and Frenchwomen") (*S* 2:13).

126. Given the impossibility of escape, the solution becomes, first, the opposition of "Judaic chaos" to the classical Russian "order"; and second, the transformation of the chaos itself into a principle of order, *khaos iudeiskii* 'Judaic chaos' into *iudeiskie zaboty* 'Judaic cares.'

127. The smell of musk is another link between the descriptions of his Jewish home and the Sukharevka market; cf. "Now the smell of the fresh slaughterhouse hits you in the head with musk and health—the smell of animal corpses" (*S* 2:297).

128. *S* 2:13.

129. See the essay called, provisionally, "Skriabin i khristianstvo" ("Scriabin

and Christianity") (*S* 2:157) (in *Ss* the essay is given as "Pushkin i Skriabin" ["Pushkin and Scriabin"], not Mandelstam's title).

130. Otsup 1933, 238–39. Similarly, Ronen has called the descent to the primitive source the "secret theme" of Mandelstam's lyrics (Yale University seminar, spring 1975).

131. Uspenskii 1990, 93 n. 13. Cf. "Obrastu prisoskami i v penu / Okeana zavitkom vop'ius'" ("I will grow suckers and stick / A tendril into the ocean foam") with "Ostan'sia penoi, Afrodita, / I slovo v muzyku vernis'" ("Remain foam, Aphrodite, / And word, return to music"). In the "Octaves," the attraction to that primordial state is part of the poet's attempt not to abandon culture but to preserve it, though facing something uncertain and unknown.

132. Ronen (1983, 208 n. 172) quotes Mandelstam's "namesake," L. I. Mandelstam, on his own writing: "Chuvstvuiu temnye vyrazheniia i nedostatok lovkosti po slogu; a mrachnyi mucheknicheskii prizrak dukha bez tela, tak zhe kak iudaizm, v'etsia po vsemu khodu etogo sochineniia" ("I feel the dark expressions and an insufficiency of adroitness in style; but the gloomy martyr's ghost of a spirit without a body, just like Judaism, winds along the entire course of this composition"). Yet Annenskii's similar description of his own stilted language in "Drugomu" ("To the Other"), "A po strokam, kak prizrak na pirakh, / Ten' dvizhetsia tak delanno i vialo" ("But along the lines, like a ghost at a feast, / A shade moves so affectedly and sluggishly"), suggests that such difficult speech may be the poet's condition.

133. "Tell me, draftsman of the desert."

134. Ronen 1983, 112, 205. In my article on "The sound, discreet and muted," the first poem in the second edition of *Stone,* I suggest that the "sound . . . of the fruit falling [*sorvavshegosia*] from the tree" recalls Tiutchev's stone, "fallen [*sorvalsia*] by itself or cast down [*nizvernut*] by a rational hand" (Pollak 1988, 103).

135. *S* 2:127.

136. "Neumolimye slova" ("Inexorable words").

137. *S* 2:106.

138. *S* 2:14.

139. Ronen 1990, 1640; Ronen 1977b.

140. Dal' notes that *styd* 'shame' is characteristic of humans, never of animals. It means modesty, sensitivity to baseness; it presumes a moral sense (*Tolkovyi slovar'*, 8th ed., s.v. *stud*). It is what distinguishes the poet from mortals and requires that he go to the underworld to recover the word. In this respect mortals are comparable to lower forms of life: neither know what they are lacking, while the poet's glory and his shame is his awareness. Only the poet can descend, in "The Swallow" as in "Lamarck."

141. Ronen 1983, 168; Ronen 1990, 1624.

142. M. B. Meilakh's discussion of Akhmatova's name provides a parallel to Mandelstam's case: "Thus, the poetic gift of the author, of the heroine of Akhmatova's lyrics, is recognized as intimately connected to the meaning of the author's name" (Meilakh 1975, 44–45).

143. *S* 2:21.

144. Ronen 1977a, 175 n. 34. Cf. the "Jewish staff" or "crozier" (*evreiskii posokh*) that the poet takes with him to Armenia, that "little sister of the Judaic land," in *Fourth Prose*. On this staff as a transformation of the "crozier" in Mandelstam's 1914 poem "Posokh" ("The Staff") and his 1915 essay "Petr Chaadaev," see Harris 1986, 2–3, and Cavanagh 1990, 609. Mandelstam refers to the flowering rod also in "Est' tsennostei nezyblemaia skala" ("There is an unshakeable hierarchy of values" [1914]): "Kak tsarskii posokh v khizhine prorokov, / U nas tsvela torzhestvennaia bol'" ("Like the royal staff in the hut of the prophets, / A solemn pain blossomed among us").

145. In Jeremiah, too, the flowering almond rod (*zhezl mindal'nogo dereva*) appears in the context of difficult speech (1:11, 6). Jeremiah, like Moses, doubted his ability to speak, while in each case the almond is a sign that God has chosen His mouthpiece.

146. "I already saw earlier in the Erevan museum a skeleton hunched up in a sitting position, placed in a large potter's amphora, with a hole in the skull [*cherep*] drilled for the evil spirit" (*S* 2:102); "By the way, I respectfully wrapped in my handkerchief the porous lime box from someone's cranium [*cherepnoi korobki*]" (*S* 2:102). See a more detailed discussion of the skull as remains in Pollak 1987, 459.

147. Ronen 1990, 1645.

148. *S* 2:126.

149. Cf. on the one hand the skulls discovered on the island of Sevan in ch. 1, and on the other the "Promethean" head of Ashot Ovanesian in ch. 2 (*S* 2:105–6).

150. *S* 2:234.

151. Lamarck [1809] 1984, 262.

152. *S* 2:122.

153. *S* 2:362. In "Ashtarak," Mandelstam draws a parallel between his nocturnal study of Marr's Armenian grammar and the miller's insomniac inspections (*vykhodit* 'he goes out') of the millstones (*S* 2:127). Again the poet's mental effort is compared to an exit into an open place (moreover, Mandelstam implies a further comparison between the Armenian language and the large crushing stones).

154. See also the "Octave" "I ia *vykhozhu* iz prostranstva" ("And I go out of space"), discussed in Chapter 4.

155. *S* 2:225. Just as a sixth sense draws the poet out onto the mountain, so instinct (*instinkt, genial'noe stereometricheskoe chut'e*) is the principle that directs the formation of the crystal.

CHAPTER 3. JUDAIC CHAOS, JUDAIC CARES

Epigraph: Heisenberg 1959, 105–6; Heisenberg 1979, 76.

1. *S* 2:214, 239.

2. The composition of the "Octaves" spanned three years that included the completion and appearance in print of *Journey to Armenia,* the composition of *Conversation about Dante,* the end of the "Moscow" period and the beginning of the "Voronezh" period of Mandelstam's work. Of the eleven "Octaves," all but two were begun in November 1933; one was begun in May 1932, and one in January

1934, when six were finished. Two were finished in February and three in July 1935. (See *S* 1:529; NM 1987, 187–88. These dates differ somewhat from the dates given in *Ss* 1:198–202.) In this respect, the "Octaves" can be said to have been longer in process than any other work by Mandelstam (with the exception of a few poems revised years after they were written).

3. Akhmatova 1968, 2:181. Nadezhda Mandelstam interprets Mandelstam's comment about civic verse narrowly ("But the civic theme is nevertheless a piece of stale bread, and it could not completely satisfy him" [NM 1987, 187]); in this case, her understanding may not reflect Mandelstam's.

4. See *S* 1:529; NM 1987, 187.

5. "Kvartira" ("The Apartment") was the domestic name of the poem (*S* 1:528; see NM 1987, 186).

6. "Vot i kvartira est'—mozhno pisat' stikhi." Quoted by Ronen as the report of contemporaries (1973a, 385).

7. See Ronen 1973a, 385–86. See also Freidin 1987, 239. Compare, in particular, Khodasevich's line "Ia sam nad soboi vyrastaiu" ("I myself rise up above myself") with Mandelstam's "I ia vykhozhu iz prostranstva" ("And I go out of space"); Khodasevich's "I vizhu bol'shimi glazami" ("And I see with big eyes") with Mandelstam's "S bol'shimi usami kusava . . ." ("With big eyes the biter . . .") and "S beschislennym mnozhestvom glaz" ("With a countless multitude of eyes"). Khodasevich's "Ballad" has eleven stanzas.

8. The "Octaves" account for a large part of the ternary lines in 1930–34. The proportion of amphibrachic to iambic lines in the "Octaves" (8:3) vastly exceeds the average for the period as a whole (4:3), or even for the year 1933–34 (5:4). However, in 1935–37, though iambs once again predominate, as they did to varying degrees in 1908–25, ternary meters remain more frequent than they had been before 1930 (Gasparov 1990, 339–40). The Stalin epigram, an instance of civic verse dating to the period of the "Octaves," is in anapaests.

Yet Mandelstam's interest in civic verse was not new. His lecture of March 1914, "Neskol'ko slov o grazhdanskoi poezii" ("A Few Words about Civic Poetry") (Ronen 1983, 23–24) and the "Roman" poems of 1914 and 1915, as well as the Chaadaev essay of the same period, testify to this interest.

9. Many of the motifs of the "Octaves" appear also in *Journey to Armenia* and *Conversation about Dante.*

10. Levin 1975a, 226. Levin makes similar comments in his studies of "Umyvalsia noch'iu na dvore" ("I washed at night in the yard") (Levin 1973) and "Masteritsa vinovatykh vzorov" ("Mistress of guilty glances") (Levin 1982).

11. "1 January 1924."

12. Nadezhda Mandelstam describes the genesis of those poems of the *Second Voronezh Notebook:* "Out of the 'Ode' came a multitude of verses, entirely unlike it, antithetical to it, as if the law of the recoil of a spring were at work here" (NM 1970a, 216; see the chapter "Oda" ["The Ode"] passim).

13. "All works of world literature I divide into permitted and written without permission. The first are trash, the second—stolen air" (*S* 2:92).

14. See also the variant of this poem, "Emu kavkazskie krichali gory" ("The Caucasus Mountains shouted to him").

15. Hence the July 1935 final datings of "In needlelike, plague-filled goblets" and "And I go out of space." See NM 1987, 187–88.

16. Nerler gives "I'll perform a smoke-colored rite . . ." in two stanzas, of five and three lines (*S* 2:221), rather than, like the "Octaves," as a single unit or in two quatrains. The resulting pair of stanzas is in keeping with the general tendency of the Voronezh verse away from symmetry, towards oddness (see Levin 1978, 124–25 and passim).

17. NM 1987, 187.

18. Brown 1973, 124. Cf. Natasha Shtempel''s comment on Mandelstam's words, as they were reported by Akhmatova: "'It should not be forgotten that he said in 1937: —I renounce neither the living nor the dead.' (Speaking of the dead, Osip Emil'evich had in mind Gumilev. —N. Sh.)" (Shtempel' 1987, 213).

19. Nadezhda Mandelstam alludes to echoes of Gumilev in the "Octaves," though she does not specify (NM 1972, 59). Five other octaves, grouped as "Schast'e" ("Happiness"), precede Gumilev's poem called "Octave" in the 1916 volume *Kolchan* (*The Quiver*). Samuil Schwarzband describes *The Quiver* as constructed on groups of eight poems (1987, 298). The dedicatory poem "Pamiati Annenskogo" ("To the Memory of Annenskii") may be significant in light of Annenskii's own poem that plays on 8, "∞": "Deviz Tainstvennoi pokhozh / Na oprokinutoe 8" ("The Device of the Mysterious is like / An overturned 8").

20. See also, inter alia, Gumilev's "Estestvo" ("Nature") and "Slovo" ("The Word").

21. *Apollon* 1914, 5:34–42; Gumilev 1968, 4:333–36.

22. See the advertisements in the front materials to Zenkevich's *Wild Porphyry* (Saint Petersburg: Tsekh poetov, 1912) and in the end pages of *Stone* (Saint Petersburg: Acme, 1913).

23. Gumilev 1968, 4:334.

24. NM 1987, 187.

25. Gumilev 1968, 4:334. Gumilev's own "Happiness" depends on a single "antinomy of consciousness," and almost programmatically so: the opposition between apparent contentment and actual misfortune. Thus the completest sadness is the one "amid silks" ("No net trevozhnei i zabroshennei— / Pechali posredi shelkov," in "Bol'nye veriat v rozy maiskie" ["Invalids believe in May roses"]).

26. Timenchik 1974, 39–46.

27. Ibid., 39–40. The oxymoronic possibilities implied by the two definitions of *acme*—which might suggest, roughly, both "beginning" and "end"—are implicit in two apparently antithetical analyses of Acmeism by contemporary observers. V. M. Zhirmunskii (1916) saw Acmeism as a revolutionary move, a break with the poetics of Symbolism; hence, "beginning." B. M. Eikhenbaum (1923) called Acmeism a "culmination" of the symbolists' accomplishments; hence, "ending."

28. See Lawrence L. Thomas on Marr's polysemantic clusters, to which Mandelstam refers with his derivation of the Armenian word for "head" in *Journey to*

Armenia (S 2:106). Thomas speculates on Marr's debt to L. Lévy-Bruhl (1957, 70–81). Mandelstam's "Armenia" poem "Azure and clay, clay and azure" may refer to Marr's musings on the original complex linking "sky," "sea," and "earth" (cf. the following line of the poem, "Chego zh tebe eshche? . . ." ["What more do you want? . . ."]).

29. "The Old Crimea."

30. I am grateful to Viach. Vs. Ivanov for bringing this connection to my attention.

31. "Zemlia i nebo v knige 'Shakh-name' bol'ny bazedovoi bolezn'iu—oni voskhititel'no pucheglazy" ("The earth and sky in the book *Shah-Nameh* are sick with goiter—they are ravishingly exophthalmic") (S 2:125).

32. S 2:199.

33. S 2:125. The miniature is the poetic form par excellence from the semiotic point of view. Tomas Venclova writes: "Poetry is perhaps the most complex and remarkable phenomenon in the 'informational economy' of mankind: it incorporates the maximum significance and meaning in the minimum volume. Here it is worth recalling the well-known words of Pasternak, who said that poetic thinking is the 'natural consequence of man's ephemerality and the long-range enormousness of his tasks'" (1986, 22–23); Venclova is referring to Pasternak's "Zametki k perevodam shekspirovskikh tragedii" ("Notes to the Translations of Shakespeare's Tragedies") (1961, 194).

34. In the course of the "Octaves," objects are no longer represented in three dimensions. Tiny things may appear large, as if observed from extremely close range, or enormous things may be reduced to a scale that the human eye can accommodate.

35. Cf. Gumilev's review of the first *Stone*, which appeared in *Apollon* 1914, no. 1–2: "This love for everything alive and solid brings O. Mandelstam to architecture. He loves buildings as other poets love mountains or the sea" (Gumilev 1968, 4:327).

36. Cf. the negative treatment of *vernost'* 'loyalty' in the description of life in Zamoskvorech'e—where, by "birth," Mandelstam is not at home: that neighborhood appears in *Journey to Armenia* as the antithesis of Armenia, that "little sister of the Judaic land":

> Riadom so mnoiu prozhivali surovye sem'i trudiashchikhsia. . . . Vnutri ikh komnaty byli ubrany, kak kustarnye magaziny, razlichnymi simvolami rodstva, dolgoletiia i domashnei *vernosti*. . . . I ia blagodaril svoe rozhdenie za to, chto ia lish' sluchainyi gost' Zamoskovorech'ia i v nem ne provedu luchshikh svoikh let. Nigde i nikogda ia ne chuvstvoval s takoi siloi arbuznuiu pustotu Rossii. (S 2:107–8)

> Next to me lived stern families of workers. . . . Inside their rooms were decorated like handicraft stores, with various symbols of kinship, longevity, and domestic faithfulness. . . . And I thanked my birth that I was just an accidental guest of Zamoskovorech'e and would not spend my best years

there. Never and nowhere did I feel with such force the watermelon emptiness of Russia.

The Muscovites' mechanical existence might be the object of Odysseus's protest ("Neuzheli my rozhdeny dlia skotskogo blagopoluchiia . . ." ["Surely we were not born for the well-being of beasts . . ."]).

37. Ronen 1983, 88–89. The "ambivalently antithetical" treatment of the "theme of freedom and faithfulness," as Ronen describes it, emerges again in another context mediated by Gorodetskii. "Impossible freedom" is the obverse of the "mobile fetters of being," which Timenchik has identified as a reference to Gorodetskii's octave "Ia sozertsal tebia, tumannost' Andromedy" ("I contemplated you, Andromeda's fogginess") (see OM 1987, 299). Again the poet finds freedom in subordination to an overriding law. This is the Acmeist position: laws liberate the poet.

A note by Paul Goldberger illuminates the Acmeist attachment to architecture, appropriately, with reference to poetry: "Architecture is not free verse. It's more like a sonnet: It demands creativity within a highly structured framework. Designing buildings is a struggle to make art within limits, to soar without wings, to make magic without pretending that the world is supernatural. It is the ultimate exercise in accommodating reality" ("Within Limits," *New York Times Magazine,* pt. 2, Home Design, April 7, 1991). Cf. in "The Morning of Acmeism": "We do not fly, we climb only those towers that we can build ourselves" (*S* 2:145).

38. The same rhyme confirms the subject of Arsenii Tarkovskii's much later portrait of a Mandelstamian poet, in the 1963 "Poet": "Kak boialsia on prostranstva / Koridorov! Postoianstva / Kreditorov!" ("How he feared the space / Of corridors! The constancy / Of creditors!").

39. Akhmatova 1968, 2:179.

40. Ronen 1983, 302–3.

41. *S* 2:189–90. Mandelstam's essay on Blok's death, "A. Blok (7 avgusta 21 g.–7 avgusta 22 g.), appears as "Barsuch'ia nora" ("The Badger's Hole") in *Ss* 2:270–75.

42. Khodasevich, for example, testifies to the posthumous association of Gumilev with Blok in his essay "Gumilev i Blok" ("Gumilev and Blok") (1976, 118–40).

43. Cf. Ronen on the Blokian voice in "The Apartment" (Ronen 1973a, 385–86), and on "echoes of Blok's mining and metallurgical messianism" in the "Octaves"; Ronen cites "Novaia Amerika" ("The New America"), one of Blok's "civic" poems (Ronen 1983, 279 n. 83).

44. Ryszard Przybylski writes that for Mandelstam every poem was his last (1987, 190).

45. Ronen, referring in particular to lyrics by Lermontov and Fet as well as Derzhavin, writes: "M. persistently explored the last poems of various Russian poets" (1983, 61; see also Ronen 1990, 1621). Derzhavin's last poem, "Reka vremen v svoem stremlen'i" ("The river of time in its striving"), is an octave.

46. On the level of the individual lyric, Mandelstam's idea of finality motivates the search for the word, and the despair at its loss: without the confirming appearance of the "right" word, the poet remains in the darkness and chaos of the "formless element" ("besformennaia stikhiia" ["On the Nature of the Word"]); see "The Swallow." In the absence of the one right word, the poem cannot be finished (see NM 1970, 75). In this respect, Mandelstam represents the antithesis of Pasternak, who tended to go on speaking, who never pronounced the last word, for whom there was always another possibility, another way of saying something, or anything.

47. NM 1987, 188. The order of the poems in *Den' poezii* (1981, 198–201), apparently as copied down by Mandelstam, coincides with Nadezhda Mandelstam's in the case of the first three "Octaves" (the later and then the earlier "I love . . ." variants, followed by "When, destroying the draft") and in the case of the last two: "In needlelike, plague-filled goblets" and "And I go out of space," which Nadezhda Mandelstam gives as one of two possible final pairs. The order of the intermediate poems in *Den' poezii* is "O butterfly . . ."; "Schubert on the water . . ."; "Tell me, draftsman of the desert"; "And the maple's jagged paw"; "The minute appendage of the sixth sense"; "Overcoming nature's inducacy." But Nadezhda Mandelstam's position is ultimately unclear. Nerler notes that she corroborated the order in the collected works, justified by I. M. Semenko. Yet in Semenko's explanation this order does not seem obligatory (*S* 1:529–30). Cf. NM 1987, 187–89; Baines 1976, 89–90; Brown 1968, 32–48.

48. Here I follow the text of *Ss* and OM 1973; cf. *zelenye formy* in *S* 1:200.

49. NM 1987, 188, 189.

50. The "I love the appearance of the fabric" variants represent the result of a process, a beginning (birth) that is an end (the completion of gestation); "And I go out of space" represents an end that may be a beginning (death becomes new life). In this respect, as the "Octaves" move from birth to death, the plot is a traditional one.

51. Cf. Mandelstam's comparison, in *Conversation about Dante,* of the poet to a sculptor, whose work "does not leave material traces," but who simply "removes the excess," while the "drafts are never destroyed," but remain implicit in the work (*S* 2:231).

52. Ronen 1973a, 369 and n. 6.

53. *S* 2:143. Ronen calls this passage from "The Morning of Acmeism" a key to "When, destroying the draft" (1973a, 369 n. 6).

54. At the same time, in *Conversation about Dante* Mandelstam is concerned with writing implements as a part of the physical act of composition, just as he is concerned with the activity of the scribe (*S* 2:249–50).

55. Levin observes a similar shift from personal to impersonal in the poem "In needlelike, plague-filled goblets" (1975, 227).

56. *S* 2:92.

57. *S* 2:142.

58. The mathematician's counterpart, elsewhere in Mandelstam's work, is the magician. Corresponding to the process by which the number is raised to an enor-

mous power is the process of growth that Mandelstam explores, for example, in *Journey to Armenia*. The chess game of "Moscow" has a mystical aspect: "Figury shakhmat rastut, kogda popadaiut v luchevoi fokus kombinatsii" ("The chess pieces grow when they fall into the radial focus of the moves") (*S* 2:115). With *fokus* Mandelstam refers not just to the microscope lens but also to the magician's sleight-of-hand, suggesting a conjuring act. In the library of "On the Naturalists," where the name of the book the traveler reads, Firdusi's *Book of Kings,* or *Shah-Nameh,* recalls the chess game—"*shakh*maty," the person who presides over the reading of Persian poetry, the library director Mamikon Artem'evich Gevorkian, is himself a magician: his initials give him away (*MAG* 'magician'; thanks to Eric Naiman for this observation) (*S* 2:125; see Pollak 1983, 146–47 n. 15). Cf. Gothic architecture as a combination of the rational and the mystical in "The Morning of Acmeism" and in "Notre Dame."

59. Mandelstam's "Ni razviazat' nel'zia, ni posmotret'" ("One can't undo it, or take a look"), about the note of "The minute appendage . . . ," echoes Gumilev's "Ni s"est', ni vypit', ni potselovat'" ("One cannot eat, or drink, or kiss [them]"), referring to verses; his "iashcheritsa" ("lizard") recalls Gumilev's "tvar' skol'zkaia" ("slippery creature") ("iashcheritsy temennoi glazok" ["the lizard's pineal eye"] is the vestigial organ once thought to be the seat of the soul).

60. NM 1970a, 286.

61. Levin 1978, 125.

62. The number eleven is related to the inarticulateness implied by Mandelstam's name, as one instance of the "raw" quality of his late poetry (on "raw," see Ronen 1990, 1646). Nadezhda Mandelstam discusses the odd-lined stanzas that began to appear in Voronezh (NM 1970a, 286).

63. Two of the three integers from 1 to 11 absent in the "Octaves" figure elsewhere in Mandelstam's work: 7, which Nadezhda Mandelstam refers to as Mandelstam's favorite number, speculating that he retained the "twin" octaves in the Belyi cycle in order to preserve the total of seven poems (1972, 443; but cf. *S* 1:535); and 9, a key, according to Ronen, in the "ode" and "elegy" of the mid 1920s. Ronen discusses the significance of the numbers 8 and 9 in the construction of "The Slate Ode" and "1 January 1924" (1983, 13–15).

64. Quoted in Ronen 1983, 362–63 n. 53. Mandelstam is referring to a passage from Ivanov's essay "Krizis individualizma" ("The Crisis of Individualism"), identified by Ronen: "The age of the epic has flown; so let the choral dithyramb commence. Bitter is our introit: the dirge of the self-abnegating but not yet released spirit. Let the one who does not want to sing the choral song depart from the circle, covering his face with his hands" (1909, 99–100; the translation incorporates Ronen's rendering of "plach samootrekaiushchegosia i eshche ne otreshennogo dukha" [1983, 362]).

65. Cf. Vladimir Nabokov on *The Overcoat:* "The prose of Pushkin is three-dimensional; that of Gogol is four-dimensional, at least. He may be compared to his contemporary, the mathematician Lobachevsky, who blasted Euclid and discovered a century ago many of the theories which Einstein later developed. If parallel lines

do not meet it is not because meet they cannot, but because they have other things to do" (1944, 145).

66. On Mandelstam's "twins" and "triplets," see the chapter "Dvoinye pobegi" ("Double Shoots") in NM 1970a (206–12) (this chapter does not appear in Max Hayward's translation; cf. Rayfield 1973). Among Mandelstam's other essays, "Fransua Villon" ("François Villon") is a twin to "On the Interlocutor."

67. *S* 2:167. "The Word and Culture" (*Drakon*, May 1921) was republished in the almanac *Tsekh poetov* (Berlin, 1922) along with thematically kindred pieces, including Gumilev's "Word" and "Poema nachala" ("Epic of the Beginning").

68. *S* 2:171–72. The possibility of new life implicit even in the opening scene of "The Word and Culture," with its vision of the "world without people," is more clearly evident in a similar passage, also dating to 1921, in Ehrenburg's portrait of Pasternak: "Maybe people will cover the whole earth with asphalt, but still somewhere in Iceland or in Patagonia a crack will remain. Some blades of grass will sprout [*Prorastet travka*] and pilgrimages of scholars and lovers to this miraculous phenomenon will begin. Maybe, too, lyric poetry will be abolished as unnecessary, but somewhere Pasternak's grandson and Lermontov's great-great-grandson will start up with amazement, open their mouths, exclaim an 'oh!' tormenting for them, clear and bright for everyone" (1922, 130).

69. *S* 2:175.

70. Cf. Ronen's summation, in a different regard, at the end of *An Approach to Mandel'štam:* "I believe that M. meant to ask this question rather than to answer it" (1983, 362).

71. Ivanov 1909, 100. Discussing Mandelstam's relation to Herzen ("Omnia mea mecum porto"), Nadezhda Mandelstam notes: "For him the path lies not away from people, but to people—he felt himself not a person standing above the crowd, but one of the crowd" (NM 1970a, 178; see Ronen 1983, 273–74). The Voronezh poem "Eshche ne umer ty, eshche ty ne odin" ("You have not yet died, you are not alone") confirms the equivalence of "death" and "solitude."

72. Ronen 1983, 362 n. 59.

73. Nesbet 1988, 120–22.

74. Brown 1968, 43. Baines seems to think that the "Judaic cares" belong to the "Jewish poet." She is almost right, although her conclusion—that the "Jewish poet is made to sound querulous and pernickety"—is not (1976, 96).

75. Gumilev's "On podozritel'nym vzgliadom / *Smeril* menia vsego" ("He, with a suspicious look, / Took my whole *measure*") might be compared with "Sypuchikh peskov *geometr*" ("*Geometer* of the shifting sands"). See also, in Gumilev's fourth octave: "Akh, ia ne zhivu v *pustyne*" ("Ah, I don't live in the *desert*") ("Ved' ia ne greshnik, o bozhe"). Gumilev's fifth and last octave can be compared with Mandelstam's last: "Mne vdrug pochudilos', chto, nem, / Izranen, nag, lezhu ia v chashche" ("It suddenly seemed that mute, / Wounded, naked, I was lying in a thicket") ("V moi samyi luchshii, svetlyi den' "); in "And I go out of space," the poet is alone, ill, in a garden.

76. NM 1987, 321.

77. Taranovsky 1976, 66–67.

78. "Chertezhnik pustyni" is the domestic name of the octave about the drafts-man of the desert (see NM 1987, 188).

79. Cf. Baines 1976, 96.

80. "The Admiralty." Gumilev refers to an activity like the geometer's in "The Word": "Patriarkh sedoi, sebe pod ruku / Pokorivshii i dobro i zlo, / Ne reshaias' obratit'sia k zvuku, / *Trost' iu na peske chertil chislo*" ("The hoary patriarch, having subjugated / Both good and evil, / Unable to bring himself to turn to sound, / Traced number in the sand with his staff"). Number "communicates all the nuances of meaning." But the word, in Gumilev's poem, does more: the word stops the sun, the word destroys cities—the word is God. Mandelstam does not share Gumilev's view of number; but he establishes a similar opposition between the geometer's sketch and the more powerful activity of the poet.

81. NM 1987, 60.

82. Nadezhda Mandelstam's usage often echoes Mandelstam's, even when she is not explicitly quoting or referring to his words. If we do not always accept her interpretations, we can generally trust her as to representations of Mandelstam's thought, because she is extremely attentive to the word (her role as scribe and later as memorizer of his work may have facilitated this). Thus when she uses a word that Mandelstam would not have, she is careful to point that out; see, for example, the reference to *sobornost'* in her discussion of the "Octaves" (1987, 189).

83. Nesbet identifies a subtext of "Draftsman of the desert" in Goethe's "An-klage," pointing out that the lines "Er versteht nicht was er sagt, / Was er sagt wird er nicht halten" are a model for the last two lines of the octave (in Nesbet's translation, "He understands not what he says, / What he says he'll not retain") (1988, 121). The parallel is striking. But Mandelstam's lines have a truly circular structure, and they concern an alternation between unconscious and conscious activity; Goethe's lines lack true circularity, and they concern not a cycle but a singular, purely unconscious state. Goethe's romantic portrait is antithetical to Mandelstam's poet, who understands what he says, and retains everything.

84. "Rebellions and Frenchwomen" (*S* 2:13).

85. In one typed copy of Mandelstam's letter to Tikhonov of December 31, 1936, the word *zabota* 'care' is substituted for *rabota* 'work': "dazhe zabota nad svoim stikhom" ("even care [concerning] my verse") (Poliakova 1991, 30). Cf. *zabota* as the poet's activity in *Conversation about Dante:* "Ved' u nego nemalaia zabota" ("Indeed, he has no small care").

86. Annenskii's "Vecherom" ("In the Evening") is a subtext, too, of "O vre-menakh prostykh i grubykh" ("[Tales] of times simple and crude"): "Kogda, s driakhleiushchei liubov'iu, / Meshaia v pesniakh Rim i sneg, / Ovidii pel arbu volov'iu / V pokhode varvarskikh teleg" ("When, with decrepit love, / Mingling Rome and snow in songs, / Ovid sang of an oxcart / Among the barbarian wag-ons"); cf. Annenskii's "Svivaia medlenno s liuboviiu pechal', / Ochami zhadnymi poet ukhodit v dal'" ("Slowly weaving together sadness and love, / With greedy eyes the poet goes off into the distance").

87. Mandelstam's distinction between the child and the adult contrasts with Pasternak's. Pasternak's child is the bearer of poetic understanding; the adult is uncomprehending of poetry. Mandelstam's groggy "child that hasn't gotten enough sleep" (*nevyspavsheesia ditia*), who can blame circumstances for his troubles, is opposed to the fully conscious adult, who must travel out his course alone, taking responsibility not just for himself but "for everyone." However, the child opposed to the adult, as in "Oh, how we love to dissemble'" and "I am no longer a child," is not the same as the child of the "Octaves," who possesses the knowledge that the adult (the multitude) cannot grasp.

88. The word *opasnyi* 'dangerous' appears in both the first and the fourth stanzas of "Mistress . . ." (thus, in the first stanza of each half of this six-stanza poem). It refers in the first case to the world of articulate speech—"Usmiren muzhskoi opasnyi norov, / Ne zvuchit utoplennitsa-rech'" ("The dangerous masculine obstinacy has been tamed, / Speech-the-drowned-woman does not sound"); and in the second to the underwater world of "dark speeches," indicated, it seems, by signs from creatures of instinct: "Makom brovki mechen put' opasnyi. / Chto zhe mne, kak ianycharu, liub / Etot kroshechnyi, letuche-krasnyi, / Etot zhalkii polumesiats gub?" ("The dangerous path is marked by the poppy-seed of the brow. / Why do I, like a janissary, love / This tiny, fleetingly red, / This pitiful half-moon of the lips?"). (Cf. "Ia s toboi v glukhoi meshok zash'ius'" ["I will sew myself up in a deep sack with you"] and "Rasporot', razorvat' meshok / V kotorom tmin zashit" ["Tear, rip the sack / In which the caraway is sewn"] in the 1922 "Hayloft" poem "Iu ne znaiu, s kakikh por" ("I don't know since when"); "caraway" is recalled in the "poppy-seed" of "Mistress. . . .")

89. Here is another examination of the possibility of transformation into a creature without consciousness. Cf. the "dark soul of a beast" ("Temnaia zverinaia dusha") that in the 1909 poem "Ni o chem ne nuzhno govorit'" ("One need not speak of anything") "swims like a young dolphin through the hoary universal deep" ("I plyvet del'finom molodym / Po sedym puchinam mirovym") (but Taranovsky refers to this as a poem of Mandelstam's "symbolist period" [1976, 75]).

90. *S* 2:276. Cf. also, in "Literary Moscow," "Invention and recollection are the two elements that move the poetry of B. Pasternak" (*S* 2:277).

91. In "The Greek flute . . . ," recollection is compared to an act of imbibing: "Vsled za nim my ego ne povtorim, / Kom'ia gliny v ladoniakh moria, / I kogda ia *napolnilsia morem*, / Morom stala mne mera moia" ("After him we will not repeat him, / Wearing out lumps of clay in the palms, / And when I was filled with the sea, / My measure became a plague for me").

92. Cf. Jakobson on *pit'* 'to drink' / *pet'* 'to sing' as a "traditional etymological figure," with reference to Maiakovskii's "Radosti pei. Poi" ("Drink joy. Sing") in "Nash marsh" ("Our March") (1987, 302 n. 37).

93. Ronen (1977a, 172) suggests that the match that appears in the following line—"I spichka sernaia menia b sogret' mogla" ("And a sulphur match could keep me warm")—has a subtext in Annenskii's "Preliudiia" ("Prelude"): "I ia drozhu sred' vas, drozhu za svoi pokoi, / Kak spichku na vetru zagorodiv rukoi" ("And I

tremble among you, I tremble for my peace, / Sheltering it with my hand like a match in the wind"). The echo supports the association of *zabota* with the intimate moments of the poet's soul.

94. The reflexive *tianut'sia,* which supports the reciprocal sense of *zabota,* links the act of reaching out, and the more explicit references to communication in the poem, with drinking, as represented by the verb *tianut'* 'imbibe' or 'inhale', as in "Eshche obidu tianet s bliudtsa" ("Still imbibes insult from the saucer"). In "Ne u menia, ne u tebia—u nikh . . ." ("Not I, not you—they have . . ."), a form of the same verb, *potianut* 'they [will] draw', refers to inhaling (the object is *dyshashchaia tiazhest'* 'breathing heaviness'). Thomson, too, notes a connection between drinking and breathing in Mandelstam (1991, 505 n. 14).

95. See Levin on the importance of the conative and phatic and also the expressive function in later Mandelstam (1978, 137–38).

96. Jakobson 1960, 356.

97. *Ss* 3:281.

98. Wolkonsky and Poltoratzky 1961.

99. With reference to the second quatrain of "Schubert on the water," Viach. Vs. Ivanov writes that Mandelstam "has in mind a familiar universe that already potentially exists (in the future)" (1990, 359).

100. *S* 2:208.

101. The close connection between *shepot* and *lepet,* and the fact of *lepet* as a positive principle (and the poet's source) is evident in the 1937 Voronezh poem "O, kak zhe ia khochu" ("Oh, how I want"). "Babble" and "whisper" are the means by which the poet enters the future. Pace Marina Glazova, who finds a "contradiction in the poem" (1984, 293), the light and its ray do not cease to exist without the poet, who wants to "fly after the ray / Where I am not at all." The light and ray are constituted of the poet's whisper, which now has an autonomous existence: "On tol'ko tem i luch, / On tol'ko tem i svet, / Chto shopotom moguch / I lepetom sogret" ("It is a ray, / It is light, only because / It's made powerful by a whisper / And warmed by babble").

102. The "Requiem" shares a number of images with the "Octaves," including the "hard-blue eye" (*golubotverdyi glaz*), the poet wandering winding paths with frightened steps, and the theme of the poet and the crowd: "Shel chuia razgovor beschislennoi tolpy" ("Went sensing the conversation of the countless crowd"; the conversation of the crowd is babble). (Cf. "We live, not sensing the country beneath us," another poem about a man of the mountains ["the Kremlin mountaineer"].)

103. Desert places are a potential meeting place between the poet-prophet and the universe—nature or God. Russian poetry has precedents in Lermontov, whose "wilderness [*pustynia*] harkens to God" ("Vykhozhu odin ia na dorogu" ["I go out alone onto the road"] is a subtext of the last "Octave") and in Tiutchev, who refers to the biblical voice crying in the wilderness (*pustynia,* in "Pevuchest' est' v morskikh volnakh" ["There is melodiousness in the sea waves"]). The Sinai desert is the place of revelation in Annenskii's "Poeziia" ("Poetry"): "Nad vys'iu plamennoi Sinaia . . . / Iskat' sledov Ee sandalii / Mezhdu zanosami pustyn'" ("Above the

height of the fiery Sinai . . . / To search for the traces of Her sandals / Amid the drifts of the deserts"); this immediately precedes the poem "∞".

104. Ronen 1983, 173.

105. See Jakobson 1990.

106. See Jaynes 1976, 100–125. Cf. Gumilev's "Nature": "Poet, lish' ty edinyi v sile / Postich' uzhasnyi tot iazyk / Kotorym sfinsky govorili / V krugu drakonovykh vladyk" ("Poet, you alone have the power / To comprehend that terrible language / That the sphinxes spoke / In the circle of the dragon sovereigns"). The poet understands the sphinxes' riddling, which is not ordinary propositional language.

107. *S* 2:171.

108. Ronen 1983, 186.

109. In *Journey to Armenia* Mandelstam refers to an "arched extension" (*dugovaia rastiazhka*) with reference to the embryonic nasturtium leaf, as the end of the process of growth (*S* 2:114).

110. Viach. Vs. Ivanov has discussed the possible etymological connection between *veter* 'wind' and *vitiia* 'orator' (Ithaca, N.Y., February 20, 1991; he cites Thieme 1954). Thus the wind that is implied in the second quatrain is connected to the poet's breath in the first (*zadykhaniia, vzdokh*). Cf. *vzdokh* 'sigh' with *ston* 'groan' in "Overcoming nature's inducacy."

111. Ronen refers to the "straightening" of the dead body as "M.'s stable leitmotif"; he interprets it as the "posthumous growth of artist the redeemer" [*sic*] (1983, 183 n. 135). Mandelstam's reference to the poet's body growing younger as it "endlessly straight[ens]" anticipates recent hypotheses about human life expectancy, which, some scientists now think, may increase after a certain point, producing a curve similar to the one Mandelstam suggests (see Gina Kolata, "Study Challenges Longevity Theory," *New York Times,* October 16, 1992, sec. A). Mandelstam describes Darwin's *Origin of Species* as "slowly straightening out" ("medlenno vypriamliaiushchaiasia" [*S* 2:371]; cf. *vypriamitel'nyi vzdokh*).

112. Born 1962, 27.

113. Cf. Mandelstam's comments in "The Morning of Acmeism" about the law of identity:

A = A: what a beautiful poetic theme. Symbolism languished, grew bored with the law of identity, Acmeism makes it its slogan and proposes it in place of the dubious *a realibus ad realiora*. The capacity for astonishment is the poet's chief virtue. But how then can one not be astonished at that most fruitful of laws—the law of identity? The one who is filled with reverential astonishment before this law is indubitably a poet. (*S* 2:144)

The law of identity, for the Acmeist, is another version of the spiral: it has to do with the perpetual novelty of the past. The Symbolists' trajectory is linear and unidirectional, as opposed to the Acmeists' recursive path.

114. See "Moscow" (*S* 2:115).

115. With reference to the "Octaves" and *Journey to Armenia*, Ronen writes that "horn signifies the hard spiral path of growth in respect to a somatic awareness

of the 'inner excess of space'" (1983, 360 n. 49). (Cf. the helices of "The minute appendage of the sixth sense" and "The Birth of a Smile.")

116. *Fourth Prose* (S 2:92).

117. "On dirizhiroval kavkazskimi gorami" ("He conducted the Caucasus Mountains"); "Blue eyes and burning frontal bone"; "10 ianvaria 1934" ("10 January 1934").

118. S 2:232.

119. Mandelstam quotes Tsvetaeva's "ustupchivost' rechi russkoi" ("the pliancy of Russian speech," from her poem "Nad sinevoiu podmoskovnykh roshch" ["Above the blueness of the groves outside of Moscow"]) (S 2:235). Senderovich identifies "evasion" (*uklonenie*) as an important process in Pasternak's work (*Georgii Pobedonosets*, 326, 337). Cf., in a Pasternakian poem of the *Second Voronezh Notebook*, "Tvoi zrachok v nebesnoi korke, / Obrashchennyi vdal' i nits, / Zashchishchaiut ogovorki / Slabykh, chuiushchikh resnits" ("Your pupil in the heavenly coating, / Turned to the distance and down, / Is defended by the reservations / Of the weak, perceptive lashes").

120. S 2:231–32. See also the description of the Ulysses canto as the epitome of Dante's "sailing" composition (S 2:233).

121. The typical Byzantine pendentive is a "spherical triangle" (cf. *kruglye ugly* 'round corners' or 'angles'), that is, a triangular area marked out in a sphere (a dome). Nerler notes that such structures were first used in Hagia Sophia (S 1:462).

122. As the "Octave" about this embodiment of circularity, "And the maple's jagged paw" is the still center of the "Octaves," a moment of repose.

123. S 2:127.

124. Bertrand Russell writes: "Arabic philosophy is not important as original thought. Men like Avicenna and Averroes are essentially commentators" (1945, 427). Other writers put the matter in a different perspective: "Averroes was to enjoy an extensive influence for many centuries after his death through the tendency of many thinkers to regard him as *the* commentator on Aristotle" (Leaman 1988, 163); "by the middle of the thirteenth century there was a tendency for the doctrine of the Philosopher to be identified with that of the Commentator, as Averroes soon became metonymically known: Aristotle meant, for some, neither more nor less than the Commentator and his interpretations" (Mohammed 1984, 4).

125. S 2:217–18.

126. Oliver Leaman notes that Averroes "had a far more successful afterlife among the Jewish communities in the medieval world" than within Islam (1988, 5).

127. Russell 1945, 428.

128. Kaganskaia 1977, 180.

129. Thus cf. Epstein's observation that both Mandelstam and Pasternak were compared, by contemporaries, "to exotic animals—inhabitants of roughly the same southern Arabian world where their common historical homeland was located"; Epstein is referring to the camel in Mandelstam's case and to the Arabian steed in Pasternak's, on which see Chapter 4 (Epstein 1991, 200).

130. Cf. Mandelstam's 1920 poem "Kogda Psikheia-zhizn' spuskaetsia k ten-

iam" ("When Psyche-life descends to the shades"). The ancient image of the soul as a woman ("Dusha ved' zhenshchina . . .") and as a butterfly arose at about the same time, around the fifth century B.C.

131. However, this problem is not a new one in Mandelstam's work. Aristotle's definition of the soul as the "form" of the body, and the consequent inseparability of the two, has resonances in Mandelstam's description of the word as a "complex," a " 'system,' " in "On the Nature of the Word": "The meaning of a word can be seen as a candle burning from within a paper lantern, and, conversely, the sound representation, the so-called phoneme, can be placed within the meaning, like the same candle in the same lantern" (*S* 2:183). In a passage about the relation between the word and its meaning in "The Word and Culture," Mandelstam calls the word a Psyche, "wander[ing] freely like a soul around an abandoned but not forgotten body" (*S* 2:171).

132. Ronen, personal communication, winter 1977–78; Levin 1975, 228. With "V igol'chatykh, *chumnykh bokalakh,* / My *p'em* navazhden'e prichin" ("In needlelike, plague-filled goblets, / We drink the delusion of causes") compare also Pushkin's "*Bokaly* penim druzhno my, / I devy-rozy *p'em* dykhan'e,— / Byt' mozhet . . . polnoe *Chumy*" ("We froth the goblets in friendship, / And drink the breath of the maiden-rose— / Perhaps . . . full of the Plague").

133. Cf. Gumilev's "Zalog bessmertiia dlia smertnykh, / Pervonachal'nye slova" ("The guarantee of immortality for mortals, / The original words").

134. Cf. the butterfly called *traurnyi plashch* (*Vanessa antiopa* in Brokgaus-Efron 1896, s.v. *babochki*), known in English as the mourning cloak.

135. See *Purgatorio* 24. 61–66. See also Dobrokhotov 1990, 70–71. Pasternak's idea of universal subjectivity is closer to Averroes's possible intellect than is Mandelstam's distinction between the collective and the individual consciousness. See Pasternak's 1913 lecture "Simvolizm i bessmertie" ("Symbolism and Immortality"); Pasternak describes the lecture in the *Autobiographical Sketch* (1982, 438–39); the theses are reprinted in Pasternak 1990b, 255–56.

136. *S* 2:144.

137. Levin 1975a, 227. Levin defines a "real connection" in terms of common denotation (1975a, 226 n. 2).

138. Brown notes: "In *biriul'ki* the figures are small wooden goblets, spoons, and other common objects" (1968, 45). The word *igol'chatyi* 'needlelike' suggests the size and shape of the figures.

139. *S* 2:177.

140. *S* 2:142.

141. Levin 1975a, 231.

142. *S* 2:144.

143. "Do not attempt foreign tongues . . ."

144. Heraclitus, Fr. 52; see Marcovich 1967, 490.

145. Levin 1975a, 230 n. 10.

146. Marcovich 1967, 493, 494.

147. Ronen, personal communication, winter 1977–78.

148. Cf. "Glücklicher Säugling! Dir ist ein unendlicher Raum noch die Wiege, / Werde Mann, und dir wird eng die unendliche Welt" ("Happy infant! You still have endless space in the cradle, / Become a man, and the endless world will be narrow for you").

149. In his article about "In needlelike, plague-filled goblets," Levin writes: "The last two lines are permeated by relativistic conceptions: here one can see allusions to the relativity of space (*a big universe in the cradle*) and time (*of a small eternity*) and even to the correlation of space-time" (1975a, 230).

150. Marcovich, too, suggests that Heraclitus's *aiōn* is the human lifetime, though beyond that his interpretation diverges from Mandelstam's; he see the image of the child as reflecting the foolishness of maturity (1967, 493–95).

151. The "small eternity" is comparable to the "moment" in "I love the appearance of the fabric," the only other direct temporal reference in the "Octaves" (and again the child appears, in the corresponding second quatrain in the later "I love" variant): "I tak khorosho mne i tiazhko, / Kogda priblizhaetsia *mig*" ("And it's so good and so hard for me / When the moment's near"); cf., in "Tristia," *uznavan'ia mig* 'the moment of recognition', the creative moment.

152. Semenko comments: "out of what is understood as space, which is the main thing (the universe is greater than eternity) there is an exit not into eternity, but into infinity" (quoted in *S* 1:530).

153. Ronen 1983, 168.

154. Taranovsky observes a similar process when he notes that the verbs *nabukhaet* 'swells' and *rastet* 'grows' in "On a step ladder I [climbed] . . ." mean "'increase from within'"; he comments: "I believe that these two images are also connected with the process of creation" (1976, 43 n. 20).

155. "V allee kolokol'chik mednyi" ("In the lane a small brass bell").

156. *S* 2:105, 127–28. Cf. Darwin as gardener in "Literaturnyi stil' Darvina" ("Darwin's Literary Style") (*S* 2:371).

157. In *Journey to Armenia,* another apocalyptic image echoes the description of the garden, the subject of the "pointless" conversation at the Moscow send-off for Kuzin, on his way to Armenia: "[govor] ob aviatsii, o *mertvykh* petliakh, kogda ne zamechaesh', chto tebia oprokinuli, i zemlia, kak *ogromnyi korichnevyi* potolok, rushitsia tebe na golovu" ("[talk] of aviation, of loops, when you don't notice that you've been overturned, and the earth, like an enormous brown ceiling, collapses on your head") (*S* 2:110–11).

158. Segal 1968, 163.

159. "Solominka" (1916); "Meganom" (1917); "Sumerki svobody" ("The Twilight of Freedom") (1918); "V Peterburge my soidemsia snova" ("In Petersburg we will meet again") (1920); "Kontsert na vokzale" ("Concert at the Railroad Station") (1921); "Kholodno roze v snegu" ("The rose is cold in the snow") in "Armenia" (1930).

160. Ronen 1977a, 175.

161. Toporov 1991, 24.

162. *S* 2:125. The reference to Adam and Eve indicates that this is not just any

garden but the original garden, Paradise: "Adam and Eve confer, dressed in the latest paradisial fashion." Laurence Binyon comments on the unusual perspective of Persian miniatures, and specifically of the image of the garden in those paintings (Binyon and Wilkinson 1931, xv–xvi). E. Bertel's notes that the garden is the central point in descriptions of nature in tenth-century Persian poetry (1935, 44).

163. *S* 2:92.

164. *Bezlistvennyi* occurs also in "When Psyche-life descends to the shades": "I les bezlistvennyi prozrachnykh golosov / Sukhie zhaloby kropiat, kak dozhdik melkii" ("And the leafless forest of transparent voices / Is sprinkled with dry complaints, like a light drizzle"). This is the realm of the dead, to which unexpressed—unborn—thoughts return; cf. "I mysl' besplotnaia v chertog tenei vernetsia" ("And the incorporeal thought returns to the palace of the shades") in the twin poem "The Swallow." But whereas in that earlier poem leaflessness suggests loss, in the "Octaves" it suggests the possibility of cure.

165. The "Octaves" have the riddling quality that Ronen has associated with Acmeism and with Mandelstam's poetics in particular (1990, 1633–34).

166. A garden, an enclosed space, contains a universe. Compare also the Greek *paradeisos* 'park', which refers inter alia to the Garden of Eden in the New Testament. In this respect, it is both a first place and a final place: the place from which man has come and to which he returns. It represents both a birth and a death.

167. The earth is a book in the last two poems of the "Armenia" group: "I uzhe nikogda ne raskroiu / V biblioteke avtorov goncharnykh / Prekrasnoi zemli pustoteluiu knigu, / Po kotoroi uchilis' pervye liudi" ("And I will never again open, / In the library of potter authors, / The hollow book of the beautiful earth, / Which the first people studied") ("Ia tebia nikogda ne uvizhu" ["I will never see you"]); "Nad knigoi zvonkikh glin, nad knizhnoiu zemlei, / Nad gnoinoi knigoiu, / nad glinoi dorogoi, / Kotoroi muchimsia, kak muzykoi i slovom" ("Over the book of ringing clays, over the book earth, / Over the rotting book, over the dear clay / That torments us like music and the word") ("Lazur' da glina, glina da lazur'" ["Azure and clay, clay and azure"]). (Cf. the related images in the 1937 poem "Goncharami velik ostrov sinii" ["The dark blue island is great with potters"], where the earth holds the potters' craft much as it held coins—the poet's words—in "Nashedsii podkovu" ["The Finder of a Horseshoe"].) But the metaphor in the "Octaves" is of the type that Mandelstam describes in *Conversation about Dante* as "Heraclitian," where it is impossible to tell which is the tenor, which the vehicle—in this case, whether the book is the cosmos (cf. earth) or the cosmos the book (*S* 2:232–33).

168. NM 1972, 131–32, 545–46.

169. I am grateful to Omry Ronen for this suggestion. Cf. Heisenberg on the Pythagorean conception of number as a universal descriptive tool in "Abstraction in Modern Science" (1990, 80).

170. Marcovich 1967, 105.

171. *S* 2:218.

172. Schiller 1968, 195.

173. See Paulos 1988, 14.

174. *S* 2:372. In *Conversation about Dante* Mandelstam gives predatory birds, like children, only distant vision; cf. Ronen on that vision as the "opposite pole" to the vision of the cat's eye (1968, 260–61).

175. Mandelstam refers to Favorskii in two poems of the Belyi "Requiem," as the "engraver" amid the crowd of mourners ("A posredi tolpy stoial graviroval'shchik . . ."; "A posredi tolpy, zadumchivyi, bradatyi, / Uzhe stoial graver—drug mednokhvoinykh dosk" ["While amid the crowd stood the engraver . . ."; "While amid the crowd, pensive, bearded, / The engraver already stood—friend of copper-needled plates"]), and in the *Second Voronezh Notebook* ("Kak derevo i med'—Favorskogo polet" ["Like wood and copper is Favorskii's flight"]). Nerler mentions Favorskii's engraving "Andrei Belyi in His Coffin" (*S* 2:536).

176. Florenskii explicates Favorskii's engraving as a graphic translation of his mathematical description of the imaginary realm; in the "Octaves," Mandelstam attempts a poetic translation of the two texts. In addition to the more general rendering of aspects of the imaginary realm, some of the particulars of the "Octaves" reflect Florenskii's discussion. In light of his geometry, the second quatrain of the first "Octave," the later "I love the appearance of the fabric," might be conceived of as a representation of the "imaginary" obverse of the "fabric" that appears in the first quatrain. The arcs are characteristic of the underside of the geometric representation: "Glavnaia liniia mnimoi storony est' duga *raspriamliaiushcheisia* giperboly—mnimogo *pridatka* deistvitel'nogo. ellipsa, kakovoi *pridatok* dolzhno predstvliat' sebe kasaiushchimsia ellipsa u ego vershine" [*sic*] ("The main line of the imaginary side is the arc of a straightening hyperbola—the imaginary appendage of the true ellipsis, which appendage must be conceived as tangent to the ellipsis at its apex") (Florenskii [1922] 1985, 61); the variant "green forms" ("Zelenye formy chertia") recalls one of Florenskii's illustrations of the idea of the abstract plane: the image of spring green, which appears both a tangible object and an evanescent curtain (ibid., 59). The attribution of *sprosonok* 'half-asleep' to the activity of space suggests the sense of imperfect visual focus that the glimpse of the imaginary realm evokes. Florenskii does not refer to the designation of the publishing house on the title page of the engraving, but *Pomor'e* 'Seaside' may have prompted the sea imagery of this first "Octave."

177. Florenskii [1922] 1985, 61.

178. In mathematics, *mnimaia velichina* refers to an imaginary number, such as the square root of a negative quantity; cf. the reference to numerical roots in the last line of the poem. The term *mnimyi* has more specialized meanings, referring to other semantic fields of the poem. In optics (cf. the references to eyes and vision throughout the "Octaves"), *mnimoe izobrazhenie* is an image formed by cutting across the geometrical extensions of a bundle of light rays with a common center that have been passed through a mirror or lens; the resulting figure recalls the "salience" (*vypuklost'*) of the word, which Mandelstam describes as a geometrical

figure in *Journey to Armenia* (*S* 2:114); cf. Florenskii's characterization of the imaginary realm as "salient" (*vypuklyi*).

179. Florenskii [1922] 1985, 52.

180. *S* 2:237 and passim.

181. *S* 2:173.

182. *S* 2:145. The theme of the Gorodetskii subtext of these lines, "Menia uchila ty vol'nei i veselee / Nosit' podvizhnye okovy bytiia" ("You taught me to bear more willingly and gaily / The mobile fetters of being") ("I contemplated you, Andromeda's fogginess"), is the poet's apprenticeship, in a cosmic context (cf. "chtoby vsia tsep' prichin i sledstvii . . . sodrogalas'" ["so that the entire chain of causes and consequences . . . trembles"] in "The Morning of Acmeism"). Thus as early as 1913, Mandelstam had reason to associate the problem of the dimension beyond space with the octave form. Cf. Gumilev's lines in "Nature": "Chtob shar zemnoi, tebia rodivshii, / Vdrug vzdrognul . . . na svoei osi" ("So that the earthly sphere that gave birth to you / Suddenly shudders on its axis").

183. This is the same paradoxical situation that Mandelstam found in Joachim du Bellay's sonnet "Nouveau venu, qui cherches Rome en Rome," where, Ronen has shown, constancy is defined by change (1983, 127).

184. *S* 2:173.

185. Florenskii [1922] 1985, 48–49. In the essay "Scientific and Religious Truth," Heisenberg discusses the conflict between Galileo and the Catholic Church over the issue of the structure of the universe, and the incompatibility of the idea of relativity with totalitarian thought (he refers specifically to the Soviet system) (1990, 221–24).

186. *S* 2:247.

187. *S* 2:247.

188. Viach. Vs. Ivanov suggests that "it is not necessary to speak about the fourth dimension" with reference to the place outside of space in "And I go out of space." He writes: "Modern scholars might have interpreted [the 'neglected garden of numbers'] in the sense of Green-Schwartz supergravity superstring theory suggesting 10 dimensions. It is not absolutely impossible that Mandelstam should have known about the early predecessors of such theories. Suffice it to mention that Mandelstam used to visit ['The Stray Dog,'] where in the time of the World War I Kul'bin had a talk on the possibility of a larger number of dimensions" (note to the author, April 1993; cf. Parnis and Timenchik 1985, 224). Mandelstam's discussion of the complex figure of the beehive might support such an argument. Indeed, Mandelstam does not refer to a "fourth" dimension as such. Rather, he implies the existence of a dimension beyond three, for example, in "The Admiralty," where, referring first to the dominion of the four elements, and the "fifth," created by man (cf. "quintessence"), he writes, "Ne otritsaet li prostranstva prevoskhodstvo / Sei tselomudrenno postroennyi kovcheg" ("Does not this chastely constructed ark / Deny the supremacy of space?").

189. *S* 2:251.

190. *S* 2:225.

191. The very word *vykhozhu* (*vykhod*) incorporates a literal translation of the Latin letters that designate the axes of the geometrical model in Favorskii's engraving: *x o y*—вы́хожу; the poet departs for that "more complex mathematical dimension."

192. *S* 2:239.

193. The three actions performed in "And I go out of space" are given sequentially, but they may occur simultaneously (cf. the transformation in the order of events that occurs from a perspective outside of three-dimensional space); they may even be identical, the same act given in different terms, just as the textbook, herbal, and math book are a single "book." (The objects of *chitaiu,* the book or books the poet reads, have the function of infinitives, suggesting action that remains potential.)

194. Cf. the Voronezh eleven-liner "*Razryvy* kruglykh bukht, i khriashch, i sineva" ("Breaks of round bays, and gravel, and blueness"), where the "breaks" of the bays introduce a series of liberating recollections.

195. *S* 2:122.

196. Brown 1968, 45.

197. The search for the word, as Ronen has shown, is the search for a cure (1983, 324–27, 263). The association of the word with magical herbs, through Fet's "trav neiasnyi zapakh" ("the vague smell of grasses"), persists in the "Octaves," where the search reaches its culmination.

198. "The Morning of Acmeism" is multiply connected to the "Octaves." In addition to the image of the mathematician and exponential functions, cf. the word *ogromnyi,* which appears more than once in the essay; the problem of the relation between the poet and three-dimensional space; and the chain of causes and consequences that the poet must make "tremble."

199. *Ogromnye korni* represents the ultimate instance of the interpenetration of the antitheses "large" and "small"; here the two features are contained within the same complex, and are inseparable from each other. See Levin on the partial elimination of the opposition between *bol'shoe* 'big' and *maloe* 'small' (1969, 144).

200. See Taranovsky 1965, 116–17, on the distinctive features of the Russian stressed vowels and the corresponding sound texture.

201. See Pollak 1993.

202. Michael Hagemeister writes that *Imaginary Entities in Geometry* found a place in Soviet Dante scholarship (Florenskii [1922] 1985, 15 and n. 106). Cf. "Nazad k Ptolomeiu" ("Back to Ptolemy"), V. Ter-Oganesian's attack on Florenskii's book; among other criticisms, he objected to its cover as "somewhat futuristic for a serious mathematical monograph" (1922, 229–30). Lotman, from another point of view, raises questions about some particulars of Florenskii's account of Dante's journey, though he embraces the general problem posed about the relation between various kinds of space in the *Divine Comedy* (1986, 27–28).

203. Lotman 1986, 33.

204. In "The Teachings of Goethe and Newton on Colour in the Light of Modern Physics," Heisenberg compares the processes of scientific discovery to the

flourishing of navigation and the "daring feats of the circumnavigators of the earth" (1979, 71–72).

205. *S* 2:234.

206. See the interpretation of "I go out alone onto the road" (Lermontov's last poem), suggested over the course of Ronen 1983 (13, 75, 359, and passim).

207. Ronen 1983, 13; see also 44–45, 53.

208. Cf. the lines from the folk song that appear as the epigraph to Blok's "Dym ot kostra strueiu sizoi" ("Smoke from the bonfire in a blue-gray stream"): "Ne ukhodi. Pobud' so mnoi, / Ia tak davno tebia liubliu" ("Don't leave. Stay with me, / I have loved you so long").

CHAPTER 4. ROD = РОД

1. "I am really very sick and it's doubtful that anything could help me: approximately since December I have been getting steadily weaker and now it is even difficult for me to leave my room. For the fact that my 'second life' [cf. Pasternak's *Second Birth*] still continues I am entirely obliged to my sole and invaluable friend—my wife" (*Ss* 4:139).

Cf. "Ia dolzhen zhit', khotia ia dvazhdy umer" ("I must live, though I've died twice" [April 1935]), which might imply that Voronezh is a "third" life. The two deaths Mandelstam refers to here may be his two silences: the first, long silence between 1925 and 1930; the second, ending with these and other recent lines, that began after the Belyi "Requiem" and the journey "out of space" in the winter of 1933–34. "Ia dolzhen zhit'" is the second poem in the *First Voronezh Notebook;* it was written almost simultaneously with the first poem, "Chernozem" ("Black Earth") (see Shtempel' 1987, 231 n. 20).

2. *Ss* 3:277; cf. Mess-Baehr 1991, 273 n. 115.

3. Zenkevich et al. 1991, 96.

4. NM 1970a, 190.

5. Cf. "Zdorovo li vino? Zdorovy li mekha? / Zdorovo li v krovi Kolkhidy kolykhan'e?" ("Is wine wholesome? Are furs? / The fluttering of Colchis in the blood?"), in "Poiu, kogda gortan' syra, dusha—sukha" ("I sing when the throat is damp, the soul is dry"), a poem of February 8, 1937.

6. Zenkevich et al. 1991, 96.

7. The years in Voronezh comprised three poetic "impulses" (three periods of writing) and gave rise to three "notebooks." The first of the *Voronezh Notebooks* includes poems of April through July 1935; the second, poems of December 1936 through February 1937; the third, poems of March through May 1937.

8. See, e.g., Taranovsky 1976, 10–14, 33–34, and Ronen 1983, 80, 130, 131–32 and n. 76. Mess-Baehr returns to this theme in her study of the Stalin "Ode" (1991, 298–99 and nn. 113, 115); see also Thomson 1991, 505 and n. 14.

9. Taranovsky 1976, 10. While more than half of the thirty-two examples adduced by Taranovsky come from the 1930s, seven of them come from the *Second Voronezh Notebook* alone (see, e.g., "O etot medlennyi, odyshlivyi prostor" ["Oh, this slow, winded expanse"]; "What am I to do with myself this January?"): thus,

more than one-fifth of the examples arose in a period of approximately two months (December 6, 1936–February 12, 1937).

10. "Notre Dame" (1912).

11. Ronen 1983, 1.

12. Dale Plank diagnoses the protagonists' trouble in *My Sister Life,* seeing the title "Dushnaia noch'" ("A Sultry Night") as a reference to a nocturnal asthma attack (1972, 329, 332, 334); cf. explicit references to asthma in "Popytka dushu razluchit'" ("The attempt to separate the soul") and "Konets" ("The End").

13. *S* 2:210.

14. *S* 2:208.

15. Ten years later, in *Conversation about Dante,* Mandelstam called for a renewal of syntax: "In other words, syntax messes us up. All nominative cases should be replaced by datives indicating direction" (*S* 2:254).

16. E. B. Pasternak suggests that Pasternak anticipated Mandelstam's description of the affective force of his work in a letter to his parents of summer 1914, where he mentions his hope of writing a book that is "as fresh as your summer rain," where "every page threatens the reader with a cold" (1989, 389).

17. A. Lezhnev echoed Mandelstam in a 1927 essay: "It is the freshness and tension in Pasternak, I think, that chiefly makes for the fascination of his poems, of which Ehrenburg says that one could breathe them before dying, like bags filled with oxygen" (1970, 107).

18. *S* 2:291.

19. Levin 1971, 284, 285.

20. Mandelstam's attention to Pasternak was not unprecedented. Taranovsky suggests with surprise that Pasternak's verse had little influence on Mandelstam despite his response to *My Sister Life* (1987, 122), but Mandelstam's work in the early 1930s reflects a deep interest in Pasternak, as it had ten years earlier and would again a few years later.

21. "Zametki o peresechenii biografii . . . ," 322, 323, 297. Cf. Barnes on Pasternak's extremely positive response, in a letter to Mandelstam of September 24, 1928, to his recent collected *Verses,* which made Pasternak rethink his own earlier work (1989, 409).

22. "Naushnichki, naushniki moi" ("My little informers, my earphones").

23. Dated December 23–27 and the first of the trochaic tetrameter poems in the *Second Voronezh Notebook,* "This region's covered with dark waters" introduces a new section or cycle, including "The cause of all failures" and "Your pupil in the heavenly coating." A subtext of "This region's covered with dark waters" is "Besy" ("Demons"), which Mandelstam quotes in the 1922 essay "'Grotesk'" ("The 'Grotesque'"), among other Pushkin verses in trochaic tetrameter; these poems share, too, the picture of the wintry plains and the protagonist anguished by plaintive sounds. Meter links "This region's covered with dark waters" to the "Drozhzhi mira dorogie" ("The dear yeast of the world") variants (begun January 12), which themselves have Pushkinian subtexts in trochaic tetrameter, including "Zimniaia doroga" ("Winter Road") (see also "Zimnii vecher" ["Winter Evening"]

and "Stikhi, sochinennye noch'iu vo vremia bessonnitsy" ["Verses Composed at Night During a Time of Insomnia"]).

In his comments on the *Second Voronezh Notebook,* Pasternak put "This region's covered with dark waters," along with a few other poems, "beyond category" ("Zametki o peresechenii biografii . . . " 324).

24. Mandelstam refers to Kol'tsov twice in the *Second Voronezh Notebook:* "Ia okolo Kol'tsova / Kak sokol zakol'tsovan" ("Close to Kol'tsov, / I am ringed like a falcon"); "Eto machekha Kol'tsova, / Shutish': rodina shchegla!" ("This is Kol'tsov's stepmother, / You're joking: it's the homeland of the goldfinch!") ("This region's covered with dark waters"). Cf. Natasha Shtempel' on Mandelstam's pleasure in reading Nikitin in Voronezh (1987, 216).

25. Barnes notes: "Pasternak's first glimpse of the Urals thus coincides closely with his first glimpse of a way ahead to the poetics of 1917" (1989, 211).

26. "Razryvy kruglykh bukht, i khriashch, i sineva" ("Breaks of round bays, and gravel, and blueness").

27. "Stanzas," May–June 1935.

28. Yet Pasternak interceded for Mandelstam with Bukharin after his arrest, ostensibly as a consequence of the epigram, in May 1934; he interceded again in early 1936 in an attempt to lighten Mandelstam's exile.

29. Gershtein 1987, 194.

30. Mandelstam may have had in mind the last three stanzas of "Summer" when he wrote the "Octaves"; here Pasternak quotes *Feast in a Time of Plague* ("Na pire Platona vo vremia chumy" ["At Plato's feast in time of plague"]), including the same passages that Mandelstam alludes to in "In needlelike, plague-filled goblets" and "Draftsman of the desert" (in 1932 Mandelstam translated into German two songs from Pushkin's drama; see Ronen 1994, 182). "Summer" is in amphibrachic tetrameter; cf. the amphibrachs (trimeter) of the "Octaves." Pasternak's "I arfoi shumit uragan araviiskii" ("And the Arabian hurricane resounds like a harp") echoes Pushkin's "uragan araviiskii" ("Arabian hurricane"); cf. Mandelstam's "Arabskikh peskov geometr" ("Geometer of the Arab sands"). Pasternak's "Bessmert'ia, byt' mozhet, poslednii zalog" ("The final guarantee, perhaps, of immortality") echoes Pushkin's "Bessmert'ia, mozhet byt', zalog" ("The guarantee, perhaps, of immortality"); again cf. "I lepestka i kupola zalog" ("The guarantee of the petal and the cupola"). Cf. Ronen on the connection between "Summer," with its "pungent patience of tar," and "the tar of all-round patience" in "Preserve my speech forever . . ." (1977a, 176).

31. Pasternak, it seems, remained skeptical about Mandelstam, work and man. Viach. Vs. Ivanov recounts evidence from his own experience: "In September of 1958 I was present at a conversation of Pasternak with two foreign guests—Michel Aucouturier and Roman Jakobson. Pasternak complained that in his early years (in Mandelstam's lifetime) he did not like the kind of poetry that Mandelstam wrote, only later he saw his mistake" (communication to the author, April 1993).

32. Shtempel' 1987, 216.

33. *S* 2:234.

34. *S* 2:217, 234.

35. "'The Whistle' affected him most of all" ("Zametki o peresechenii . . . ," 324).

36. Along with "Gudok" ("The Whistle"), the domestic names of the poems of the cycle include "Ulybka" ("The Smile"), "Shchegol" ("The Goldfinch"), and "Kumir" ("The Idol"), referring to "Rozhdenie ulybki" ("The Birth of a Smile"), "Moi shchegol, ia golovu zakinu" ("My goldfinch, I'll throw my head back"), and "Vnutri gory bezdeistvuet kumir" ("Inside the mountain the idol idles"). The sequence of the five poems varies from edition to edition, and there is no indication that Mandelstam determined an order for the cycle. Nadezhda Mandelstam puts "The Whistle" first, and "The Idol" third, but she may be referring to order of composition (NM 1987, 221–22). Cf. Meilakh 1990, 417.

37. Pasternak conflates the microcosm with the macrocosm in the cycle "Tema s variatsiiami" ("Theme and Variations"), where the sea and the human body are the main terms of the comparison. He mentions *otliv* 'ebb' and *guby* 'lips'; the sea seems the medium out of which the poet arises (cf. Venclova 1986, 125–26).

38. "Vooruzhennyi zren'em uzkikh os" ("Armed with the vision of narrow wasps").

39. Mess-Baehr 1991, 290.

40. NM 1970a, 217, 188, 192.

41. "On this occasion he added that Pasternak could write only in his study at a desk, while he, Mandelstam, did not write at all, but as it were carved in stone" (Gershtein 1987, 194). Cf. Nadezhda Mandelstam's account: "In Pasternak's novel, too, an 'apartment,' or rather a desk, appeared in passing, so that a thinking person could work at it. Pasternak could not get along without a desk—he was a writing person. O. M. composed on the go [*na khodu*], and then sat for a moment to jot down [what he had composed]. Even in their method of work they were antipodes. And Mandelstam would hardly have defended a special writer's right to a desk at a time of large-scale deprivation among the people" (NM 1970a, 157–58). See also Mandelstam's description of his friend Kuzin: "B. S. was in no way a bookworm. He did science on the go [*na khodu*]" (*S* 2:110). Viach. Vs. Ivanov cautions against assuming the accuracy of the anecdote about the apartment (note to the author, April 1993). But even if apocryphal, the story is valuable as an illustration of a general tendency, much like the accounts of Mandelstam's comments about the desk, and it is consistent with the literary evidence, for example the quotation of Pasternak in "The Apartment."

42. "O. M. cursed the apartment and proposed returning it to the ones it was designated for: the honest traitors, the daubers, and suchlike gold diggers" (NM 1970a, 157).

43. The word *khudozhnik* 'artist' appeared four years later as the title of one of Pasternak's New Year's poems, where the poet is compared both to the "artist" and to the leader.

44. Barnes 1989, 10; Leonid Pasternak 1987. Guy de Mallac refers to Leonid Pasternak's early, "typically impressionistic studies," though he argues that "im-

pressionist," in the sense of the French school, is not quite accurate as applied to the work of Pasternak's father (1981, 24, 28–29). Dasha Di Simplicio discusses the complicated relations of Leonid and of Boris Pasternak to impressionism; especially interesting is her suggestion that both artist and poet came to consider impressionists realists (1989, 200).

45. In an autobiographical statement of 1924, Pasternak wrote: "I owe much if not everything to my father, Academician Leonid Osipovich Pasternak, and to my mother, an outstanding pianist"; cf., in a 1926 letter to his parents: "Sometimes it seems to me that . . . if I ever achieved something, then somewhere in the depths of my being I had been doing it for you" (quoted in Gifford 1977, 2).

46. Cf. Vladimir Markov on impressionism as a first stage of Futurism (1967, 8). The techniques of impressionism are not alien to Pasternak (see Barnes 1989, 202, 218–19, 233–34; see also Kozhinov 1980, 230). Cf. Di Simplicio on Pasternak's evolving attitude towards impressionism (1989, 200–201).

Along with "Impressionism," other Mandelstam poems about paintings may be associated with Pasternak: "Kak svetoteni muchenik Rembrandt" ("Like Rembrandt, martyr of chiaroscuro"), through Leonid Pasternak and his study *Rembrandt i evreistvo v ego tvorchestve* (*Rembrandt and Jewry in His Work*); and "Ulybnis', iagnenok gnevnyi" ("Smile, angry lamb"), which, as one of Pasternak's favorites in the *Second Voronezh Notebook* ("Zametki o peresechenii . . . ," 324), may reveal further links to his own work.

47. Pasternak's mother, Rozaliia Kofman Pasternak, had given up a career as a concert pianist when she married (see Barnes 1989, 6–7, 26). Cf. Pasternak's description of his own beginnings in music in "Tak nachinaiut. Goda v dva" ("So they begin. At about age two") and in the *Autobiographical Sketch* (1982, 416).

48. BP 1982, 437.

49. BP 1961, 159–60.

50. Venclova 1986, 133.

51. Fleishman refers to Pasternak in terms of "izobrazitel'nost'" (1977b, 33). Cf., however, Pasternak's suggestion in *Safe Conduct* that a too-literal image-making is antithetical to the goals of art: "[Art's] image embraces life, but does not seek a viewer. Its truths are not representational [*izobrazitel'ny*], but are capable of eternal development" (1982, 223). Thus Max Hayward's translation of the noun *izobraziteli* as "portrait-painters" in his rendering of Nadezhda Mandelstam's reference to "The Apartment" is unsatisfactory (NM 1970b, 150).

52. Various readers comment on Monet's "Lilas au soleil" as the inspiration for "Impressionism" (see Khardzhiev in OM 1973, 292; Langerak 1980, 146; Langerak 1991, 84). Cf. "The French," the chapter of *Journey to Armenia* about the visit to the impressionist exhibition.

53. Cf. Pasternak's recent "Summer," stanzas from which Mandelstam recited to Emma Gershtein, and also his earlier poem of the same title in *My Sister Life*.

54. Timenchik notes the association of "lilac" with Annenskii, especially through his "Ametisty" ("Amethysts"), in the minds of readers of the 1910s (1981,

179); Pasternak would be included among them (on Annenskii as an early influence on Pasternak, cf. Trenin and Khardzhiev 1976, 10, 14–15).

Elliot Mossman comments on "the color purple and its tones, violet and lilac" in *Doctor Zhivago* (1972, 285–86). The passage Mossman quotes from part 10 of the novel reveals a link between lilac and revolution ("The color of happiness, the color of memories, the color of Russia's tumbling pre-revolutionary virginity was also light-lilac") that confirms the fundamental importance of the color in *My Sister Life*, and its connection to the origins of poetry (hence the association with storms). Mossman observes also connections between shades of purple and the theme of resurrection in *Doctor Zhivago*. His account illuminates the complex relation between poetry and illness in Pasternak's work: "One need only think of Zhivago's death in a crowded, stifling trolleycar under a lilac, threatening sky, to complete a regenerative cycle, the start of which has been lost in a plethora of smothering violets in the florists' quarter of Moscow." Thus, too, in Mandelstam's work the theme of difficult breathing recurs along with references to new life as poetry returns.

55. Mandelstam shares with Pasternak the association of storms and poetry: "Poeziia, tebe polezny grozy" ("Poetry, storms are good for you") ("To the German Speech"). In a note dating to the 1910s, citing Tiutchev as the expert on the stormy life, Mandelstam calls the storm the "prototype of the historical event" ("proobraz istoricheskogo sobytiia"), which is essential to poetry (*S* 2:375).

56. In Mandelstam's work, as in Pasternak's, distorted, feverish vision often accompanies artistic inspiration (see, for example, Isenberg's comments about "delirium" in *The Egyptian Stamp* [1986, 128–31]). The painting is the product of the artist's fevered brain, which "distends" the "parched [coagulated] summer" ("Ego zapeksheesia leto / Lilovym mozgom razogreto"); *rasshirenie* 'dilation', 'distension' ("Rasshirennoe v dukhotu") is a medical term, referring to the circulatory system or the pupils. Langerak distinguishes in "Impressionism" a "subfield" of terminology associated with unpleasantness, injury, illness (*obmorok* 'swoon', *strup'ia* 'scabs', *zapeksheesia* 'parched', *lilovym mozgom* 'lilac brain'), and suggests that these items give information about the creative process (1980, 143).

57. *Dukhota* is prominent in *My Sister Life* in the chapters "Romanovka" and "The attempt to separate the soul": see, for example, "Dushnaia noch'" ("A Sultry Night"), "Eshche bolee dushnyi rassvet" ("A Still More Sultry Dawn"); see also, earlier in that book: "Ploshche dosok v vode—dukhota" ("Flatter than boards in the water is the sultriness") ("Opredelenie poezii" ["Definition of Poetry"]).

58. In her memoirs of Mandelstam in Voronezh, Shtempel' writes that Batiushkov was one of Mandelstam's most beloved poets, and that Mandelstam spoke of him as a contemporary. She juxtaposes references to "Batiushkov" and comments about Pasternak as the contemporary whom Mandelstam most valued (1987, 215–16). Akhmatova echoes "Batiushkov" in her Pasternakian "Poet": "Svist parovoza, khrust arbuznoi *korki*, / V dushistoi laike robkaia ruka" ("The whistle of a steamboat, the crunch of watermelon rind, / A timid hand in fragrant kidskin"). Cf. "V *svetloi perchatke kholodnuiu ruku* / Ia s likhoradochnoi zavist'iu zhmu" ("The

cold hand in the bright glove / I grasp with feverish envy"). See also Mandelstam's "Tvoi zrachok v nebesnoi *korke*" ("Your pupil in the heavenly coating"), another poem with connections to Pasternak.

59. *S* 2:291. Cf. the images of blood and circulation that reappear in the "Whistle" cycle.

60. Ronen 1983, 261–62.

61. See, for example, "Kuda mne radost' det' moiu? / V stikhi, v graflennuiu os'minu?" ("What am I to do with my joy? / [Put it] into verses, into a lined notebook?") in "Nasha groza" ("Our Storm").

62. *S* 2:291.

63. S. S. Averintsev suggests that Mandelstam is referring to himself in this line (1990, 55). Ronen shows that in the 1931 poem "Noch' na dvore . . ." ("Night in the courtyard . . ."), Mandelstam both identifies with and distances himself from the city-dwellers—the audience at a theatrical performance (1991, 11).

64. Gershtein 1987, 194.

65. NM 1970a, 158, 161.

66. NM 1987, 176. Cf. the variant "Po pereulkam . . ." ("Along the side streets . . .").

67. Taranovsky 1976, 2.

68. *S* 2:208; *S* 2:180; *S* 2:171.

69. See Ronen 1983, 259.

70. The "torture of ebb and flow" (in Ronen's translation) is not just a physical torment; it is also, as Ronen makes clear, the torment of the word, Mandelstam's constant theme (1983, 274 n. 74; 257–59).

71. Gifford 1977, 12. Pasternak's letter to Yashvili was written on July 30, 1932, less than two months after the composition of "Batiushkov."

72. Senderovich 1994, 310–11.

73. *Blagodarnost'* 'gratitude' appears in a fragment of Mandelstam's notes to "Darwin's Literary Style"; the passage seems to refer to the pre-Darwinian naturalists. The note that follows includes a second phrase that will appear in "Not I, not you": "*Prilivy i otlivy* dostovernosti kak ritm v izlozhenii (Proiskh. vidov)" ("The ebb and flow of authenticity, like the exposition of rhythm [Orig. of Species]"); see also, in the text of that essay: "*Prilivy i otlivy* dostovernosti ozhivliaiut kazhduiu malen'kuiu glavu 'Proiskhozhdeniia vidov'" ("The ebb and flow of authenticity enliven every little chapter of *The Origin of Species*) (*S* 2:460, 372).

74. *S* 2:248.

75. *S* 2:211.

76. Ronen 1968, 255.

77. See also Baratynskii's "Serdets liudskikh pred nami obnazhivshi" ("Baring people's hearts to us") in "Blagosloven sviatoe vozvestivshii" ("Blessed is the one who proclaims the holy"), to which Ronen compares the last four lines of "Not I, not you" (1983, 216 n. 180); Ronen comments on "On Sowing a Forest" (1983, 262, 323).

78. *S* 2:186.

79. *Ss* 4:140. The manuscript of this letter is reproduced in *S* 2, between pp. 96 and 97. The New Year's greeting is squeezed in at an angle at the very top, opposite the date and above the salutation; it appears to have been a last rather than a first word.

80. According to Nadezhda Mandelstam, "Your pupil" was written on January 2 (1987, 233), not, like "Ulybnis', iagnenok gnevnyi . . ." ("Smile, angry lamb") on January 9, as initially suggested (cf. *Ss* 1:235–36).

81. Here and elsewhere, I follow Ronen's translation of "nebesnaia korka" (1983, 359).

82. In Ronen's excellent translation: "Luminous, iridescent, discarnate, suppliant for the time being" (1983, 359).

83. *S* 2:554.

84. NM 1987, 233; Shtempel' 1987, 224; cf. *S* 2:553.

85. Ronen 1983, 359 n. 46.

86. "Mne v sumerki ty vse—pansionerkoiu" ("In the twilight you are still a schoolgirl to me"). Anna Ljunggren, referring to this passage, finds the eye at the center of the poet's self-portrait in "Zerkalo" ("The Mirror"), in *My Sister Life* (Ljunggren 1989, 231).

87. "Pasternak's external materialization is wonderful: something in his face of the Arab and of his horse at the same time: guardedness, attentiveness—and, any second. . . . Complete readiness for flight.—A huge, also equine, wild and timid garrulousness of the eyes. (Not eye, but oculus [*Ne glaz, a oko*])" (Tsvetaeva 1979, 136). "A Downpour of Light" is dated 1922; Pasternak's poem, published in that year, was written, apparently, in 1920 (BP 1965, 643).

88. Eyewitness accounts as summarized by Barnes suggest an eye that could be described by Mandelstam's "omut oka": Pasternak's "most remarkable trait was the dark, vitreous gaze of his eyes—more prominent than in his brother and sisters, who also inherited this feature from their mother. As a young teenager Pasternak was thus assuming the striking and slightly equine appearance (something both of the Arab and of his stallion, as Tsvetaeva put it) which distinguished him through life" (1989, 34). Ehrenburg continues the equine comparison: "Pasternak's rhythm is the rhythm of our day, violent and wild in its speed. Who would have thought that these good old solid-rumped iambs could leap over the barriers like Arab steeds?" (1970, 40).

Several observers describe Pasternak's eyes as dark. Ehrenburg writes: "Byli ochevidny lish' smuglaia chernota i bol'shie pechal'nye glaza" (1922, 127) ("All I could see clearly was a swarthy darkness [literally, blackness] and large sad eyes" [(1922) 1970, 39]); but cf. Ol'ga Ivinskaia: "Glaza orlinogo iantarnogo tsveta" (1978, 17) ("His eyes were the amber color of an eagle's" [1978a, 7]). The eye of "Your pupil" is light: "Svetlyi, raduzhnyi, besplotnyi" ("Luminous, iridescent, incorporeal"). A variant specifies: "Seryi, iskrenne-zelenyi" ("Gray, sincerely green") (*S* 2:554); cf. Ann Pasternak Slater's description of the "sly greenish-blue eyes" of Pasternak's brother Alexander (Alexander Pasternak 1984, xxi). The memoirs of one contemporary reconcile these descriptions: the sculptor Zoia Maslennikova, who must have observed Pasternak closely in modeling his bust, describes Pasternak's ability to transform himself in mimicking others, and the consequent variability of his appearance: "v eto mgnovenie karie glaza Borisa Leonidovicha mne pokazalis' sero-golubymi" ("at that moment Boris Leonidovich's brown eyes seemed to me gray-blue") (1990, 8; thanks to Savely Senderovich for this reference). As the rejected variant indicates, Mandelstam, too, is not giving a literal portrait but recording the impression produced by the extraordinary eye. (Cf. ". . . Slabykh, chuiushchikh resnits" [". . . Of the weak, perceptive lashes"] with *robkaia* 'timid' in "Batiushkov.")

89. Note Pasternak's predeliction for the root *kos-* (hence Akhmatova's "Kositsia . . ." ["Looks aslant . . ."]), as in "Kosykh kartin . . ." ("Slant pictures"), as opposed to *kosn-,* as in "I to, chto vsiakoi kosnosti kosnei" ("And what is more stagnant than any stagnation"), or "tilted" as opposed to "stilted."

90. This trait might be associated with the well-documented status of the subject in Pasternak's verse, its dissolution in the landscape (see Erlich 1964); and with his revisions, his perpetual search for a better version, at times through questions to readers (cf. the apparent indifference to the presence of a reader in the poems; Pasternak's stance is opposed to the stance of his lyrical subject).

91. Cf. Pasternak's "Gde dal' *pugaetsia*" ("Where the distance is frightened") in "Vesna, ia s ulitsy . . ." ("Spring, I've come from the street . . ."), and Akhmatova's "on / *Puglivo* probiraetsia po khvoiam, / Chtob ne *spugnut'* prostranstva chutkii son" ("he / Fearfully steals through the pine needles, / So as not to scare away the sensitive dream of space").

92. "After he wrote down the poem 'Your pupil in the heavenly coating,' he said in astonishment [*udivlenno*] that only he and Baratynskii wrote poems to their wives" (NM 1972, 277). The word *udivlenno,* which must be considered in light of Nadezhda Mandelstam's tendency to echo the lexicon of the Mandelstamian text she is commenting on (so that in some cases we can guess at what Mandelstam might have said on the basis of her phrasing), not only suggests Mandelstam's amazement but also supports the possibility of another addressee.

93. "So they begin . . ." is the third poem in the *Themes and Variations* cycle "Ia ikh mog pozabyt'" ("I Could Forget Them"), possible connections of which to the "Whistle" cycle should be explored.

94. Cf. Akhmatova's "Zvenit vdali smertel'nyi bubenets" ("The fatal sleigh bell rings in the distance") ("The Poet").

95. The pupil will live as long as the word continues to sound: "Budet on . . . / *Dolgo* zhit' v *rodnoi* strane" ("It will . . . / Live long in its native land"); cf. "Nam ostaetsia tol'ko imia, / Chudesnyi zvuk, na *dolgii* srok" ("Only a name remains to us, / A miraculous sound, for a long time"); see also Pushkin's "I *dolgo* budu ia liubezen tem *narodu* . . ." ("And long will I be beloved of the people because . . .") ("Ia pamiatnik sebe vozdvig nerukotvornyi" ["I raised a monument to myself not built by human hands"]). The poet's future life—the life of the word—is long enough.

96. Ronen 1983, 359.

97. Gasparov 1987, 303.

98. Barnes comments on Pasternak's September 24, 1928 letter to Mandelstam: "Pasternak's self-deprecation and compliments to Mandelstam were characteristically exaggerated" (1989, 409). The tone of excessive praise appears typical, to some extent, of the poets' dialogue.

99. Freidin, too, suggests that Mandelstam's letter to Pasternak is connected to the "Ode" (1987, 261). See also, in the "Ode": "Khudozhnik, pomogi tomu, kto *ves'* s toboi" ("Artist, help the one who is entirely with you"); "Na *vsekh* gotovykh zhit' i umeret' / Begut, igraia, khmurye morshchinki" ("Toward everyone prepared to live and die / The lowering wrinkles run, playing").

100. In his own poem of thanks, Pasternak may echo Mandelstam: cf. "Ia ponial: vse zhivo" ("I understand: everything's alive"); "Ia molvil: spasibo" ("I muttered: thanks").

101. He is writing on another anniversary, not just the New Year. The letter recalls the poems in praise of the great people's poet that poured forth in this year, the hundredth anniversary of Pushkin's death.

102. Fleishman gives the last three stanzas of this six-stanza version of the poem, as it was published in *Novyi mir* 1936, no. 10 (1984, 385–86; cf. stanzas 7–9, published in BP 1990, 2:13–14).

103. Fleishman 1984, 386, 382–83.

104. See ibid., 386 and n. 113. Barnes attributes a similar motivation to Pasternak's letter to Mandelstam of September 24, 1928: "By 1928 Mandelstam was increasingly the target of attack in the literary press and of administrative reprisals, and he was becoming increasingly embittered. In his September letter Pasternak was doubtless consciously trying to support and encourage him" (1989, 409).

105. See Pasternak's letter to his cousin Ol'ga Freidenberg of August 7, 1949: "In the final analysis, what am I worth—and indeed can I be of any worth, however slight, if the obstacle of blood and origin remains unsurmounted . . .?" (BP 1981, 280; cf. Dreizin 1990, 142).

106. I translate *narod* 'the people', as distinct from *liudi* 'people'.

107. Fleishman 1984, 288.

108. V. N. Al'fonsov discusses the problem of the new poetic voice in terms of audience, address: "In the period of *Second Birth* the question of 'type of expression' arose before Pasternak also in the concrete social and moral plane, as the need for a relation to a new reader. It became a question of his own evolution, or, as it was said then, 'remaking.' Here too it did not remain confined to style and had its contradictions" (in BP 1990, 1:34).

109. The association with *prostota* and *pravota* might favor the abstract *priamota* as the middle member; cf. Pasternak's description of Lenin, in the autobiographical sketch "My Sister Life," using the metaphysical term: "ego v glaza brosavshaiasia priamota" ("his striking directness") (BP 1965, 655). But the modifier *priamei,* the only lexical manifestation of the motif in *Second Birth,* has a physical as well as a metaphysical aspect. Thus Pasternak's limp, the result of the

childhood fall from a horse, comes to imply more than a physical difference, as Fleishman points out.

110. "Liubimaia,—molvy slashchavoi" ("Beloved, the fumes of sickly-sweet talk").

111. In his memoirs of Pasternak, recalling the beginnings of the romance, N. Vil'mont confirms that Pasternak's thoughts about writing "simply" were connected to his feeling for "Neigauzikha" (1989, 147–51). Gifford comments: "The peculiar stamp of these poems to Zinaida [in *Second Birth*] is their greater simplicity and restraint" (1977, 142).

112. NM 1987, 155.

113. Gifford translates: "alone lays the road of escape from likelihood to simple truth" (1977, 142); the interpolated "simple" supports the argument for the relation between simplicity and rightness.

114. *Pravota* (*pravda*) appears also in the first cycle of *Second Birth*, "Waves," which, published in *Novyi mir* in January 1932, may have prompted Mandelstam's abandoned stanza about "waves of inner rightness" ("*Volny* vnutrennei *pravoty*") (quoted in *Ss* 1; see also NM 1987, 155).

115. See Mallac 1981, 331; Dreizin 1990, 135. However, cf. a further twist on Pasternak's already complicated relation to Judaism; Pasternak wrote in a letter of 1929 to a family friend, quoted by Fleishman: "Very little was necessary for me to become [an] orthodox [Jew]—it would have been enough for me to marry an Orthodox Christian" (1981, 196 n. 82).

116. Cf. "Schastliv, kto . . . / Bez teni chuzhe*rod*'ia . . . / Vsei kroviiu v na*rode*. // Ia v *riad* ikh ne popal. / No i ne *radi* forsa, / S sherengoi prikhlebal, / V *rod*niu chuzhuiu vtersia"; the poem is orchestrated around the reiterated *rod* 'kin', 'family' (*gens*).

117. "Beloved, the fumes of sickly-sweet talk."

118. Mandelstam's association of Pasternak with Belyi was not idiosyncratic. On the importance of Belyi's rhythms for early Pasternak, see Trenin and Khardzhiev 1976, 10. Viach. Vs. Ivanov notes that in his early autobiographical statements, Pasternak called Belyi his teacher; Pasternak's rhythmical experiments in *Bliznets v tuchakh* (*The Twin in the Clouds*) indicate familiarity with Belyi's theories (1988, 72, 73–74). Cf. the lines from the first poem of the "Requiem," ". . . Kakovo tebe tam—v pusto*te*, v chisto*te*,—siro*te*" (". . . How things are with you there, orphan—in the emptiness, in the clearness"), with Pasternak's "Estestvenno stremit'sia k chistote" ("It's natural to strive for purity"), in "Neskol'ko polozhenii" ("A Few Propositions" [BP (1931) 1982, 113]).

119. Mandelstam gives *priamizna* a metaphysical sense, although, like Pasternak, he also has in mind a physical quality.

120. "Mne stydno i den' oto dnia stydnei, / Chto v vek takikh tenei / Vysokaia odna bolzen' / Eshche zovetsia pesn'" ("I'm ashamed, and more ashamed each day, / That in an age of such shadows, / One sublime malady / Is still called song") (lines 17–20). Ronen suggests a connection between the appearances of *bolezn'* 'illness' in "Blue eyes and burning frontal bone" and in *A Sublime Malady* (per-

sonal communication, April 1992; cf. his comments on the interconnections between "1 January 1924" and *A Sublime Malady,* in Ronen 1983, 252 n. 35).

121. BP 1965, 38–39.

122. Cf. Ronen on *prostaia pesen'ka* 'the simple ditty' of "1 January 1924,"
opposed, as is *prostaia sonatinka* 'the simple sonatina', to [*te*] *sonaty moguchie*
'those powerful sonatas'. On the second poem of the "Requiem," "10 January
1934," as a sequel to "1 January 1924," see Ronen 1983, 327–28, 233–34. Both
Ronen and Taranovsky discuss the connection between singing and dying in Mandelstam's work (Ronen 1983, 254–55; Taranovsky 1976, 128–29).

123. Ronen points out the reference to Pasternak's 1915 poem "Zimnee nebo"
("Winter Sky") in "Blue eyes and burning frontal bone" and "10 January 1934"
(personal communication, April 1992).

124. Cf. Alexander Zholkovsky on the "ecstatic mediation between the upper
and the lower" that occurs, typically, in Pasternak's "From the floor . . ." (1991,
62–63).

125. Cf. the moon that presides over the events of "From the floor . . ." with
the "ebb and flow" that, in Mandelstam's poem, hints at the tides as well as the
process of respiration.

126. "Kogda dushe i toropkoi i robkoi / Predstanet vdrug sobytii glubina, /
Ona bezhit *viiushcheiusia tropkoi,* / No smerti ei tropina ne iasna" ("When the
depth of events suddenly appears / Before the timorous and timid soul, / It runs
along a winding track, / But the path of death is not clear to it"); cf. "I Gete,
svishchushchii *na v'iushcheisia trope*" ("And Goethe, whistling on the winding
path").

127. Fleishman interprets the last stanza of Pasternak's "simplicity" poem as a
characteristic twist on the poet's account of the "heresy" of simplicity ("No my
poshchazheny ne budem, / Kogda ee ne utaim. / Ona vsego nuzhnee liudiam, / No
slozhnoe poniatnei im") ("But we will not be spared / Unless we hide it. / People
need it most of all, / But what's complicated is more comprehensible to them").
Pasternak's mode is no simplistic "simplicity," but a simplicity concealed, appearing (to the uninitiated) as complexity (Fleishman [1984] cites examples of other
artists in Pasternak: Scriabin, Chopin).

Cf. "No ty prekrasna bez *izvilin,* / I prelesti tvoei sekret / Razgadke *zhizni*
ravnosilen" ("But you are splendid without convolutions, / And the secret of your
charm / Equals the solution to the riddle of life")—as if *izviliny* represented art as
opposed to the simple truth of life. Gifford, commenting on these lines, suggests that
Pasternak's strength lies in the "convolutions" (1977, 143–44).

128. NM 1970a, 214.

129. See Levin 1981, 168–70. As the authors of "Zametki o peresechenii
biografii . . ." note (321–22), the second part of Pasternak's poem is clearly a
dialogue with Mandelstam. But Mandelstam responds to the first part of the poem
too.

130. Cf. Mandelstam's *vsia sila* with Pasternak's *vse* and *sila, sily.*

131. Pasternak refers to features of the verb, Mandelstam to substantives. The

categories they select are characteristic of their respective poetics. Pasternak's is a poetry of verbs. He defines the soul, for example, in terms of movement above all: "Akh! narech'e smertel'noe 'zdes'' / Nevdomek sodrogan'iu srashchennomu" ("Ah! the fatal adverb 'here' / Never occurred to the spliced shuddering") ("Definition of the Soul"). Mandelstam's is a poetry of nouns; the poet's task is to give names, to find the one right word.

132. Cf. not only the parallel, noted by Levin, between nature in the first part of the poem and "the people" in the second (Levin 1981, 168), but also the comparison, in the second part of the poem, of the people to elements of nature ("kopnoi cheremukh belogrozdykh" ["a heap of white-clustered bird cherry"]; "vetok" ["the branches"]).

133. NM 1970a, 161–62. The perpetual struggle for the poet's position, which Nadezhda Mandelstam sees as crucial to Mandelstam's life and work (ibid., 214), links him, by contrast, with Fet, another Russian poet of doubtful origins. In "Notes on Poetry" Mandelstam called Pasternak's verse an "important patriarchal manifestation of Fet's Russian poetry" (S 2:210). Boris Gasparov comments on Mandelstam's association of Pasternak and Fet with particular reference to "Stikhi o russkoi poezii" ("Verses about Russian Poetry"); he mentions in this regard Fet's possible Jewish ancestry (1987, 300–304).

134. "Komissarzhevskaia" (S 2:41–42).

135. NM 1987, 197, 224.

136. Meilakh, referring to Nadezhda Mandelstam's commentary, writes that the motif of the petrification of the idol is opposed to the motifs of the child and of ancestral origins (1990, 417–18).

137. NM 1987, 219; cf. NM 1970a, 211–12.

138. Thus for Pasternak, too, the concept of the ages of man (vozrasty) was important; see also Safe Conduct (BP [1931] 1982, 199).

139. The possible etymological relation, noted by Vasmer, between klevetat' 'to slander' on the one hand and klevat' 'to peck' and kliuv 'beak' on the other supports the juxtaposition of the bird with slander.

140. Cf. the extended discussion of the spiteful goldfinch by Mess-Baehr (1991, 271–74).

141. "Stikhi moi, begom, begom" ("My verse, hurry, hurry").

142. NM 1987, 220.

143. See Herbert Friedmann's magisterial study The Symbolic Goldfinch (1946). Friedmann's source for the appearance of the goldfinch in Russian painting is N. P. Kondakov's The Russian Icon (trans., 1927); he also makes use of Kondakov 1910.

144. Cf. v zrachke tvoem 'in your pupil' with tvoi zrachok 'your pupil', that Pasternakian protagonist.

145. Friedmann 1946, 9, 24.

146. NM 1987, 219.

147. See Friedmann 1946, 12, 60. Cf. Kondakov on a Florentine Madonna, as quoted in Friedmann: "This picture represents at the same time the play of the Child

and also the preservation from illness because in ancient times the goldfinch was brought to sick children with the belief that the cheerful little bird had a 'lucky eye' and protected the patient from illness" (Friedmann 1946, 20; Kondakov 1910, 30).

148. Friedmann 1946, 11, 24 n. 48.

149. NM 1987, 220.

150. "O, etot medlennyi, odyshlivyi prostor!— / Ia im presyshchen do otkaza" ("Oh, this slow, winded expanse!— / I'm sated with it to revulsion"); "I neba krug mne byl nedugom" ("And the circle of the sky was my illness"). Cf. "A solntse shchuritsia v krakhmal'noi nishchete— / Ego prishchur spokoen i uteshen" ("While the sun squints in starched poverty— / Its squint is calm and comforted") with "V roskoshnoi bednosti, v moguchei nishchete / Zhivi spokoen i uteshen" ("In luxurious poverty, in mighty indigence / Live calm and comforted"): the landscape and the poet are characterized in identical terms.

151. The association of the goldfinch with the Passion (and perhaps also the Resurrection) cannot be ignored (cf. Mandelstam's poem of early February about the artist's martyrdom, "Like Rembrandt, martyr of chiaroscuro"), but other aspects of the Christian myth appear more important. Indeed, the motif of the goldfinch as augur of illness has been interpreted with reference to Christ's relation to Christians, on the one hand, and to Jews, on the other, where Jews are like the incurably ill subject: the goldfinch as Christ turns away from them (Friedmann 1946, 12).

152. "The Idol" and "The Smile" may have a common source in Pasternak. Mandelstam echoes the description of the laughter of the Sphinx in Pasternak's "Tema," the first poem of the cycle "Theme and Variations": ". . . samyi strannyi, samyi tikhii, / Igraiushchii s epokhi Psammatikha / Uglami skul pustyni detskii smekh" (". . . the strangest, quietest / Childish laughter, playing since the epoch of Psammetichus / With the corners of the desert's cheekbones"). He splits the Pasternakian laughter into the smile of the child and the smile of the inscrutable statue: "Uglami gub ono [ditia] igraet v slave" ("With the corners of its lips it [the child] plays in glory") ("The Smile"); "On ulybaetsia svoim tishaishim rtom" ("It smiles with its very quiet mouth") ("The Idol").

Venclova describes the movement of the third poem of Pasternak's cycle, "Mchalis' zvezdy . . ." ("The stars raced . . ."), from night to dawn, and the poet's movement from unconsciousness and silence to consciousness and speech (1986, 129, 132). These are the terms, too, of the "Whistle" cycle.

153. Ronen compares the anatomical term raduzhnaia obolochka 'iris' (1983, 359), which appears in Mandelstam's Petrarch translations: "O, raduzhnaia o-bolochka strakha! / Efir ochei, gliadevshikh v glub' efira" ("Oh, iridescent covering of fear! / Ether of eyes looking into the depth of the ether").

154. On the idol or Kashchei, or both, as Stalin, see Zeeman 1988, 138, 141–42; Baines 1976, 161; Thomson 1991, 519–20; Chinnov 1967, 127–28. Cf. Meilakh's more subtle study of the Stalin myth in relation to "The Idol" (1990), and Ronen's refutation of Chinnov's identification of Kashchei as Stalin (1968, 257). Mandelstam suggested, then rejected the possibility that the model for the idol was V. K. Shileiko (NM 1987, 222–23; cf. Meilakh 1990, 417). I suggest that there may

be a parallel to a poet whom Mandelstam came to see as a sycophant, as Shileiko apparently saw Mandelstam (see NM 1972, 507; cf. Ronen 1983, 333 n. 6).

155. The reader must avoid attributing to Mandelstam the allegory rejected by Ronen, who notes that Mandelstam made his political points plain (1968, 253).

156. Cf. Mandelstam's direct reference to Stalin, in "We live, not sensing the country beneath us," as "the Kremlin mountaineer" (*kremlevskii gorets*), a phrase Meilakh cites as evidence of a connection to the idol inside the mountain (1990, 420–21).

157. NM 1970a, 252.

158. Poliakova 1991, 29–30.

159. In the letter to Tikhonov, Mandelstam envisions his own place in Russian poetry: "My rhyme among others will be published some day, and it will belong to the people of the Soviet land, to whom I am in endless debt."

160. NM 1970a, 250, 325, 253.

161. NM 1972, 606.

162. *S* 2:109–10, 112–13.

163. "To the German Speech."

164. *S* 2:209. Cf. Tsvetaeva's comment in "A Downpour of Light" on becoming acquainted with *My Sister Life:* "with it [the book] open on my chest—with the first ray of sun—I awaken [*prosypaius'*]" (1979, 135). In the two "Hayloft" poems, poetry means awakening the nocturnal universe: ". . . plechom / Rastolkat' noch', razbudit'"; "I podumal: zachem budit' / Udlinennykh zvuchanii roi . . . " (". . . with a shoulder / Shove the night, awaken [it]"; "And I thought: why awaken / The swarm of lengthened sounds . . .").

165. *S* 2:209, 181, 46.

166. Cf. Pushkin's "Eshche ustalye lakei / Na shubakh u pod"ezda spiat" ("Tired lackeys still / Sleep on fur coats by the entrance") (*Eugene Onegin* 1.22).

167. *S* 2:223. Cf. Annenskii's "Toska pripominan'ia" ("Anguish of Recollection"): "Ia uidu ot liudei, no kuda zhe / Ot nochei mne kuda zh skhoronit'sia?" ("I go away from people, but where / Oh, where can I bury myself from the nights?"). The poet's nocturnal vigil is implicit in this picture of the impossibility of oblivion.

168. Another image of awakening occurs in a poem dated January 20, the following day: "Kak zemliu gde-nibud' nebesnyi kamen' budit, / Upal opal'nyi stikh, ne znaiushchii ottsa" ("As somewhere the stone of the sky awakens the earth, / A disgraced verse fell, knowing no father").

169. Ronen 1983, 359. "Lines Composed at Night During a Time of Insomnia"; "I go out alone onto the road . . ."

170. The last word of "Now I'm in a web of light," *umyvalsia,* echoes the first word of Mandelstam's 1921 poem on the death of Gumilev, "Umyvalsia noch'iu na dvore" ("I washed at night in the yard"). Ronen contrasts "the wide-awake performer of the ablution" in that poem with Akhmatova's "hallucinating insomniac" in "Strakh, vo t'me perebiraia veshchi" ("Fear, picking out things in the darkness") (Ronen 1977a, 167). The themes of awakening and washing are joined in the final rhyme of "Now I'm in a web of light . . ." (*prosypalsia* 'awakens' / *umyvalsia*

'bathes', 'washes'). The "ritual of purification" accomplished, according to Ronen, in "I washed at night in the yard," is repeated in "Now I'm in a web of light," with light, not water, as the medium.

Levin distinguishes "I washed at night in the yard" from Mandelstam's earlier verse in its experience of the earthly, its fusion of "low" and "high" and its setting in contemporary life rather than in a mythic realm (1973, 270). Ronen, who suggests that Mandelstam does not abandon his earlier poetics of quotation in this poem (1977a, 159), cites "I washed . . ." as one of Mandelstam's attempts, prior to the 1930s, to elaborate a Russian voice (1994, 182). Thus the theme of "the people," explicit in "Now I'm in a web of light," is latent here.

171. Mess-Baehr 1991, 314.

172. "The Idol," with thirteen lines, like "Not I, not you," with eleven, is an instance of the odd-lined poems that arose in Voronezh; Nadezhda Mandelstam refers to "The Idol" in calling attention to the appearance of these irregular verse forms (1987, 224).

173. See NM 1987, 221. *Iz* occurs less frequently than *ikh;* but other dentals (and palatals) are abundant (see also unstressed *es, se,* where the vowel is reduced to *i*).

174. *S* 2:208.

175. Ronen 1983, 186.

176. *Khriashch* as "cartilage" is also implied in "On Sowing a Forest," given *zarodyshi* as "embryos." Ronen writes that in Baratynskii's poem, *khriashch* "signifies the sandy wood soil and the hardened hearts of the new generation" (1983, 323). In "Not I, not you," "cartilage" is the primary sense of *khriashch*.

177. Trenin and Khardzhiev [1932] 1976, 24.

178. *S* 2:210. The birds in "Notes on Poetry" (the nightingale and the "woodgrouse on the mate"), like the images of breathing, are derived from Pasternak (cf. "Definition of Poetry," which Mandelstam quotes here, and "A Few Propositions"). Birds, too, are central to Mandelstam's self-representation, though, at least in the case of the goldfinch, the origins of the image are not so clearly independent.

179. For contemporary descriptions of the primacy of vowels in the sound texture of Mandelstam's earlier verse, and the influence of Mandelstam's teacher on his idea of the role of consonants, see Timenchik 1974, 24–25 n. 6; Timenchik 1981, 288–89.

180. *S* 2:46.

181. *S* 2:48.

182. *S* 2:45.

183. *S* 2:44.

184. Cf. Blok's "Prostim ugriumstvo—razve eto / Sokrytyi dvigatel' ego" ("Let's forgive the moroseness—surely that isn't / His hidden motive force"), which invokes one of Nekrasov's characteristic epithets (*ugriumyi* 'gloomy', 'morose' appears three times, for example, in "Edu li noch'iu . . ." ["Whether I ride at night . . ."]); Blok takes up the "malice" or "spite" of the tradition of Nekrasov and Lermontov.

185. On the salt–star "nexus," see Ronen 1983, 278–79; see also Ronen

1977a). Cf. Mandelstam's discovery of "burning salt" in the verse of Fet and of Fet's heir, Pasternak ("Notes on Poetry" [S 2:209–10]).

186. S 2:270.

187. Levinton 1989, 40–41. Commenting on "Yes, I loved them . . . ," Timenchik discusses the "joke" as "the Word" (1975, 222–25). Elsewhere he considers the historical and cultural context of Akhmatova's poem (Timenchik 1988).

188. S 2:270.

189. Ronen 1990, 1646; see also Ronen 1983, 87, 313.

190. Harris implies the importance of malice as an approach to literature (1982, 112–30).

191. "Eto byla surovaia i prekrasnaia zima 20–21 goda. Posledniaia stradnaia zima Sovetskoi Rossii, i ia zhaleiu o nei, vspominaiu o nei s nezhnost'iu. Ia liubil etot Nevskii, pustoi i chernyi, kak bochka, ozhivliaemyi tol'ko glazastymi av-tomobiliami i redkimi, redkimi prokhozhimi, vziatymi na uchet nochnoi pustynei. Togda u Peterburga ostavalas' odna golova, odni nervy" ("That was the severe and beautiful winter of 1920–21. The last harrowing winter of Soviet Russia, and I miss it, I recollect it with tenderness. I loved that Nevsky, empty and black as a barrel, enlivened only by big-eyed automobiles and rare, rare passersby, registered by the nighttime desertedness. Then Petersburg had only a head, only nerves left") (S 2:274).

192. S 2:274, 271.

193. The poem can be described as a body of five stanzas plus a sixth as coda: the anaphoric Komu of stanza 1 recurs in stanza 5, and perhaps the fact that it is repeated twice, instead of three times as in the first stanza, leaves the poem open to a final quatrain.

194. NM 1970a, 213.

195. This coat is nothing to be ashamed of ("Nel'zia zveriu stydit'sia push-noi svoei shkury" ["A beast should not be ashamed of its furry hide"]). Cf. the fur coat in "The Fur Coat" and in Fourth Prose as an image of luxury, of which the owner is ashamed. The fur coat of "In a Fur Coat above One's Station" is Akakii Akak'evich's "overcoat" and the protective fur of the beast of litera-ture; indeed, Akakii Akak'evich, who acquired his coat because of the Peters-burg climate, is a prime example of the beast of literature furred by night and winter. Moreover, Akakii Akak'evich's overcoat was taken away because it was "above his station"—the low-level civil servant had no right to such a coat ("it's mine").

196. The photograph, reproduced in S 2 (between pp. 96–97), of V. V. Gippius as a student might be a portrait of the "beast of literature": the subject has thick hair, a prickly mustache and beard, beetling brows, a pronounced scowl; cf., in the last chapter of The Noise of Time: "so literature rages [zlitsia] for a century and looks askance [kositsia] at the event" (S 2:44). In a letter to Gippius of April 1908, Mandelstam writes that his addressee had been, for him, a friend-foe (drugo-vrag): "But I always saw in you the representative of a precious and at the same time

hostile principle, where the duality of this principle constituted its very charm" (*S* 2:483).

197. The rhyme scheme of "Not I, not you" is one example of such nonclassical rhymes; see also the other eleven-liners of the *Second Voronezh Notebook,* "Like Rembrandt, martyr of chiaroscuro" and "Breaks of round bays, and gravel, and blueness."

198. NM 1970a, 214.

199. Freidin discusses the Phaedra story as the model for a Mandelstamian incest myth, with Russia as stepmother (1987).

200. "Zametki o peresechenii biografii . . . ," 324.

201. Senderovich identified this subtext during an informal seminar at Cornell University in the summer and fall of 1989.

202. Ronen 1983, 6 n. 9, 70 n. 10; Ronen 1991, 41.

203. Ivanov, note to the author, April 1993.

204. Consonants are crucial not only as the basis of Hebrew roots in general but also as the substance of the tetragrammaton, the four letters that represent the name of God, out of which the Torah is conceived to have been constructed (see Scholem 1971, 293–95). Epstein, too, observes a parallel between the consonantal basis of Hebrew roots and Mandelstam's description of Russian in terms of consonants (1991, 189).

205. Ronen writes: "The black and yellow colors of the *tallit* are associated in [Mandel'shtam's] poetic vocabulary with Judaism" (1973b, 295). See also the extended discussion of Mandelstam's Judaism in the chapter titled "The Black-Yellow Light" in Taranovsky 1976, 48–67. According to Donald Rayfield, the goldfinch is Mandelstam's alter ego, and the last bearer of the Jewish black and yellow in his work (1973, 10).

206. Tynianov 1929, 573. In one contemporary's account, in a talk at the Mandelstam evening of March 14, 1933, in Moscow, Eikhenbaum echoed Tynianov with his comments on Mandelstam's "Latin" lexicon and the contrast between Pasternak's word as "thing" and Mandelstam's word as "shade of the thing." Eikhenbaum, too, notes Mandelstam's departures from Russian syntax (Sokolova 1990, 440).

207. Uspenskii writes that the "milieu in which [Mandelstam] was educated was extremely indeterminate in a linguistic regard," and he quotes Mandelstam's comment in *The Noise of Time* about "our language" as a fusion of the maternal and the paternal speech (1990, 93).

208. Uspenskii 1990, 91. Nakhimovsky makes a similar point: "One cannot imagine, say, Akhmatova delighting in her possession of Russian. For her it was a birthright; for Mandelshtam a conscious gift" (1992, 25). Mandelstam treats Russian as an objective entity, for example, in the letter to Tikhonov accompanying "Kashchei": "The Russian language is capable of miracles, if only the verse obeys it, learns from it and—boldly struggles with it. How any language honors the poet's struggle with it and with what coldness it repays indifference and despicable submission to it!" (Poliakova 1991, 29).

209. See Ronen 1983, 186.

210. Bloomfield 1933, 247; emphasis in original.

211. Pasternak, using the same pronominal form without an antecedent, does not tell everything he knows. In "Spasskoe," for example, an anaphoric third person plural pronoun (*ikh, imi* 'them') appears without an antecedent, though the antecedent can be reconstructed on the basis of information given in the text.

212. Participants in the Hunter College Mandelstam Conference (November 16, 1991) suggested that Mandelstam was Khlebnikov's and Pasternak's contemporary more than Akhmatova's. Cf. Ronen on Mandelstam and trans-sense language (1991). Mandelstam's idea of the consonant as "seed" may derive from Khlebnikov. The use of *ikh* is the epitome of Tynianov's conception of Mandelstam's word as a "verse abstraction," as opposed to Pasternak's "verse thing" (1929, 572).

213. NM 1987, 221.

214. Cf. Levinton on Mandelstam's "linguistic theme" (1979, 31). In another respect, however, Mandelstam considered his "Spanish" as he had Italian in *Conversation about Dante,* where he wrote: "Chudesno zdes' obilie brachushchikhsia okonchanii. Ital'ianskii glagol u*si*livaetsia k kontsu i tol'ko v *okonchanii* zhivet" ("Marvelous here is the abundance of marrying endings. The Italian verb grows more intense towards the end and lives only in the ending") (*S* 2:216). Cf. his 1912 poem about Greek: "I glagol'nykh *okonchanii* kolokol, / Mne *vdali ukazyvaet put'* . . ." ("And the bell of verbal endings / Shows me the way into the distance"). In 1936, too, endings mark out a distant journey.

215. Ronen 1994, 182.

216. NM 1970a, 225–26; NM 1972, 563–64; NM 1987, 221; cf. Shtempel' 1987, 222. Recounting Mandelstam's conversation with the Voronezh commandant (so Max Hayward translates *nachal'nik* [NM 1970b, 206–10]; cf. "inquisitor") about his Spanish studies, Nadezhda Mandelstam uses Mandelstam's imagery in yet another instance: "emu [nachal'niku] zakhotelos' posmotret', kakaia ptitsa sidit u nego v kletke" ("he [the commandant] wanted to see what kind of bird he had in his cage") (NM 1970a, 224). The metaphor of the caged bird is central in the Goldfinch poems, to which this conversation is closely related.

217. Referring to Nadezhda Mandelstam's comments, Boris Gass, who writes about Pasternak's ancestry, notes that Mandelstam "similarly traced his genealogy to the Spanish Jews, denying their European continuation" (1985, 59; cf. NM 1972, 563).

218. Valentin Parnakh, "Les Poètes russes d'aujourd'hui," *Europe* 8, 40 (15 April 1926). Fleishman, who refers to Parnakh's article (1977a, 312 n. 23), discusses the story of the Pasternak ancestry and Boris Pasternak's awareness and use of it (1990, 17–19). Parnakh was a model for Parnok, the hero of *The Egyptian Stamp* (Brown 1965, 47–48; Timenchik 1974, 37; Nakhimovsky 1992, 26).

219. See Parnakh 1934, 38–41. Cf. the commentary to Mandelstam's letter to his father of December 12, 1936 (Zenkevich et al., 1991, 96 n. 2). The quincentenary of the birth of Pasternak's ancestor Isaac Abravanel fell in 1937. Among the celebrations was a conference at Tartu (see Trend and Loewe 1937, vii–viii), plans

for which could have come to the attention of Mandelstam, who was studying and "writing" his Spanish at least the year before.

Pasternak's father was the author of a monograph on Rembrandt as the most Jewish of painters. Leonid Pasternak's *Rembrandt and Jewry in His Work* was published in Berlin in 1923 (see Gibian 1983). Mandelstam may have recollected that book in writing "Like Rembrandt, martyr of chiaroscuro," another eleven-line poem (dated February 4, 1937, along with the third eleven-liner in the *Second Voronezh Notebook*, "Breaks of round bays, and gravel [*khriashch*] and blueness").

220. Taranovsky 1976, 66 n. 21. Mess-Baehr has come to conclusions similar to mine about the identity of Mandelstam's Sephardic poet and, therefore, about some of the references in the "Whistle" cycle, though she does not refer to Parnakh's study (1991, 273 n. 55).

221. De León was arrested "due to intrigues of scholarly [*uchenye*] colleagues" (Parnakh 1934, 59–60). Shtempel' suggests that the recent "Spanish events" may have inspired the last lines of "When the goldfinch in the airy pastry" (1987, 222). Cf. Mess-Baehr on the possibility of topical allusions in that poem, and with particular reference to the image of the "scholarly cape" (1991, 272–73). Pasternak, according to Fleishman (1984), may have exploited parallels between the situation in Soviet Russia and the Spanish Inquisition. Cf. Lermontov's use of such a device in his early play *Ispantsy* (*The Spaniards* [1830]).

222. NM 1970a, 225. This account not only recalls de León's fate, it anticipates Mandelstam's own fate: both the second arrest and the doubt about the continuation of verse afterwards. The fate of the verse, too, is similar. According to Parnakh, de León's poems were published only forty years after his death. Mandelstam's poems appeared in Soviet Russia in 1973, thirty-five years after his death in 1938.

223. NM 1970a, 214. Mess-Baehr, too, disagrees with Nadezhda Mandelstam about *lesnaia Salamanka* (1991, 272–74).

224. Poliakova 1991, 29.

225. "Chto delat' nam s ubitost'iu ravnin?" ("What are we to do with the deadness of the plains?").

226. That tradition continues today. An innovation introduced in the early 1930s made possible a renewed interest in *vinkensport:* a box "that lets in light and air but blocks a bird's vision" (James Pressley, "How Many Songs Can a Caged Finch Sing in a Flemish Accent?" *Wall Street Journal,* August 6, 1993, sec. A).

227. "I vse na svete naiznanku" ("And everything in the world is inside out"), the middle line of the second stanza, is "extra," giving it five lines and making the poem a nine-liner.

228. In her comments on the goldfinch poems, Nadezhda Mandelstam implies a contrast between the stubbornness and disobedience of the goldfinch and the behavior advised by a Voronezh neighbor: "Kretova, for her part, tried to convince O. M. to be sensible and understand what contemporary literature is and what demands are made on the Soviet writer and poet" (NM 1987, 220).

229. De León's lyric, which dates from 1576 or 1577, is untitled; the first line is "Aquí la envidia, y mentira" ([1953] 1961, 48, 96).

230. The motif of slander emerges in B. Dubin's translation, "Pokidaia temnitsu" ("Leaving the Dungeon"): "Zdes' odno neizmenno: / Zavist' i *kleveta*" ("Here one thing is unchanging: / Envy and slander"). But Parnakh's *lozh'* 'falsehood' is closer than *kleveta* is to de León's *mentira*.

231. "You have not yet died, you are not yet alone." In Dubin's translation, de León's poem is still closer to Mandelstam's: "I so vseiu vselennoi / Ia proshchaius', smirennyi, / Pust' so mnoi—nishcheta. // V sel'skoi khizhine s sadom / Za stolom nebogatym / Bog—moi sud i sovet" ("And I bid farewell / To the whole universe, humble, / If poverty's with me, so be it. // In a rural hut with a garden / At a poor table / God is my judge and counsel") (Stolbov 1990, 141).

232. NM 1972, 563.

233. See Ronen 1973a, 372 and n. 11.

234. Taranovsky 1976, 57–59; Ronen 1990, 1623.

235. Black and yellow appear, for example, in "Dvortsovaia ploshchad'" ("Palace Square"): "Tol'ko tam, gde tverd' svetla, / Cherno-zheltyi loskut *zlitsia*" ("Only where the firmament is bright, / A black and yellow rag rages"). Just as black and yellow have double connections, with Russianness and Jewishness, so Mandelstam links with his Jewish ancestors the features of honesty and sternness that appear in "I washed at night in the yard" (Ronen translates "I zemlia po sovesti surova" as "And the earth is honestly stern" [1977a, 158]), where Levin and Ronen identify a new concern with a Russian reality: "Otets chasto govoril o *chestnosti* deda kak o vysokom dukhovnom kachestve. Dlia evreia *chestnost'* —eto mudrost' i pochti sviatost'. Chem dal'she po pokolen'iam etikh *surovykh* goluboglazykh starikov, tem *chestnee* i *surovee*" ("My father often spoke of my grandfather's honesty as a sublime spiritual quality. For a Jew, honesty is wisdom and almost holiness. The further back in the generations of these stern blue-eyed old men, the more honest and stern they were") ("The Judaic Chaos," *S* 2:21).

The interpenetration of features associated with Mandelstam's black and yellow is reflected in the phonological structure of *chërnyi* and *zhëltyi,* both two-syllable words with initial stress, which correspond and nearly overlap, phoneme for phoneme. The first phonemes are the voiceless affricate (*ch*) and the voiced fricative (*zh*), alveopalatal and palatal, respectively; these are followed by the identical stressed vowel (*o*); third are the dental (*r*) and alveolar (*l*) resonants; fourth, two dentals, the voiced nasal (*n*) and the voiceless stop (*t*).

236. "A. Blok" (*S* 2:189).

237. In the drafts to *Conversation about Dante,* Mandelstam himself implies the importance of alien intrusions for the life of the poet's language: "Dante's verbal circles are thoroughly barbarized. To keep his speech healthy, he always adds a barbarian admixture to it" (*Ss* 3:185). Although in this passage Mandelstam is speaking of onomatopoeic effects, elsewhere he refers specifically (and in similar terms) to foreign language, including Slavicisms; the principle is the same ("Here's

an example for you. Canto 32 of the *Inferno* suddenly falls ill with a barbarian Slavicitis" [*Ss* 3:184]).

238. Turbin 1985, 95. Pushkin established a model for later poets. The poet's non-Russian heritage is rather more typical than not; see also the examples of Nekrasov, Fet, Pasternak, and to some extent Tiutchev, Blok, Tsvetaeva, Akhmatova, Khodasevich; in retrospect, Zhukovskii, too, might be considered here.

Ronen refers to Lermontov and Pushkin in commenting on the Mandelstamian theme of the poet's foreign birth, and with particular reference to "I haven't heard Ossian's tales"; he notes that Lermontov echoes Pushkin's line "Pod nebom Afriki moei" ("Beneath the sky of my Africa") in his "Grob Ossiana" ("Ossian's Tomb") (1973a, 372 and n. 11).

239. See Ronen 1973a, 371.

240. Anatoly Liberman discusses the possible Spanish origins of the Scottish Learmonths (1993, 477, 573). Lermontov's reflections on his Scottish and, apparently, his "Spanish" forebears were related to his sense of the lowly social position of his father, who was disdained by his mother's well-born family (see Viskovatov 1987, 93). In Lermontov's *The Spaniards,* the "Spanish" and "Jewish" themes are conjoined: the model of the "young man . . . of 'ungentle birth'" (Eikhenbaum 1961, 162) is the abandoned foundling Fernando, who is revealed to be a Jew, a circumstance confirming his outcast state. In Mandelstam's case, Jewishness plays a double role in the "struggle for the poet's dignity in society, . . . and his position" (NM 1970a, 214). This becomes clear in *Fourth Prose,* where Mandelstam's Jewishness accounts for both his separation from society and his identity as a poet and, therefore, his sense of rightness (cf. the Jewish staff of *Fourth Prose,* that later version of the pilgrim's crozier in "The Staff").

241. Nesbet 1988, 109–10.

242. Ginzburg 1988, 222–25. Nesbet remarks, with reference to Mandelstam, "'Longing to belong' and 'wanting to be special' are not . . . mutually exclusive" (1988, 122 n. 11).

243. Levin 1969, 115–16.

244. Brown 1973, 232–33.

245. *S* 2:14.

246. "Rozu kutaiut v mekha"; "Nichego, golubka Evridika, / Chto u nas studenaia zima. // Slashche pen'ia ital'ianskoi rechi / Dlia menia rodnoi iazyk" ("A rose is muffled in furs"; "Never mind, dear Eurydice, / That it is freezing winter here. // Sweeter than the singing of the Italian speech / For me is my native language").

But as Mandelstam reconsidered the sense of these words, as he attributed to "Spanish" features he had associated with Russian in the 1923 essays, he also transferred features such as "crudeness," earlier associated with *rodnoe,* to *rodovoe* (cf. Segal on *grubost'* and *prostota* associated with *rodnoi iazyk* 'the native language' in "The spectral stage barely glimmers" [1975, 92]).

247. Uspenskii, too, suggests a connection between the grammatical theme and the theme of return to origins, though his emphasis is different: "[T]he play with

grammatical categories can be understood as a return to the first principles of *language,* and, consequently, to the first principles of being" (1990, 94).

248. Ronen 1983, 99.

249. *S* 2:213. Ronen sees the sleep of literature as another "image of the ancestral symbolist poetry" (1983, 102); again, the poet enters the dormant medium to arouse it.

250. *S* 2:238, 239, 120.

251. Cf. Ronen 1983, XV.

252. *S* 2:366; Mandelstam's emphasis.

253. *S* 2:366, 213. Mandelstam comments on the activity of the "poetically literate" reader, who fills the gaps in the work "as if extracting them from the text itself"; "[b]ut all these signs are no less precise than musical notations or the hieroglyphs of dance" (*S* 2:212–13). Reading means the discovery of what is already there.

254. *S* 2:188. Mandelstam's own scientific interests, and his "biological poetics," are a peculiar illustration of the function of the poet's ancestral inheritance. In a letter to his father of late December 1932, he writes: "I am becoming more and more convinced that we have a lot in common specifically in an intellectual respect, something I did not understand when I was a child. It's almost absurd: for example, I am rummaging around now in the natural sciences—in biology, in the theory of life, i.e., I am repeating, in some sense, the developmental stages of my father. Who would have thought it?" (Zenkevich and Nerler 1987, 205). Cf. the remarks in unpublished memoirs by Mandelstam's youngest brother, Evgenii, about the transformation in Mandelstam's relation to his father, his new wish for spiritual closeness (the editors quote Mandelstam's brother in a note to a letter of early 1929 [ibid., 202]).

255. *S* 2:48.

256. Translation from "The Life of Verse" in Gumilev 1977, 14; cf. Gumilev 1968, 162. On James's theory of emotion (and the parallel with Gumilev) see Winton 1990, 652–53. I. I. Lapshin's Russian translation of James's *Principles of Psychology* (1890) was published as early as 1896 (*Psikhologiia Dzheimsa* [Saint Petersburg: Zapiski Istoriko-filosoficheskogo fakul'teta Imperatorskogo S.-Peterburgskogo universiteta], ch. 39), with a second edition in 1898; frequent further editions appeared over the next two decades. The theory of emotion was similarly important for early Formalist ideas of the articulatory and acoustical aspects of verse (see, e.g., Jakubinskii 1919, 41–42, 43; cf. Erlich 1965, 182 n. 49).

257. Ronen 1983, 178–79.

258. See the testimony of his fellow student K. V. Mochul'skii about Mandelstam's difficulties with Greek and his relation to it—in particular, to the grammar—as poetic material (quoted in *S* 1:594).

259. I am grateful to Savely Senderovich for this suggestion.

260. Levinton 1979, 32.

261. Ronen 1990, 1621–22.

262. In "V ogromnom omute prozrachno i temno" ("In the enormous pool it's

transparent and dark"), the heart is compared to a "straw" (*solominka*).

263. "In the enormous pool it's transparent and dark"; "Inexorable words." Cf. the reed of the 1914 poem "Ravnodenstvie" ("Equilibrium") ("Est' ivolgi v lesakh . . ." ["There are orioles in the woods . . ."]): ". . . i zolotaia len' / Iz trostnika izvlech' bogatstvo tseloi noty" (" . . . and a golden indolence / Makes it hard to draw from the reed the wealth of a whole note"). In this poem, too, "heaviness" is implicit (see also "trudnye dlinnoty" ["difficult longueurs"]), though the luminous coloration and classical thematics contrast with the darkness of the poems about the Jewish pool.

264. See Thomson on the association between "heaviness" and inspiration in *Stone* (1991, 517 n. 43).

265. Ronen 1973b, 296; see also Ronen 1983, 130–31.

266. *S* 2:19–20.

267. Ronen 1968, 258.

268. Ronen juxtaposes Mandelstam's account of Gippius's speech to his discussion of *Inferno* 32 in considering "the symbolic value [Mandelstam] attributed to stridency and acuteness" (1968, 258).

269. *S* 2:243.

270. See Lotman 1980, 225.

271. Ibid., 222.

272. Thus Vygotskii, in his "Defectology," cites the example of Demosthenes as, at least according to legend, overcoming a speech defect to become the greatest orator of Athens (1983, 36).

273. *Ss* 3:280–81.

274. See also in "The Bookcase," with reference to Pushkin: "Ved' posle 37-ogo goda i krov' i stikhi zhurchali inache"; "Kakoi tsvet podobrat' k zhurchaniiu rechei" ("You see, after '37 both blood and verse murmured differently"; "What color can be compared to the murmuring of speech?") (*Ss* 2:58, 59; cf. Ronen 1983, 105–6). Commenting on Mandelstam's association of poetry with water, E. A. Toddes compares the water metaphors in the letter to Tynianov with, among others, the image of poetry as a wave (*volnoi*) in "Now I'm in a web of light," written two days earlier (1986, 93–94 and n. 33). Khardzhiev, too, compares the letter and the poem (OM 1973, 302–3).

275. See ". . . son i smert' minuia" ("Armed with the vision of narrow wasps").

References

Akhmatova, Anna. 1968. "Mandel'shtam (Listki iz dnevnika)" ["Mandelstam (Leaves from a Diary)"]. In *Sochineniia*, 2: 166–87. N.p.: Inter-Language Literary Associates.

Alter, Robert. 1978. "Osip Mandelstam: The Poet as Witness." In *Defenses of the Imagination: Jewish Writers and Modern Historical Crisis*, 25–46. Philadelphia: Jewish Publication Society of America.

Averintsev, S. S. 1990. "Sud'ba i vest' Osipa Mandel'shtama" ["Osip Mandelstam's Fate and Fame"]. In *S*, 1: 5–64.

Avins, Carol. 1983. *Border Crossings: The West and Russian Identity in Soviet Literature, 1917–1934*. Berkeley and Los Angeles: University of California Press.

Baines, Jennifer. 1976. *Mandelstam: The Later Poetry*. Cambridge: Cambridge University Press.

Barnes, Christopher. 1989. *Boris Pasternak: A Literary Biography*. Vol. 1, *1890–1928*. Cambridge: Cambridge University Press.

Bergson, Henri. 1908. *L'Évolution créatrice*. Paris: Félix Alcan.

———. 1959. "Le Rire." In *Oeuvres*, 383–485. Paris: Presses universitaires de France.

Bertalanffy, Ludwig von. 1933. *Modern Theories of Development*. Translated and adapted by J. H. Woodger. London: Oxford University Press.

Bertel's, E. 1935. *Persidskaia poeziia v Bukhare X veka* [*Persian Poetry in Tenth-Century Bukhara*]. Trudy Instituta vostokovedeniia 10. Moscow: Akademiia Nauk SSSR.

Berthelot, René. 1932. *Science et philosophie chez Goethe*. Paris: Félix Alcan.

Binyon, Laurence, and J. V. S. Wilkinson. 1931. *The Shah-Namah of Firdausi: The Book of the Persian Kings*. Oxford: Oxford University Press.

Bloomfield, Leonard. 1933. *Language*. Holt, Rinehart & Winston. Reprint, Chicago: University of Chicago Press, 1984.

Bobrov, Sergei. 1922. "Zaimstvovaniia i vliianiia" ["Borrowings and Influences"]. In *Pechat' i revoliutsii* 8: 72–92.

Boris Pasternak and His Times: Selected Papers from the Second International Symposium on Pasternak. 1989. Edited by Lazar Fleishman. Modern Russian Literature and Culture, Studies and Texts, vol. 25. Berkeley: Berkeley Slavic Specialties.

Born, Max. 1962. *Einstein's Theory of Relativity*. New York: Dover Publications.

Brokgauz, F. A., and I. A. Efron. 1896. *Entsiklopedicheskii slovar'* [*Encyclopedic Dictionary*]. Edited by I. E. Andreevskii. Saint Petersburg: Tipo-Litografiia I. A. Efrona.

Brown, Clarence. 1968. "Mandelstam's Notes towards a Supreme Fiction." *Delos*
       1: 32–48.

———. 1973. *Mandelstam*. Cambridge: Cambridge University Press.

Cavanagh, Clare Adele. 1988. "Osip Mandel'shtam and the Modernist Creation of
       Tradition." Ph.D. diss., Harvard University.

———. 1990. "Synthetic Nationality: Mandel'shtam and Chaadaev." *Slavic Re-
       view* 49, 4 (Winter): 597–610.

Chapman, H. Perry. 1990. *Rembrandt's Self-Portraits: A Study in Seventeenth-
       Century Identity*. Princeton, N.J.: Princeton University Press.

Chinnov, Igor. 1967. "Pozdnii Mandel'shtam: Nekotorye obrazy v ego poezii"
       ["Late Mandelstam: A Few Images in His Poetry"]. *Novyi zhurnal* 88: 125–
       37.

Chukovskaia, Lidiia. 1976. *Zapiski ob Anne Akhmatovoi* [*Notes about Anna
       Akhmatova*]. Vol. 1. Paris: YMCA Press.

Cohen, Arthur A. 1974. *Osip Emilievich Mandelstam: An Essay in Antiphon*. Ann
       Arbor, Mich.: Ardis.

Dal', Vladimir. [1880–82] 1981. *Tolkovyi slovar' zhivogo velikorusskogo iazyka*
       [*Interpretive Dictionary of the Living Great Russian Language*]. 8th ed. Mos-
       cow: Russkii iazyk.

Dante Alighieri. 1961. *The Divine Comedy*. Translated by John D. Sinclair. 3 vols.
       New York: Oxford University Press.

Di Simplicio, Dasha. 1989. "B. Pasternak i zhivopis'" ["B. Pasternak and Paint-
       ing"]. In *Boris Pasternak and His Times*, 195–211.

Dobrokhotov, A. L. 1990. *Dante Alig'eri*. Moscow: Mysl'.

Dreizin, Felix. 1990. *The Russian Soul and the Jew: Essays in Literary Ethnocriti-
       cism*. Lanham, Md.: University Press of America.

Ehrenburg, Ilya. 1922. "Boris Leonidovich Pasternak." In *Portrety russkikh poetov*.
       Berlin: Tsentrifuga. Reprint, Munich: Wilhelm Fink Verlag, 1972.

———. 1970. "Boris Leonidovich Pasternak." Translated by Angela Livingstone.
       In *Pasternak: Modern Judgements,* ed. Donald Davie and Angela Livingstone,
       39–41. Nashville, Tenn.: Aurora Publishers.

Eikhenbaum, B. M. 1923. *Anna Akhmatova: Opyt analiza* [*Anna Akhmatova: An
       Essay in Analysis*]. Petrograd: Petropechat'. Reprint, Paris: Lev, 1980.

———. 1961. *Stat'i o Lermontove* [*Articles about Lermontov*]. Moscow and
       Leningrad: Akademiia Nauk SSSR.

Epstein, Mikhail. 1991. "Tsadik i Talmudist: Sravnitel'nyi opyt o Pasternake i
       Mandel'shtame" ["The Tsaddik and the Talmudist: A Comparative Essay
       about Pasternak and Mandelstam"]. *Dvadtsat' dva* 77 (June–July): 186–209.

Erlich, Victor. 1964. "'Life by Verses': Boris Pasternak." In *The Double Image*,
       133–54. Baltimore: Johns Hopkins University Press.

———. 1965. *Russian Formalism: History—Doctrine*. New Haven, Conn.: Yale
       University Press.

Fersman, A. E. 1920. *Dragotsennye i tsvetnye kamni Rossii* [*Precious Stones and
       Minerals in Russia*]. Petrograd: ?-aia gosudarstvennaia tipografiia.

Fleishman, L. S. 1977a. "K publikatsii pis'ma L. O. Pasternaka k Bialiku" ["On the Occasion of the Publication of L. O. Pasternak's Letter to Bialik"]. *Slavic Hierosolymitana* 1: 309–16.

———. 1977b. *Stat'i o Pasternake* [*Articles about Pasternak*]. Bremen: K-Presse.

———. 1981. *Boris Pasternak v dvadtsatye gody* [*Boris Pasternak in the 1920s*]. Munich: Wilhelm Fink Verlag.

———. 1984. *Boris Pasternak v tridtsatye gody* [*Boris Pasternak in the 1930s*]. Jerusalem: Magnes Press.

———. 1989. "Pasternak and Bukharin in the 1930s." In *Boris dPasternak and His Times*, 171–80.

———. 1990. *Boris Pasternak: The Poet and His Politics.* Cambridge, Mass.: Harvard University Press.

Florenskii, P. A. [1922] 1985. *Mnimosti v geometrii* [*Imaginary Entities in Geometry*]. Introduction by Michael Hagemeister. Munich: Otto Sagner.

Freidin, Gregory. 1987. *A Coat of Many Colors: Osip Mandelstam and His Mythologies of Self-Presentation.* Berkeley and Los Angeles: University of California Press.

Friedmann, Herbert. 1946. *The Symbolic Goldfinch: Its History and Significance in European Devotional Art.* [Washington, D.C.:] Pantheon Books.

Gasparov, Boris. 1987. "Son o russkoi poezii (O. Mandel'shtam, 'Stikhi o russkoi poezii,' 1–2)" ["A Dream about Russian Poetry (O. Mandelstam, 'Verses about Russian Poetry,' 1–2"]. In *Stanford Slavic Studies,* 1: 259–306. Stanford, Calif.: Department of Slavic Languages and Literatures, Stanford University.

Gasparov, M. L. 1990. "Evoliutsiia metriki Mandel'shtama" ["The Evolution of Mandelstam's Metrics"]. In *Zhizn' i tvorchesto O. E. Mandel'shtama,* 336–46. Voronezh: Izdatel'stvo voronezhskogo universiteta.

Gass, Boris. 1985. *Pasynki vremennykh otchizn* [*Stepchildren of Temporal Fatherlands*]. Tel Aviv: Iakov-Press.

Gershtein, Emma. 1987. "Slushaia Mandel'shtama" ["Listening to Mandelstam"]. *Novyi mir* 10: 194–96.

Ghyka, Matila. 1977. *The Geometry of Art and Life.* New York: Dover Publications.

Gibian, George. 1983. "*Doctor Zhivago,* Russia, and Leonid Pasternak's *Rembrandt.*" In *The Russian Novel from Pushkin to Pasternak,* ed. John Garrard, 203–24. New Haven, Conn.: Yale University Press. Cornell Soviet Studies Reprints, 52. Ithaca, N.Y.: Committee on Soviet Studies, n.d.

Gifford, Henry. 1977. *Pasternak: A Critical Study.* Cambridge: Cambridge University Press.

———. 1979. "Mandelstam and the Journey." Foreword to *Journey to Armenia* by Osip Mandelstam. Translated by Sidney Monas. San Francisco: George F. Ritchie.

Ginzburg, L. Ia. 1988. "'I zaodno s pravoporiadkom . . .'" ["And at one with the established order . . ."]. In *Tynianovskii sbornik: Tret'i Tynianovskie chteniia,* ed. M. O. Chudakova, 218–30. Riga: Zinatne.

Glazova, Marina. 1984. "Mandel'štam and Dante: The *Divine Comedy* in Mandel'štam's Poetry of the 1930s." *Studies in Soviet Thought* 28: 281–335.

Goethe, Johann Wolfgang von. [1810] 1949. *Schriften zur Farbenlehre.* Vol. 16 of *Gedenkausgabe der Werke, Briefe und Gesprache.* Zurich: Artemis-Verlag.

———. [1816–17] 1950. *Italienische Reise.* Vol. 11 of *Gedenkausgabe der Werke, Briefe und Gesprache.* Zurich: Artemis-Verlag.

———. [1810] 1970. *Goethe's Theory of Colours.* Translated by Charles Lock Eastlake. London: John Murray, 1840. Reprint, Cambridge, Mass.: MIT Press.

Gorodetskii, Sergei. 1914. *Tsvetushchii posokh: Verenitsa vos'mistishii* [*The Flowering Staff: A Sequence of Octaves*]. Saint Petersburg: Griadushchii den'.

Gould, Stephen Jay. 1982. *The Panda's Thumb: More Reflections in Natural History.* New York: Norton.

Grigor'ev, A., and I. Petrova. 1977. "Mandel'shtam na poroge tridtsatykh godov" ["Mandelstam on the Threshold of the 1930s"]. *Russian Literature* 5–2 (April): 181–99.

Gumilev, Nikolai. 1968. *Sobranie sochinenii v chetyrekh tomakh* [*Collected Works in Four Volumes*]. Vol. 4. Washington, D.C.: Victor Kamkin.

———. 1977. *On Russian Poetry.* Edited and translated by David Lapeza. Ann Arbor, Mich.: Ardis.

Gydov, V. N. 1991. "'Dyshat' ne dlia sebia . . .' (voronezhskii period Osipa Mandel'shtama)" ["'To breathe not for oneself . . .' (Osip Mandelstam's Voronezh Period)"]. In *Slovo i sud'ba. Osip Mandel'shtam: Issledovaniia i materialy,* 278–86. Moscow: Nauka.

Hanfmann, George M. A. 1970. "Psyche." *Oxford Classical Dictionary.* 2d ed. Oxford: Clarendon Press.

Haraway, Donna Jeanne. 1976. *Crystals, Fabrics, and Fields: Metaphors of Organicism in Twentieth-Century Developmental Biology.* New Haven, Conn.: Yale University Press.

Harris, Jane Gary. 1986. "The 'Latin Gerundive' as Autobiographical Imperative: A Reading of Mandel'shtam's *Journey to Armenia.*" *Slavic Review* 45, 1 (Spring): 1–19.

———. 1982. "Mandelstamian *Zlost'*, Bergson, and a New Acmeist Esthetic?" *Ulbandus Review* 2, 2 (Fall): 112–30.

———. 1989. Review of *Substantial Proofs of Being,* by Charles Isenberg. *Russian Review* 48, 1 (January): 110–11.

Heisenberg, Werner. 1959. *Wandlungen in den Grundlagen der Naturwissenschaft.* Stuttgart: S. Hirzel Verlag.

———. 1979. *Philosophical Problems of Quantum Physics* [*Wandlungen in den Grundlagen der Naturwissenschaft*]. Translated by F. C. Hayes. Woodbridge, Conn.: Ox Bow Press.

———. 1990. *Across the Frontiers* [*Schritte über Grenzen*]. Translated by Peter Heath. Woodbridge, Conn.: Ox Bow Press.

Hingley, Ronald. 1985. *Pasternak: A Biography.* London: Unwin Paperbacks.

Holtz, Barry W. 1984. "Introduction: On Reading Jewish Texts." In *Back to the*

Sources: Reading the Classic Jewish Texts, ed. Barry W. Holtz, 11–29. New York: Summit Books.

Isenberg, Charles. 1986. *Substantial Proofs of Being: Osip Mandelstam's Literary Prose.* Columbus, Ohio: Slavica.

Ivanov, V. [1909] 1971. *Po zvezdam [By the Stars].* Saint Petersburg: Ory. Reprint, Letchworth, Herts.: Bradda Books.

Ivanov, Viach. Vs. 1985. "Temy i stili Vostoka v poezii Zapada" ["Themes and Styles of the East in the Poetry of the West"]. Afterword to *Vostochnye motivy: Stikhotvoreniia i poemy,* compiled by L. E. Cherkasskii and V. S. Murav'ev, 424–70. Moscow: Nauka.

———. 1988. "Pasternak i OPOIAZ (k postanovke voprosa)" ["Pasternak and OPOIAZ (Towards a Formulation of the Question)"]. In *Tynianovskii sbornik: Tret'i Tynianovskie chteniia,* ed. M. O. Chudakova, 70–82. Riga: Zinatne.

———. 1990. "'Stikhi o neizvestnom soldate' v kontekste mirovoi poezii" ["'Verses about the Unknown Soldier' in the Context of World Poetry"]. In *Zhizn' i tvorchestvo O. E. Mandel'shtama,* 356–66. Voronezh: Izdatel'stvo Voronezhskogo universiteta.

———. 1991a. "Mandelstam and Biology." MS. 34 pp.

———. 1991b. "Mandel'shtam i biologiia" ["Mandelstam and Biology"]. In *Osip Mandel'shtam: K 199-letiiu so dnia rozhdeniia. Poetika i tekstologiia. Materialy nauchnoi konferentsii 27–29 dekabria 1991 g.,* 4–7. Moscow: Gnosis.

Ivinskaia, Ol'ga. 1978a. *V plenu vremeni [A Captive of Time].* Choisy-le-Roi: Librairie Arthème Fayard.

———. 1978b. *A Captive of Time.* Translated by Max Hayward. Garden City, N.Y.: Doubleday.

Jakobson, Roman. 1960. "Linguistics and Poetics." In *Style in Language,* ed. Thomas A. Sebeok, 350–77. Cambridge, Mass.: MIT Press.

———. 1970. "Marginal Notes on the Prose of the Poet Pasternak." In *Pasternak: Modern Judgements,* ed. Donald Davie and Angela Livingstone, 135–51. Nashville, Tenn.: Aurora Publishers.

———. 1987. "Noveishaia russkaia poeziia." ["Modern Russian Poetry"]. In *Raboty po poetike,* 272–316. Moscow: Progress Publishers.

Jakubinskii, L. P. 1919. "O zvukakh stikhotvornogo iazyka" ["On the Sounds of Verse Language"]. In *Poetika: Sborniki po teorii poeticheskogo iazyka.* Petrograd: 18-ia Gosudarstvennaia tipografiia.

Jaynes, Julian. 1976. *The Origin of Consciousness in the Breakdown of the Bicameral Mind.* Boston: Houghton Mifflin.

Kaganskaia, Maiia. 1977. "Osip Mandel'shtam—poet iudeiskii" ["Osip Mandelstam—Judaic Poet"]. In *Sion* 20: 174–95.

Khodasevich, V. F. 1976. "Gumilev i Blok" ["Gumilev and Blok"]. In *Nekropol': Vospominaniia,* 118–40. Paris: YMCA Press.

Kondakov, N. P. 1910. *Ikonografiia Bogomateri: Sviazi grecheskoi i russkoi ikonopisi s ital'ianskoiu zhivopis'iu rannego Vozrozhdeniia [The Iconography of the Virgin: Connections between Greek and Russian Icon Painting and Italian Painting of the Early Renaissance*]. Saint Petersburg: Tovarishchestvo R. Golike i A. Vil'borg.

Kozhinov, V. 1980. *Stikhi i poeziia* [*Verse and Poetry*]. Moscow: Sovetskii pisatel'.

Lamarck, Jean-Baptiste de. [1809] 1984. *Zoological Philosophy*. Translated by Hugh Elliot. Chicago: University of Chicago Press.

Langerak, Thomas. 1980. "Mandel'štams 'Impressionizm.'" In *Voz'mi na radost': To Honour Jeanne van der Eng-Liedmeier*, 139–48. Amsterdam: n.p.

———. 1991. "'Kak svetoteni muchenik Rembrandt . . .' (Razgovor poeta s khudozhnikom)" ["'Like Rembrandt, martyr of chiaroscuro . . .' (The Poet's Conversation with the Painter)"]. In *Osip Mandel'shtam: K 100-letiiu so dnia rozhdeniia. Poetika i tekstologiia*, 83–86. Moscow: Gnosis.

Leaman, Oliver. 1988. *Averroes and his Philosophy*. Oxford: Clarendon Press; New York: Oxford University Press.

León, Luis de. [1953] 1961. *The Original Poems of Fray Luis de León*. Edited with an Introduction and Notes by Edward Sarmiento. Manchester: Manchester University Press.

Lermontov, Mikhail. 1983. *Major Poetical Works*. Translated by Anatoly Liberman. Minneapolis: University of Minnesota Press.

Lermontovskaia entsiklopediia. 1981. Edited by V. A. Manuilov. Moscow: Sovetskaia entsiklopediia.

Levin, Iu. I. 1969. "O nekotorykh chertakh plana soderzhaniia v poeticheskikh tekstakh: Materialy k izucheniiu poetiki O. Mandel'shtama" ["On Some Features of the Plane of Content in Poetic Texts: Materials for the Study of O. Mandelstam's Poetics"]. *International Journal of Slavic Linguistics and Poetics* 12: 106–64.

———. 1971. "O nekotorykh chertakh plana soderzhaniia v poeticheskikh tekstakh" ["On Some Features of the Plane of Content in Poetic Texts"]. In *Teksty sovetskogo literaturovedcheskogo strukturalizma*, ed. Karl Eimermacher et al., 278–94. Centrifuga: Russian Reprintings and Printings, vol. 5. Munich: Wilhelm Fink Verlag.

———. 1972. "Zametki k *Razgovoru o Dante* O. Mandel'shtama" ["Notes on O. Mandelstam's *Conversation about Dante*"]. *International Journal of Slavic Linguistics and Poetics* 15: 184–97.

———. 1973. "Razbor odnogo stikhotvoreniia Mandel'shtama" ["Analysis of a Poem by Mandelstam"]. In *Slavic Poetics: Essays in Honor of Kiril Taranovsky*, ed. Roman Jakobson, C. H. van Schooneveld, and Dean S. Worth, 267–76. The Hague: Mouton.

———. 1975a. "Leksiko-semanticheskii analiz odnogo stikhotvoreniia O. Mandel'shtama" ["Lexical-Semantic Analysis of a Poem by O. Mandelstam"]. In *Slovo v russkoi sovetskoi poezii*, 225–33. Moscow: Nauka.

———. 1975b. "Zametki o 'krymsko-ellinskikh' stikhakh O. Mandel'shtama" ["Notes on O. Mandelstam's 'Crimean-Hellenic' Poems"]. *Russian Literature* 10–11: 5–31.

―――. 1978. "Zametki o poezii O. Mandel'shtama tridtsatykh godov. I" ["Notes on O. Mandelstam's Poetry of the 1930s. I"]. *Slavica Hierosolymitana* 3: 110–73.

―――. 1981. "Zametki k stikhotvoreniiu B. Pasternaka 'Vse naklonen'ia i zalogi'" ["Notes on B. Pasternak's Poem 'All verbal moods and voices'"]. *Russian Literature* 9-2 (15 February): 163–74.

―――. 1982. "'Masteritsa vinovatykh vzorov . . .' O. Mandel'shtama" ["O. Mandelstam's 'Mistress of guilty glances . . .'"]. In *Uchenyi material po analizu poeticheskikh tekstov,* ed. M. Iu. Lotman, 168–79. Tallin: Tallinskii pedagogicheskii institut im. E. Vil'de.

Levin, Iu. I., D. M. Segal, R. D. Timenchik, V. N. Toporov, and T. V. Civ'ian. 1974. "Russkaia semanticheskaia poetika kak potentsial'naia kul'turnaia paradigma" ["Russian Semantic Poetics as a Potential Cultural Paradigm"]. *Russian Literature* 7-8: 47–82.

Levinton, G. A. 1979. "Poeticheskii bilingvizm i mezh"iazykovye vliianiia (Iazyk kak podtekst)" ["Poetic Bilingualism and Interlanguage Influences (Language as Subtext)"]. In *Vtorichnye modeliruiushchie sistemy,* 30–33. Tartu, Estonia: Tartuskii gosudarstvennyi universitet.

―――. 1989. "K voprosu o statuse 'literaturnoi shutki' u Akhmatovoi i Mandel'shtama" ["On the Question of the Status of the 'Literary Joke' in Akhmatova and Mandelstam"]. In *Anna Akhmatova i russkaia kul'tura nachala XX veka: Tezisy konferentsii,* 40–43. Moscow: Akademiia Nauk SSSR.

Lezhnev, A. 1970. "The Poetry of Boris Pasternak." Translated by Angela Livingstone. In *Pasternak: Modern Judgements,* ed. Donald Davie and Angela Livingstone, 85–107. Nashville, Tenn.: Aurora Publishers.

Ljunggren, Anna. 1989. "'Sad' i 'Ia sam': Smysl i kompozitsiia stikhotvoreniia 'Zerkalo'" ["'The Garden' and 'I Myself': The Meaning and Composition of the Poem 'The Mirror'"]. In *Boris Pasternak and His Times,* 224–37.

Lotman, Iu. M. [1970] 1971. *Struktura khudozhestvennogo teksta* [*The Structure of the Artistic Text*]. Moscow: Iskusstvo. Brown University Slavic Reprints, 9. Providence, R. I.: Brown University Press.

―――. 1977. "Stikhotvoreniia rannego Pasternaka i nekotorye voprosy strukturnogo izucheniia teksta" ["The Poems of Early Pasternak and Some Questions of the Structural Study of the Text"]. In *Readings in Soviet Semiotics (Russian Texts),* ed. L. Matejka, S. Shishkoff et al., 210–43. Ann Arbor: Michigan Slavic Publications.

―――. 1980. *Roman A. S. Pushkina "Evgenii Onegin" : Kommentarii* [*A. S. Pushkin's Novel "Eugene Onegin" : A Commentary*]. Leningrad: Prosveshchenie.

―――. 1986. "Zametki o khudozhestvennom prostranstve" ["Notes on Artistic Space"]. In *Semiotika prostranstva i prostranstvo semiotiki. Trudy po znakovym sistemam* 19: 25–43. Tartu, Estonia: Tartuskii gosudarstvennyi universitet.

Mallac, Guy de. 1981. *Boris Pasternak: His Life and Art.* Norman: University of Oklahoma Press.

Mandelstam, Nadezhda. 1970a. *Vospominaniia [Memoirs]*. New York: Izdatel'stvo imeni Chekhova.

———. 1970b. *Hope Against Hope: A Memoir*. Translated by Max Hayward. New York: Atheneum.

———. 1972. *Vtoraia kniga [Second Book]*. Paris: YMCA Press.

———. 1987. *Kniga tret'ia [Third Book]*. Paris: YMCA Press.

Mandelstam, Osip. 1955. *Sobranie sochinenii. [Collected Works]*. New York: Izdatel'stvo imeni Chekhova.

———. 1965. *The Prose of Osip Mandelstam: "The Noise of Time"; "Theodosia"; "The Egyptian Stamp."* Translated, with a critical essay, by Clarence Brown. Princeton, N.J.: Princeton University Press.

———. 1967, 1971, 1969. *Sobranie sochineniia v trekh tomakh [Collected Works in Three Volumes]*. Inter-Language Literary Associates. Vol. 1, 2d ed.: Washington, D.C. Vol. 2, 2d ed.: New York: Vol. 3: New York.

———. 1973. *Stikhotvoreniia [Poems]*. Leningrad: Sovetskii pisatel'.

———. 1979. *Mandelstam: The Complete Critical Prose and Letters*. Translated by Constance Link and Jane Gary Harris. Edited by Jane Gary Harris. Ann Arbor, Mich.: Ardis.

———. 1981. *Sobranie sochinenii [Collected Works]*. Vol. 4. Paris: YMCA Press.

———. 1981. "Vos'mistishiia" ["Octaves"]. In *Den' poezii*, 198–201. Moscow: Sovetskii pisatel'.

———. 1987. *Slovo i kul'tura [The Word and Culture]*. Moscow: Sovetskii pisatel'.

———. 1990. *Sochineniia [Works]*. Edited by P. M. Nerler. 2 vols. Moscow: Khudozhestvennaia literatura.

Marcovich, M. 1967. *Heraclitus: Greek Text with a Short Commentary*. Merida, Venezuela: Los Andes University Press.

Markov, Vladimir, ed. 1967. *Manifesty i programmy russkikh futuristov [Manifestoes and Programs of the Russian Futurists]*. Slavische Propylaen. Texte in Neu- und Nachdrucken, vol. 27. Munich: Wilhelm Fink Verlag.

Maslennikova, Zoia. 1990. *Portret Borisa Pasternaka [A Portrait of Boris Pasternak]*. Moscow: Sovetskaia Rossiia.

Mayr, Ernst. 1982. *The Growth of Biological Thought: Diversity, Evolution, and Inheritance*. Cambridge, Mass.: Harvard University Press.

Meilakh, M. B. 1975. "Ob imenakh Akhmatovoi, I. Anna" ["On Akhmatova's Names, I. Anna"]. *Russian Literature* 10–11: 33–57.

———. 1990. "'Vnutri gory bezdeistvuet kumir . . .' K stalinskoi teme v poezii Mandel'shtama" ["'Inside the mountain the idol idles . . .': On the Stalin Theme in Mandelstam's Poetry"]. In *Zhizn' i tvorchestvo O. E. Mandel'shtama*, 416–26. Voronezh: Izdatel'stvo voronezhskogo universiteta.

Mess-Baehr, Irina. 1991. "Ezopov iazyk v poezii Mandel'shtama 30-kh godov" ["Aesopian Language in Mandelstam's Poetry of the 1930s"]. *Russian Literature* 29, 3 (1 April): 243–393.

Meyer, Angelika. 1987. *"Sestra moja—žizn'" von Boris Pasternak: Analyse und Interpretation*. Munich: Otto Sagner.

Mohammed, Ovey N. 1984. *Averroes' Doctrine of Immortality: A Matter of Controversy.* Waterloo, Ont.: Wilfred Laurier University Press.

Mossman, Elliott. 1972. "Pasternak's Short Fiction." *Russian Literature Triquarterly* 2 (Winter): 279–302.

Nabokov, Vladimir. 1944. *Nikolai Gogol.* New York: New Directions.

Nakhimovsky, Alice Stone. 1992. *Russian-Jewish Literature and Identity: Jabotinsky, Babel, Grossman, Galich, Roziner, Markish.* Baltimore: Johns Hopkins University Press.

Nesbet, Anne. 1988. "Tokens of Elective Affinity: The Uses of Goethe in Mandel'štam." *Slavic and East European Journal* 32, 1 (Spring 1988): 109–25.

O'Connor, Katherine Tiernan. 1988. *Boris Pasternak's "My Sister—Life": The Illusion of Narrative.* Ann Arbor, Mich: Ardis.

Orlinsky, Harry M. 1974. "The Canonization of the Bible and the Exclusion of the Apocrypha." In *Essays in Biblical Culture and Bible Translation,* ed. H. M. Orlinsky, 257–86. New York: Ktav Publishing House.

Otsup, Nikolai. 1933. "O poezii i poetakh v SSSR" ["On Poetry and Poets in the USSR"]. *Chisla,* bk. 7–8: 236–42.

Pallas, Peter Simon. 1793. *Voyages de M. P. S. Pallas, en différentes provinces de l'empire de Russie, et dans l'Asie septentrionale.* 5 vols. Paris: Maradan.

———. 1812. *Travels Through the Southern Provinces of the Russian Empire, in the Years 1793 and 1794.* 2d ed. 2 vols. London: J. Stockdale.

Parnakh, V. 1934. *Ispanskie i portugal'skie poety, zhertvy inkvizitsii [Spanish and Portugese Poets, Victims of the Inquisition].* Leningrad and Moscow: Academia.

Parnis, A. E., and R. D. Timenchik. 1985. "Programmy 'Brodiachei sobaki'" ["The Programs of the 'Stray Dog'"]. In *Pamiatniki kul'tury. Novye otkrytiia: Pis'mennost'. Iskusstvo. Arkheologiia. Ezhegodnik 1983,* 160–257. Leningrad: Nauka.

Pasternak, Alexander. 1984. *A Vanished Present: The Memoirs of Alexander Pasternak.* Edited and translated by Ann Pasternak Slater. Oxford: Oxford University Press.

Pasternak, Boris. 1959. *Doktor Zhivago.* Ann Arbor: University of Michigan Press.

———. 1961. *Sobranie sochinenii v trekh tomakh [Collected Works in Three Volumes].* Vol. 3. Ann Arbor: University of Michigan Press.

———. 1965. *Stikhotvoreniia i poemy [Lyrics and Epics].* Introduction by A. D. Siniavskii. Moscow and Leningrad: Sovetskii pisatel'.

———. 1981. *Perepiska s Ol'goi Freidenberg [Correspondence with Olga Freidenberg].* New York: Harcourt Brace Jovanovich.

———. 1982. *Okhrannaia gramota [Safe Conduct].* In *Vozdushnye puti: Proza raznykh let,* 191–284. Moscow: Sovetskii pisatel'.

———. 1990a. *Stikhotvoreniia i poemy [Lyrics and Epics].* 2 vols. Leningrad: Sovetskii pisatel'.

————. 1990b. *Boris Pasternak ob iskusstve* [*Boris Pasternak on Art*]. Moscow: Iskusstvo.

Pasternak, E. B. 1989. *Boris Pasternak: Materialy dlia biografii* [*Boris Pasternak: Materials for a Biography*]. Moscow: Sovetskii pisatel'.

Pasternak, L. O. 1923. *Rembrandt i evreistvo v ego tvorchestve* [*Rembrandt and Jewry in His Work*]. Berlin: S. D. Saltzmann. Reprinted in Gass 1985.

————. 1987. *A Russian Impressionist: Paintings and Drawings by Leonid Pasternak, 1890–1945*. Washington, D.C.: Smithsonian Institution.

Paulos, John Allen. 1988. *Innumeracy: Mathematical Illiteracy and Its Consequences*. New York: Hill & Wang.

Pinskii, L. 1989. "Poetika Dante v osveshchenii poeta" ["Dante's Poetics in a Poet's Elucidation"]. In *Magistral'nyi siuzhet*, 367–96. Moscow: Sovetskii pisatel'.

Plank, D. L. 1972. "Readings of *My Sister Life*." *Russian Literature Triquarterly* 3 (May): 323–37.

Poliakova, S. V., ed. 1991. "Pis'ma O. E. Mandel'shtama N. S. Tikhonovu" ["O. E. Mandelstam's Letters to N. S. Tikhonov"]. In *Slovo i sud'ba. Osip Mandel'shtam: Issledovaniia i materialy*, 28–33. Moscow: Nauka.

Pollak, Nancy. 1983. "The Obscure Way to Mandel'štam's Armenia." Ph.D. diss., Yale University.

————. 1987. "Mandel'shtam's *Mandel'shtein* (Initial Observations on the Cracking of a Slit-Eyed Nut, OR, a Couple of Chinks in the Shchell)." *Slavic Review* 46, 3–4 (Fall–Winter): 450–70.

————. 1988. "Mandel'štam's 'First' Poem." *Slavic and East European Journal* 32, 1 (Spring 1988): 98–108.

———— 1993. "Sound as Vision in Lermontov's 'Vykhozhu odin ia na dorogu.'" In *Elementa* 1, 2: 159–65.

Proyart, Jacqueline de. 1964. *Pasternak*. N.p.: Gallimard.

Przybylski, Ryszard. 1987. *An Essay on the Poetry of Osip Mandelstam: God's Grateful Guest*. Translated by Madeline G. Levine. Ann Arbor, Mich.: Ardis.

Rayfield, Donald, intro. and trans. 1973. *"Chapter 42" by Nadezhda Mandel'shtam and "The Goldfinch" by Osip Mandel'shtam*. London: Menard Press.

Ronen, Omry. 1968. "Mandel'štam's *Kaščej*." In *Studies Presented to Professor Roman Jakobson by His Students*, 252–64. Cambridge, Mass.: Slavica Publishers.

————. 1973a. "Leksicheskii povtor, podtekst i smysl v poetike Osipa Mandel'shtama" ["Lexical Reiteration, Subtext, and Meaning in the Poetics of Osip Mandelstam"]. *Slavic Poetics: Essays in Honor of Kiril Taranovsky*, ed. Roman Jakobson, C. H. van Schooneveld, and Dean S. Worth, 367–87. The Hague: Mouton.

————. 1973b. "Mandelshtam, Osip Emilyevich." *Encyclopedia Judaica Year Book, 1973*, 294–96. Jerusalem: Keter Publishing House.

————. 1977a. "A Beam upon the Axe: Some Antecedents of Osip Mandel'štam's 'Umyvalsja noč'ju na dvore. . . .'" *Slavica Hierosolymitana* 1: 158–76.

————. 1977b. "The Dry River and the Black Ice: Anamnesis and Amnesia in

Mandel'štam's Poem 'Ja slovo pozabyl, čto ja xotel skazat'.'" *Slavica Hierosolymitana* 1: 177–84.

———. 1979. "K siuzhetu 'Stikhov o neizvestnom soldate' Mandel'shtama." ["On the Plot of Mandelstam's 'Verses about the Unknown Soldier'"]. *Slavica Hierosolymitana* 4: 214–22.

———. 1983. *An Approach to Mandel'štam.* Jerusalem: Magnes Press.

———. 1990. "Osip Mandelshtam." In *European Writers: The Twentieth Century,* ed. George Stade, 10: 1619–49. New York: Scribner.

———. 1991. "Zaum' za predelami avangarda" ["Trans-Sense Beyond the Limits of the Avant-Garde"]. *Literaturnoe obozrenie* 12: 40–43.

———. 1993. "Trans-Sense as a Signifier and a Signified in Non-Futurist Texts." In *Elementa* 1, 1: 43–55.

———. 1994. "O 'russkom golose' Osipa Mandel'shtama" ["On Osip Mandelstam's 'Russian Voice'"]. In *Tynianovskii sbornik: Piatye Tynianovskie chteniia.* Riga: Zinatne.

Russell, Bertrand. 1945. *A History of Western Philosophy.* New York: Simon & Schuster.

Sacks, Oliver. 1990. *Seeing Voices: A Journey into the World of the Deaf.* New York: HarperCollins.

Schiller, Friedrich. 1968. *Sämtliche Werke.* Vol. 3. Munich: Winkler-Verlag.

Scholem, Gershom. 1971. "Revelation and Tradition as Religious Categories in Judaism." In *The Messianic Idea in Judaism,* 282–303. New York: Schocken.

Schwarzband, Samuil. 1987. "*Kolchan:* 'Chetvertaia kniga' stikhotvorenii N. Gumileva" ["*The Quiver:* N. Gumilev's 'Fourth Book' of Poems"]. In *Nikolaj Gumilev, 1886–1986: Papers from the Gumilev Centenary Symposium Held at Ross Priory, University of Strathclyde, 1986,* ed. Sheelagh Duffin Graham, 293–310. Berkeley, Calif.: Berkeley Slavic Specialties.

Segal, D. M. 1968. "Nabliudeniia nad semanticheskoi strukturoi poeticheskogo proizvedeniia" ["Observations on the Semantic Structure of a Poetic Work"]. *International Journal of Slavic Linguistics and Poetics* 11: 159–71.

———. 1973. "Mikrosemantika odnogo stikhotvoreniia" ["The Microsemantics of a Poem"]. In *Slavic Poetics: Essays in Honor of Kiril Taranovsky,* ed. Roman Jakobson, C. H. van Schooneveld, and Dean S. Worth, 395–405. The Hague: Mouton.

———. 1975. "Fragment semanticheskoi poetiki O. E. Mandel'shtama" ["A Fragment of O. E. Mandelstam's Semantic Poetics"]. *Russian Literature* 10–11: 59–146.

Senderovich, Savely. 1994. *Georgii Pobedonosets v russkoi kul'ture* [*Georgii Pobedonosets in Russian Culture*]. Bern: Peter Lang.

Shtempel', N. E. 1987. "Mandel'shtam v Voronezhe" ["Mandelstam in Voronezh"]. ["Osip Mandel'shtam: Poslednie tvorcheskie gody"]. *Novyi mir* 10: 207–34.

Sokolova, Natal'ia. 1990. "14 marta 1933 g. Vecher Osipa Mandel'shtama" ["14 March 1993. Osip Mandelstam's Literary Evening"]. In O. E. Mandel'shtam, *"I ty, Moskva, sestra moia, legka . . ." Stikhi, proza, vospominaniia, materialy k biografii. Venok Mandel'shtamu*, 438–44. Moscow: Moskovskii rabochii.

Steiner, George. 1985. "Our Homeland the Text." *Salmagundi* 66 (Winter–Spring): 4–25.

Steiner, Peter. 1976. "On Semantic Poetics: O. Mandel'štam in the Discussions of the Soviet Structuralists." *Dispositio* 1, 3: 339–48.

Steinsaltz, Adin. 1976. *The Essential Talmud*. Translated by Chaya Galai. New York: Basic Books.

———. 1989. *The Talmud: The Steinsaltz Edition. A Reference Guide*. New York: Random House.

Stilman, Leon. 1974. "The 'All-Seeing Eye' in Gogol." In *Gogol from the Twentieth Century*, ed. Robert A. Maguire, 376–89. Princeton, N.J.: Princeton University Press.

Stolbov, V., ed. 1990. *Poeziia ispanskogo vozrozhdeniia* [*The Poetry of the Spanish Renaissance*]. Moscow: Khudozhestvennaia literatura.

Stora, Judith. 1968. "Pasternak et le judaisme." *Cahiers du monde russe et soviétique* 9, 3–4: 353–64.

Struve, Nikita. 1982. *Ossip Mandelstam*. Paris: Institut d'études slaves.

Taranovsky, Kiril. 1965. "The Sound Texture of Russian Verse in the Light of Phonemic Distinctive Features." *International Journal of Slavic Linguistics and Poetics* 9: 114–24.

———. 1976. *Essays on Mandel'štam*. Cambridge, Mass.: Harvard University Press.

———. 1987. "Two Notes on Mandel'štam's 'Hayloft' Poems." In *Text and Context: Essays to Honor Nils Åke Nilsson*, ed. Peter Alberg Jensen et al., 122–27. Stockholm: Almqvist & Wiksell International.

Ter-Oganesian, V. 1922. "Nazad k Ptolomeiu" ["Back to Ptolemy"]. In *Pod znamenem marksizma* 9–10: 229–30.

Thieme, Paul. 1954. "Die Wurzel *vat*." In *Asiatica: Festschrift Friedrich Weller*. Leipzig: Otto Harrassowitz, 656–66. Reprinted in *Indogermanische Dichtersprache*, ed. Rüdiger Schmitt, 187–203. Wege der Forschung, vol. 165. Darmstadt: Wissenschaftliche Buchgesellschaft, 1968.

Thomas, Lawrence L. 1957. *The Linguistic Theories of N. Ja. Marr*. University of California Publications in Linguistics, vol. 14. Berkeley and Los Angeles: University of California Press.

Thomson, R. D. B. 1991. "Mandel'štam's *Kamen'*: The Evolution of an Image." *Russian Literature* 30, 4 (15 November): 501–30.

Timenchik, R. D. 1974. "Zametki ob akmeizme" ["Notes on Acmeism"]. *Russian Literature* 7–8: 23–46.

———. 1975. "Avtometaopisanie u Akhmatovoi" ["Autometadescription in Akhmatova"]. *Russian Literature* 10–11: 213–26.

———. 1977. "Zametki ob akmeizme II" ["Notes on Acmeism II"]. *Russian Literature* 5, 3 (July): 281–300.

———. 1981. "Zametki ob akmeizme III" ["Notes on Acmeism III"]. *Russian Literature* 9, 2 (15 February): 175–89.

———. 1988. "Tynianov i 'literaturnaia kul'tura' 1910-kh godov" ["Tynianov and the 'Literary Culture' of the 1910s"]. In *Tynianovskii sbornik: Tret'i Tynianovskie chteniia,* ed. M. O. Chudakova, 159–73. Riga: Zinatne.

Toddes, E. A. 1986. "Mandel'shtam i opoiazovskaia filologiia" ["Mandelstam and OPOIAZ Philology"]. In *Tynianovskii sbornik: Vtorye Tynianovskie chteniia,* ed. M. O. Chudakova, 78–102. Riga: Zinatne.

Toporov, V. N. 1991. "O 'psikhofiziologicheskom' komponente poezii Mandel'shtama" ["On the 'Psychophysiological' Component of Mandelstam's Poetry"]. In *Osip Mandel'shtam: K 100-letiiu so dnia rozhdeniia. Poetika i tekstologiia. Materialy nauchnoi konferentsii 27–29 dekabria 1991 g.,* 7–27. Moscow: Gnosis.

Trend, J. B., and H. Loewe, eds. 1937. Paul Goodman, L. Rabinowitz et al., *Isaac Abravanel: Six Lectures.* Introduction by H. Loewe. Cambridge: Cambridge University Press.

Trenin, V. V., and N. I. Khardzhiev. [1932] 1976. "O Borise Pasternake" ["On Boris Pasternak"]. In *Boris Pasternak: Essays,* ed. Nils Åke Nilsson, 9–25. Stockholm: Almqvist & Wiksell International.

Tsvetaeva, Marina. 1979. "Svetovoi liven'" ["A Downpour of Light"]. In *Izbrannaia proza v dvukh tomakh, 1917–1937,* 1: 135–48. New York: Russica Publishers.

Turbin, V. N. 1985. "'Situatsiia dvuiazychiia' v tvorchestve Pushkina i Lermontova" ["The 'Situation of Bilingualism' in the Work of Pushkin and Lermontov"]. In *Lermontovskii sbornik,* 91–103. Leningrad: Nauka.

Tynianov, Iu. 1929. "Promezhutok." ["The Interval"]. *Arkhaisty i novatory.* Reprint, Ann Arbor, Mich.: Ardis, 1985.

Uspenskii, F. B. 1990. "K poetike O. Mandel'shtama (grammatika kak predmet poezii)" ["Towards a Poetics of O. Mandelstam (Grammar as the Subject of Poetry)"]. In *Blokovskii sbornik* 11: 90–96. Tartu, Estonia: Tartuskii gosudarstvennyi universitet.

Vasmer, Max. 1964–73. *Etimologicheskii slovar' russkogo iazyka* [*Etymological Dictionary of the Russian Language*]. 4 vols. Moscow: Progress.

Venclova, Tomas. 1986. *Neustoichivoe ravnovesie: vosem' russkikh poeticheskikh tekstov* [*An Unstable Equilibrium: Eight Russian Poetic Texts*]. New Haven, Conn.: Yale Center for International and Area Studies.

Vil'mont, N. 1989. *O Borise Pasternake: Vospominaniia i mysli* [*On Boris Pasternak: Memoirs and Thoughts*]. Moscow: Sovetskii pisatel'.

Viskovatov, P. A. 1987. *Mikhail Iur'evich Lermontov: Zhizn' i tvorchestvo* [*Mikhail Iur'evich Lermontov: Life and Work*]. Moscow: Sovremennik.

Vygotskii, L. S. 1983. *Osnovy defektologii* [*Fundamentals of Defectology*]. *Sobranie sochinenii v shesti tomakh.* Vol. 5. Moscow: Pedagogika.

West, Daphne. 1981. "Mandelstam and the Evolutionists." *Journal of Russian Studies* 42: 30–38.

Winton, Ward M. 1990. "Jamesian Aspects of Misattribution Research." *Personality and Social Psychology Bulletin* 16, 4 (December): 652–64.

Wolkonsky, Catherine A., and Marianna A. Poltoratzky. 1961. *Handbook of Russian Roots*. New York: Columbia University Press.

"Zametki o peresechenii biografii Osipa Mandel'shtama i Borisa Pasternaka" ["Notes on the Intersection of the Biography of Osip Mandelstam and Boris Pasternak"]. 1979–81. In *Pamiat': Istoricheskii sbornik*, 4: 282–337. Moscow and Paris: YMCA Press.

Zeeman, Peter. 1988. *The Later Poetry of Osip Mandelstam: Text and Context*. Amsterdam: Rodopi.

Zenkevich, E. P., and P. M. Nerler, eds. 1987. "Iz pisem O. E. Mandel'shtama rodnym" ["From O. E. Mandelstam's Letters to Relatives"]. *Novyi mir* 10: 201–7.

Zenkevich, E. P., A. A. Mandel'shtam, and P. M. Nerler, eds. 1991. "Osip Mandel'shtam v perepiske sem'i" ["Osip Mandelstam in His Family's Correspondence"]. In *Slovo i sud'ba. Osip Mandel'shtam: Issledovaniia i materialy*, 50–101. Moscow: Nauka.

Zhirmunskii, V. M. 1916. "Preodolevshie simvolizm" ["Those Who Overcame Symbolism"]. In *Russkaia mysl'*, bk. 12. Reprinted in *Teoriia literatury. Poetika. Stilistika*, 106–33. Leningrad: Nauka, 1977.

Zholkovskii, Aleksandr. 1991. "Ekstaticheskie motivy Pasternaka v svete ego lichnoi mifologii" ["Pasternak's Ecstatic Motifs in Light of His Personal Mythology"]. In *Boris Pasternak, 1890–1990*, ed. Lev Loseff, 52–74. Norwich Symposia on Russian Literature and Culture, 1. Northfield, Vt.: Russian School of Norwich University.

General Index

Akhmatova, Anna, 4, 40, 42, 45, 120–21, 151n.142, 154n.18, 185n.170, 188n.208, 189n.212, 192n.238; "Ne budem pit' iz odnogo stakana" ("We will not drink, from the same glass"), 121; "Poet," 94, 102, 176n.58, 179nn.89, 91, 94
almond, image of, 21, 34, 38, 43–44, 146n.62. *See also* geode
Annenskii, Innokentii, 55, 62, 116, 149n.108, 150n.115, 151n.132, 154n.19, 160n.86, 161n.93, 162n.103, 175n.54, 185n.167
Arab theme, 65–66

babble, 31, 75, 124, 150n.117, 162nn.101, 102; as origins of poet's speech, 33; as "pointless" activity, 53–54, 57–59
Baratynskii, Evgenii, 99, 118, 124, 145n.39, 149n.114, 177n.77, 186n.176
Batiushkov, Konstantin, 82, 96–98, 176n.58
Belyi, Andrei, 45, 61, 108, 145n.43, 181n.116
blindness and deafness, as conditions of creativity, 19, 27–30, 134. *See also* deprivation; sense
Blok, Aleksandr, 5, 45, 61, 127, 131, 156nn.42, 43, 171n.208, 186n.184, 192n.238; "Na ostrovakh" ("On the Islands"), 71, 78; "Ravenna," 69
breathing (respiration), theme of: common to Mandelstam and Pasternak, 86–88; diseased, and cure for, 85–90, 96, 135; in the "Gudok" cycle, 90–91

child, image of: in Mandelstam and Pasternak, compared, 161n.87; and swollen glands, 146n.62; in "Vos'mistishiia," 69–70, 81. *See also* babble; language
civic verse, 40–41, 44, 106, 108, 120, 153nn.3, 8, 156n.43

Dante Alighieri, 7, 9, 14, 19–24, 26, 31, 36–38, 63, 65, 66, 76–79, 82, 134,

143n.4, 144n.25, 147n.68, 148n.86, 170n.202
deprivation, 14, 27, 85, 122; of senses, 29–30, 34, 37, 126
Derzhavin, Gavriil, 156n.45

Fet, Afanasii, 71, 116, 156n.45, 170n.197, 187n.185, 192n.238; ancestry of, 183n.133
Florenskii, P. A., 76–82, 168n.176, 169n.178, 170n.202

geode, image of, 19–21, 23, 35–36, 38
Goethe, Johann Wolfgang von, 15–19, 59, 127–28, 130, 137n.12, 138n.33, 144nn.22, 27, 145n.39, 146nn.49, 55, 147n.78, 149n.101, 160n.83
goldfinch: colors of, and Judaism, 124, 188n.205; hybrid speech of, 133–34; iconography of, 112–14, 184nn.147, 151; image of, 186n.178, 189n.216, 190n.228; "Sephardic" features of, 125, 127; theme of spite and, 120
Gorodetskii, Sergei, 42–44, 156n.37, 169n.182
Gumilev, Nikolai: death of, 45, 156n.42, 185n.170; on "The Octave," 42–43; review of *Kamen'*, 155n.35; Mandelstam's "conversation" with, 42, 154n.18
—*Works:* "Estestvo" ("Nature"), 82, 154n.20, 163n.106, 165n.133, 169n.182; *Gondla*, 45; "Pamiati Annenskogo" ("To the Memory of Annenskii"), 154n.19; "Persidskaia miniatiura" ("Persian Miniature"), 44, 45; "Poema nachala" ("Epic of the Beginning"), 159n.67; "Schast'e" ("Happiness"), 53, 154nn.19, 25, 159n.75; "Shestoe chuvstvo" ("Sixth Sense"), 49, 50, 158n.59; "Slovo" ("The Word"), 49–50, 154n.20, 159n.67, 160n.80; "Vos'mistishie" ("Octave"), 34, 42, 70–71, 154n.19; "Zhizn' stikha" ("The Life of Verse"), 131–32

Works by Osip Mandelstam

Library of Congress Cataloging-in-Publication Data

Pollak, Nancy.
   Mandelstam the reader / Nancy Pollak.
      p.   cm. — (Parallax)
   Includes bibliographical references and index.
   ISBN 0-8018-5006-1 (alk. paper)
    1. Mandel'shtam, Osip, 1891–1938—Criticism
and interpretation. I. Title. II. Series: Parallax
(Baltimore, Md.)
   PG3476.M355Z876   1995
   891.71'3—dc20   94-41632